cut here

Standard Search Co

To Do This:	Use This Command:	Example:
Search for part of a word	*	mon*
Must *include* a word	+	monty + python
Must *exclude* a word	–	monty – python
Search for a complete phrase	" "	"monty python"
Only search in the title of the page	t:	t:monty python
Only search in the URL of the page	u:	u:monty python

Advanced Search Options

Option	Description
Search the Web	Searches the standard Web directory
Search Usenet	Searches Usenet newsgroups
Intelligent default	Standard Yahoo! search mode
An exact phrase match	Searches for an exact phrase
Matches on all words (AND)	Changes the default OR operator to AND
Matches on any word (OR)	Returns to the default OR mode
Search Yahoo! categories	Limits your search to Yahoo! categories only
Search Web sites	Limits your search to sites in the Yahoo! directory only
Find only new listings	Searches most recent listings
After the first page, display *XX* matches per page	Customizes the number of results listed per page

GeoCities HTML Codes

Common HTML Codes

For This Effect:	Use This Code:
Background color	`<body bgcolor="xxxxxx">`document`</body>`
Blink	`<blink>`text`</blink>`
Boldface	`<b>`text`</b>`
Center	`<center>`text`</center>`
Font color	`<font color="#xxxxxx">`text`</font>`
Font size	`<font size="xx">`text`</font>`
Font	`<font face="xxxx">`text`</font>`
Heading 1	`<h1>`heading`</h1>`
Heading 2	`<h2>`heading`</h2>`
Heading 3	`<h3>`heading`</h3>`
Insert graphic	`<img src="URL">`
Insert horizontal rule	`<hr>`
Insert hyperlink	`<a href="URL">`text`</a>`
Insert line break	` `
Insert paragraph break	`<p>`
Italic	`<i>`text`</i>`
Monospace (typewriter-style)	`<tt>`text`</tt>`
Preformatted (preserves line breaks)	`<pre>`text`</pre>`
Title	`<title>`title`</title>`
Underline	`<u>`text`</u>`

Common Color Codes

Color	Code	Example
White	FFFFFF	
Red	FF0000	
Green	00FF00	
Blue	0000FF	
Magenta	FF00FF	
Cyan	00FFFF	
Yellow	FFFF00	
Black	000000	
Light gray	DDDDDD	

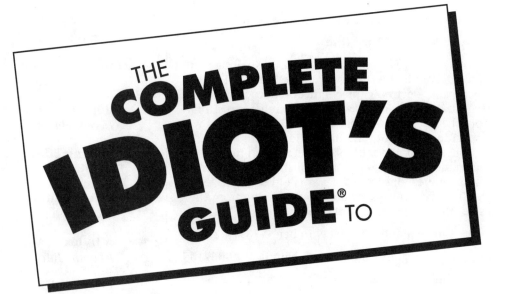

THE COMPLETE IDIOT'S GUIDE® TO

Yahoo!

by Michael Miller

A Division of Macmillan Computer Publishing
201 W. 103rd Street, Indianapolis, IN 46290

The Complete Idiot's Guide to Yahoo!

Copyright © 2000 by *Que*

International Standard Book Number: 0-7897-2277-1

Library of Congress Catalog Card Number: 99-067105

Printed in the United States of America

First Printing: February 2000

02   01   00   4   3   2   1

Trademarks

Warning and Disclaimer

Associate Publisher
Greg Wiegand

Acquisitions Editor
Angelina Ward

Development Editor
Gregory Harris

Managing Editor
Thomas F. Hayes

Project Editor
Tricia Sterling

Indexer
Deborah Hittel

Proofreader
Harvey Stanbrough

Technical Editor
Doug Dafforn

Illustrator
Judd Winick

Team Coordinator
Sharry Gregory

Interior Designer
Nathan Clement

Cover Designer
Michael Freeland

Copy Writer
Eric Borgert

Production
Darin Crone
Dan Harris

Contents at a Glance

Contents

Part 3: Make Yahoo! Work for You: Yahoo! Services — 95

10 Free Email, Anywhere, with Yahoo! Mail — 97

11 Talk Until Your Fingers Fall Off with Yahoo! Chat and Messenger — 113

20 Advertise Your Stuff (and Yourself!) with Yahoo! Classifieds and Personals   197

21 Shop 'Til You Drop with Yahoo! Shopping   205

22 Book Your Next Vacation with Yahoo! Travel   209

About the Author

Michael Miller is a writer, speaker, consultant, and the President and Founder of The Molehill Group, a strategic consulting and authoring firm based in Carmel, Indiana. More information about the author and The Molehill Group can be found at www.molehillgroup.com, and you can email the author directly at author@molehillgroup.com.

Mr. Miller has been an important force in the book publishing business since 1987, and served for more than a decade in publishing management at Macmillan Publishing, the world's largest reference publisher. As the author of 35 best-selling how-to books, Mr. Miller has written about the most popular Internet portals and topics. His most recent books include

➤ *The Complete Idiot's Guide to Online Search Secrets*

➤ *The Complete Idiot's Guide to Online Auctions*

➤ *The Complete Idiot's Guide to Surfing the Internet with WebTV*

➤ *The Complete Idiot's Guide to Microsoft Works Suite 2000*

➤ *The Complete Idiot's Guide to Fixing Your #$%@ PC*

➤ *The Official PrintMaster Guide*

From his first book (*Ventura Publisher Techniques and Applications*, published in 1988) to this, his latest title, Michael Miller has established a reputation for practical advice, technical accuracy, and an unerring empathy for the needs of his readers. Many regard Mr. Miller as the consummate reporter on new technology for an everyday audience.

Dedication

To my brother Mark and his lovely bride Stephanie: May you never lie, steal, cheat, or drink—but if you must lie, lie in each other's arms; if you must steal, steal kisses; if you must cheat, cheat death; and if you must drink, drink with us, your friends.

Acknowledgements

Special thanks to the usual suspects at Macmillan, including but not limited to Greg Wiegand, Angelina Ward, Gregory Harris, Tricia Sterling, and Doug Dafforn.

Tell Us What You Think!

As the reader of this book, *you* are our most important critic and commentator. We value your opinion and want to know what we're doing right, what we could do better, what areas you'd like to see us publish in, and any other words of wisdom you're willing to pass our way.

As an Associate Publisher for Que, I welcome your comments. You can fax, email, or write me directly to let me know what you did or didn't like about this book—as well as what we can do to make our books stronger.

Please note that I cannot help you with technical problems related to the topic of this book, and that due to the high volume of mail I receive, I might not be able to reply to every message.

When you write, please be sure to include this book's title and author as well as your name and phone or fax number. I will carefully review your comments and share them with the author and editors who worked on the book.

Fax: 317-581-4666

Email: consumer@mcp.com

Mail: Greg Wiegand, Associate Publisher
          Que
          201 West 103rd Street
          Indianapolis, IN 46290 USA

Introduction

Do you Yahoo!?

If you're connected to the Internet, chances are you do.

Yahoo! is the largest site on the Web, and the fastest growing as well. With more than 100 million users worldwide and 385 million page views per *day*, Yahoo! is visited by almost two-thirds of all Internet users at least once a month.

Although it came to prominence as the premiere Web directory, Yahoo! is now much more than a search site. With the recent addition of GeoCities and broadcast.com to the Yahoo! family, Yahoo!'s range of content and services has grown to include

- ➤ Chat rooms
- ➤ Children and family focused content
- ➤ Downloadable MP3 music files
- ➤ Email
- ➤ Full-service financial news and stock quotes
- ➤ Instant messaging
- ➤ Local news, information, and events
- ➤ Message boards and clubs
- ➤ News, weather, and sports
- ➤ Online auctions
- ➤ Online bill paying
- ➤ Online shopping
- ➤ Personal calendar and scheduling
- ➤ Personal Web pages
- ➤ Real-time online music and talk programming
- ➤ Small business services and Web site hosting
- ➤ Stock quotes and personal financial services
- ➤ Television schedules and entertainment news
- ➤ Travel information and reservations

This broad variety of content and services positions Yahoo! as a portal that is as broad and as deep as traditional commercial online services, such as America Online. Theoretically, you could do everything you want to do on the Internet without ever leaving the Yahoo! network of sites!

Who This Book Is For

If you've ever used Yahoo!—and you probably have—then this book is for you. *The Complete Idiot's Guide to Yahoo!* is written for anyone using Yahoo!—whether you're just starting out with the basics, or you're an experienced user who wants to get more out of this terrific site. No matter what parts of Yahoo! you use, you'll find a treasure trove of useful information here.

If you're searching for information on the Internet, you'll want to turn to Part 2, "Find Anything and Anyone: Yahoo! Search." In particular, Chapter 5, "Search the Web with the Yahoo! Directory," will show you inside tips and tricks to improve your searching with the Yahoo! directory.

If you're a big communicator, you'll want to turn to Part 3, "Make Yahoo! Work for You: Yahoo! Services." Here you'll learn how to set up your own free Web-based Yahoo! Mail account, and how to use Yahoo! Chat, Messenger, Message Boards, and Clubs.

If you like to buy or sell things online, you'll want to turn to Part 5, "Buy and Sell Online: Yahoo! Auctions and Shopping." This section includes the most comprehensive coverage available of Yahoo! Auctions, one of the top online auction sites on the Internet.

And if you want to create your own personal Web pages, you'll *definitely* want to turn to Part 7, "Create Personal Web Pages: Yahoo! GeoCities." This section covers everything you need to know about building and hosting Web pages on Yahoo! GeoCities—information you won't find in any other Yahoo! book currently on the market!

What You'll Find in This Book

The Complete Idiot's Guide to Yahoo! is composed of 32 chapters, organized into seven major sections:

➤ Part 1, "Can You Yahoo?: Yahoo! Basics," is your introduction to the wild and wonderful world of Yahoo! Start here to learn how to navigate Yahoo!—and how to personalize your Yahoo! experience.

➤ Part 2, "Find Anything and Anyone: Yahoo! Search," gets to the core of Yahoo!—finding stuff on the Internet. Turn to this section to learn the best ways to search for things, people, businesses, and images using the massive Yahoo! directory.

➤ Part 3, "Make Yahoo! Work for You: Yahoo! Services," shows you how to use Yahoo's various services to make your life online—and offline—that much easier. Here you'll learn all about Yahoo! Mail, Chat, Messenger, Clubs, Message Boards, Calendar, Address Book, and Briefcase.

➤ Part 4, "Get Smart, Have Fun: Yahoo! News, Information, and Entertainment," covers all the information-gathering aspects of the Yahoo! network of sites, from news headlines to television listings to digital music downloading.

➤ Part 5, "Buy and Sell Online: Yahoo! Auctions and Shopping," shows you the *best* ways to spend your money online—from auctions to electronic retailers to online real estate listings.

➤ Part 6, "Make More Money: Yahoo! Finance and Careers," shows you how to use Yahoo's investor services, career services, and business services to help you make more money and further your career.

➤ Part 7, "Create Personal Web Pages: Yahoo! GeoCities," tells you everything you need to know to create great-looking Web pages at Yahoo's sister site, Yahoo! GeoCities.

At the back of the book you'll find "The Yahoo! Glossary" where all the fancy phrases in the book are defined in plain English. And if you turn to the inside of the front cover, you'll see a tear-out card with Yahoo!'s most powerful search commands— along with the most popular HTML codes for your Yahoo! GeoCities Web pages. Finally, look at the inside front and inside back covers of the book for the direct Web addresses of Yahoo!'s most popular sites and services.

How to Do the Things You See in This Book

To get the most out of this book, you should know how it is designed. I've tried to put things together in such a way as to make reading the book both rewarding and fun. So, here's what to do when you see any of the following:

➤ Web page addresses (URLs) are presented in `computer type (monospace)`; you can enter the text into your browser's Address box to go to that page. For example, Yahoo's main page would appear as `www.yahoo.com`.

➤ Any information you need to enter—into a search box, for example, or into a form—is presented in **`bold computer type`** as well; enter this text as-written to proceed. For example, "Enter **`Batman`** in the search box to begin searching."

➤ Anything you need to click, select, or choose appears in **bold** text. For example: "Click the **Search** button."

➤ New terms are presented in *italicized text*; pay close attention to these terms.

Extras

To pack as much information as possible into *The Complete Idiot's Guide to Yahoo!*, you are presented with additional tips and advice as you read the book. These elements enhance your knowledge, or point out important pitfalls to avoid. Along the way, you'll find the following elements:

Y! Tips!

These tips offer you advice on how to work more efficiently and effectively on the Yahoo! network of sites.

Y! Traps!

These warnings point out common problems and pitfalls that—with a little foresight—you can hopefully avoid.

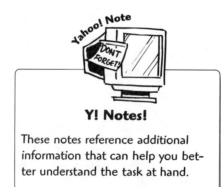

Y! Notes!

These notes reference additional information that can help you better understand the task at hand.

Get Ready to Yahoo!

Still here? It's time to get started, so turn the page and prepare to go online—with the most comprehensive site on the Internet!

Part 1
Can You Yahoo?: Yahoo! Basics

Turn here to learn all about the Yahoo! network of sites—from basic site navigation to customizing Yahoo! for your own personal use.

Chapter 1

Essential Yahoo!: How to Use the World's Most Popular Web Site

In This Chapter

➤ Discover how Yahoo! got started

➤ Find out how to jump to and link to Yahoo!'s sites

➤ Learn how to navigate from Yahoo!'s home page

➤ Discover how to make Yahoo! part of your Web browser

➤ Find out how to get help on the Yahoo! site—and how to contact Yahoo!

Yahoo! is *the* most popular site on the Internet. More people visit Yahoo! every day than visit America Online or Amazon.com or eBay or GeoCities or any other Internet destination. Every month, more than 100 million people visit one or more of the Yahoo! sites.

So if you're like most users, you can answer yes to the question, "Do you Yahoo?" But do you know *everything* you can do at Yahoo? Do you know all about Yahoo! services, including free email and online scheduling and shopping and auctions and personal ads and stock quotes and TV schedules and travel reservations and interactive games and downloadable music and Internet radio and real-time chat and instant messaging and...well, *do you?*

If you *don't* know about everything Yahoo! has to offer, you've come to the right place. Read on to learn more about Yahoo!—and how *you* can use Yahoo! for everything you do online!

Getting to Know Yahoo!

Yahoo! has an interesting history—it came into being almost in spite of itself. David Filo and Jerry Yang were students at Stanford University in 1994, in the early days of the World Wide Web. As a convenience to themselves, they started keeping track of their favorite sites on the Web, collecting and classifying hundreds and then thousands of different Web pages. As their little hobby grew more time-consuming, Filo and Yang created a custom database to house their Web links, and they made the database available for free on the Web. They named the database Yahoo! (supposedly an acronym for Yet Another Hierarchical Officious Oracle) and, after about a year, moved their site from the overloaded Stanford servers to the larger-capacity servers of Netscape Corporation.

In the spring of 1995, Yang and Filo began to realize the commercial appeal of their increasingly popular site; they accepted some venture capital and turned Yahoo! into a full-time business. Since going public in 1996, Yahoo! has become one of the highest-flying Internet stocks on the market—and one of the first Internet-related companies to actually turn a profit. (Figure 1.1 shows Yahoo's stock performance over the years.) If you had invested $100 in Yahoo! stock when it first went public, that stock would have been worth more than $1,500 less than three years later!

Figure 1.1

The performance of Yahoo! stock since 1996—all I can say is, "Yahoo!."

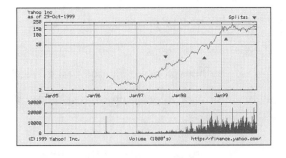

Track the Stock

Yahoo! is still a great investment in today's hot technology-driven stock market. If you want to track the performance of Yahoo! stock, follow the ticker YHOO.

Of course, the Yahoo! of today is a far cry from the database that resided on Filo and Yang's personal workstations at Stanford. Yahoo! has expanded well beyond a simple Web directory (even though most Yahoo! visitors still use the site primarily for searching). Today, Yahoo! is a full-fledged Web *portal*, a site that not only directs you to content across the Internet, but also contains its own proprietary content and services—everything from stock quotes to online auctions to interactive chat to free email.

In addition, international versions of Yahoo! are available for more than twenty countries, from Australia to the United Kingdom. As you can see, Yahoo! is more like America Online than it is a simple search site—although the Yahoo! directory is still its main claim to fame.

Getting to Yahoo!

Okay, you're sold. Yahoo! is the greatest thing since sliced bread. Now how do you get there from here?

The Main Page (Remember This Address!)

Remember this address. Write it backward on your forehead so you can read it when you look in the mirror. Have it engraved on the front of your computer monitor. (Or just save it in your browser's bookmark file. Whatever.)

The Chief Yahoo!s

Today, Yahoo! is run by a team of professional managers, including Chairman/CEO Timothy Koogle (ex-Motorola) and President/COO Jeff Mallett (ex-Novell). Filo and Yang remain on board as "Chief Yahoo!s," providing important strategic and technical direction for the rapidly expanding company.

The URL for Yahoo! is (drum roll, please): www.yahoo.com.

Okay, so it isn't that hard to figure out—and with most browsers, you can get there just by entering **yahoo** in your address box, without even the www. or the .com. Still, it's an important address!

Make Yahoo! Your Browser's Home Page

If you *really* want to Yahoo!, you can make Yahoo! the first page to load when you launch your Web browser. If you're using Internet Explorer, just drag Yahoo!'s URL and icon from the **Address** box and drop it onto the **Home** button on the Standard toolbar. If you're using Netscape Navigator, pull down the **Edit** menu, select **Preferences**, and enter www.yahoo.com in the **Home Page Location** box.

Figuring Out Other Yahoo! Addresses

As you'll learn all throughout this book, Yahoo! has a complete network of sites— local sites, service sites, topic-specific sites, you name it. Although you can link to all these sites from the main Yahoo! page, each of the sites also has its own unique address. If you know the address, you can jump directly to the page without hitting the main Yahoo! page first.

A list of the most popular Yahoo! addresses is included on the inside front cover of this book. Even if you don't know the address for a specific site, you probably can figure it out on your own. All you have to do is construct a URL that looks like this: *sitename*.yahoo.com. That is, Yahoo! almost always puts the site name first, then follows it with a yahoo.com.

For example, the address for Yahoo! Auctions is auctions.yahoo.com, and the address for Yahoo! Movies is movies.yahoo.com.Although this scheme doesn't work for every Yahoo! site, it works more often than it doesn't.

Linking to Yahoo!

If you've created your own personal Web page, you might want to put a link to Yahoo!—or one of the Yahoo! sites—on your page. It's easy enough to insert the www.yahoo.com URL as a hyperlink within your document, but you can also link directly to any other Yahoo! page. If you want to add a Yahoo! button to your link, go to docs.yahoo.com/docs/yahootogo/buttons.html for a page full of Yahoo! button graphics.

Yahoo! also has HTML code that lets you insert search boxes for the Yahoo! directory, Yahoo! News, Yahoo! Maps, and Yahoo! Yellow Pages right on your own home page. Yahoo! even lets you code your page to include Yahoo! stock tickers and weather reports! For more information about these and other ways of linking to Yahoo!, go to docs.yahoo.com/docs/yahootogo/index.html.

Crack the Code

To learn more about creating your own personal Web pages with HTML code, see Chapter 30, "Create Sophisticated Pages with HTML."

Getting to Yahoo!'s Sister Sites

In addition to the main Yahoo! network, Yahoo! also owns two other large Web sites—Yahoo! GeoCities and Yahoo! Broadcast (formerly Broadcast.com). Surprisingly, there are no links to these sites from the Yahoo! home page, so you have to go to geocities.yahoo.com for GeoCities or broadcast.yahoo.com for Yahoo! Broadcast.

More About Yahoo! GeoCities and Yahoo! Broadcast

To learn more about Yahoo! GeoCities, see Chapter 28, "Learn to Homestead with Yahoo! GeoCities." For more about Yahoo! Broadcast, see Chapter 17, "Listen to Internet Radio—and Download CD-Quality Music—with Yahoo! Radio, Broadcast, and Digital."

Getting Around Yahoo!

When you go to www.yahoo.com, you see the main Yahoo! page. This is the page you use to access most other Yahoo! sites and services, as well as search or browse through the Yahoo! directory.

As you can see in Figure 1.2, the Yahoo! page is divided into just a few major sections.

Basically, you find a link you want to go to, and then click it. (It's not that hard, really!) The question is—what's behind all those links? Read on to learn more about the various parts of Yahoo!

Yahoo! New and Interesting

When you click the **What's New?** link (or go directly to dir.yahoo.com/new/), you go to the What's New... On the Web page, shown in Figure 1.3. This page includes links to a lot of new and cool sites, including

➤ **Daily Picks**—Hot sites picked by the Yahoo! staff.

➤ **Today's Top Net Events**—A listing of today's hottest live chats and broadcasts on the Internet.

➤ **New Additions to Yahoo!**—A listing of new sites just added to the Yahoo! directory.

➤ **In the News**—Today's major news headlines.

➤ **Daily Entertainment**—Comics, crosswords, and horoscopes—plus David Letterman's Top Ten List!

Getting Back Home

On most Yahoo! pages you can return to the main Yahoo! page by clicking the **Yahoo!** logo or link, typically found somewhere at the top of the page.

11

➤ **Other Starting Points**—Including Yahoo!'s Picks of the Week, *X* of the Day
(which isn't X-rated stuff, it's things like Cards of the Day, Jokes of the Day,
Song of the Day, and so on), and Project Cool Sightings (a list of hand-picked
"cool" Web sites) .

Figure 1.2

*The Yahoo! main page—
it all starts here!*

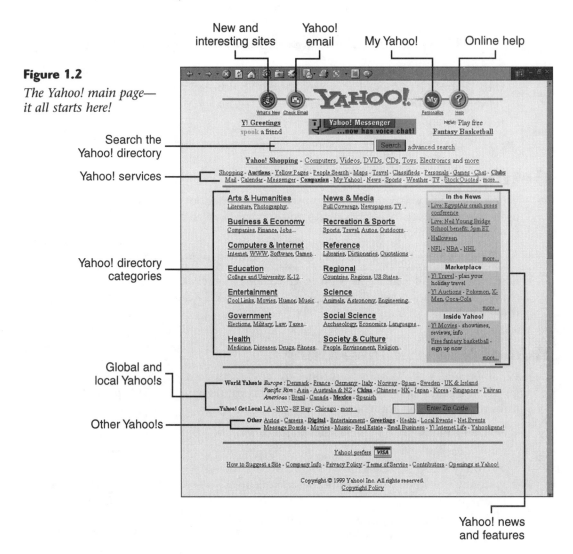

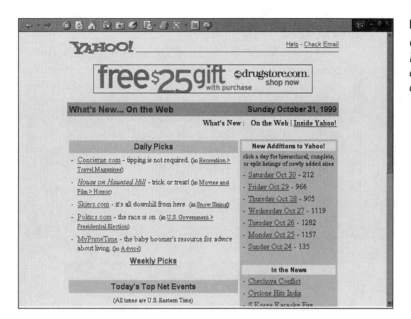

Figure 1.3
*Click the **What's New?** link to see the newest and coolest Web sites and events.*

Yahoo! Mail

When you click the **Check Mail** link (or go directly to mail.yahoo.com), you go to Yahoo! Mail, Yahoo!'s free email service. If you already have a Yahoo! Mail account, you are prompted to sign in so you can retrieve mail from your inbox, as shown in Figure 1.4. If you haven't signed up yet, you can register to start sending and receiving email from any Web browser.

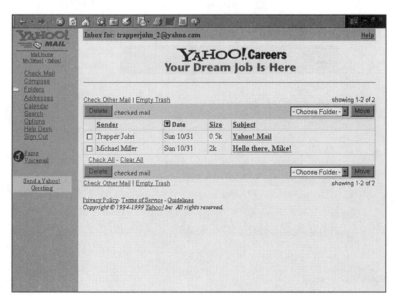

Figure 1.4
*Click the **Check Mail** link to write and receive email via Yahoo! Mail.*

More About Mail

To learn more about Yahoo! Mail, see Chapter 10, "Free Email, Anywhere, with Yahoo! Mail."

Yahoo! for You

When you click the **Personalize** link (or go directly to my.yahoo.com), you access My Yahoo!, a page you can configure for your own personal likes and dislikes. With My Yahoo! (shown in Figure 1.5), you can select the kinds of items you want to see—news, weather, sports, financials, and so on—as well as change the layout and color of the page. Many users prefer to make My Yahoo! their start page—because it's personalized.

Figure 1.5

Custom-build your own personal My Yahoo! page when you click the **Personalize** *link.*

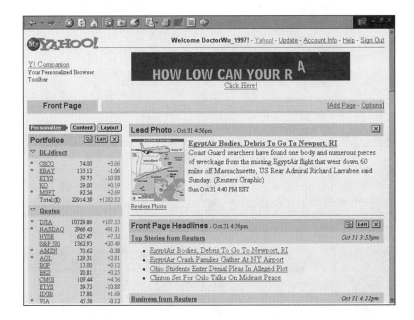

More About My Yahoo!

To learn more about My Yahoo!, see Chapter 2, "Create Your Own Personal Yahoo! with My Yahoo!."

Yahoo! Help

When you click the **Help** link, you don't actually go to Yahoo!'s main Help section. Instead, you go to the Yahoo! How-To (also accessible directly at howto. yahoo.com), an online tutorial for using Yahoo! and the Internet. If you want to go to Yahoo! Help Central (discussed in the "Getting Help with Yahoo!" section later in this chapter), go directly to help.yahoo.com.

Yahoo! Search

The big text box at the top of the main Yahoo! page is Yahoo!'s Search box. You use this box to search the Yahoo! directory; just enter your query into the **Search** box and press **Enter**, and Yahoo! returns a list of Web sites and categories that match your query.

Click the **Advanced Search** link to access Yahoo!'s advanced search options.

More About Searching

To learn more about searching the Web, see Chapter 5, "Search the Web with the Yahoo! Directory."

Yahoo! Services

The links directly underneath the Search box take you to several of Yahoo!'s many services. Among the links you'll find here are links to

➤ My Yahoo! (see Chapter 2 for more information)
➤ Yahoo! Auctions (see Chapter 19)
➤ Yahoo! Calendar (see Chapter 13)
➤ Yahoo! Chat (see Chapter 11)
➤ Yahoo! Classifieds (see Chapter 20)
➤ Yahoo! Clubs (see Chapter 12)
➤ Yahoo! Companion (discussed later in this chapter)
➤ Yahoo! Games (see Chapter 16)
➤ Yahoo! Mail (see Chapter 10)
➤ Yahoo! Maps (see Chapter 22)
➤ Yahoo! Messenger (see Chapter 11)
➤ Yahoo! News (see Chapter 15)
➤ Yahoo! People Search (see Chapter 6)
➤ Yahoo! Personals (see Chapter 20)
➤ Yahoo! Shopping (see Chapter 21)
➤ Yahoo! Sports (see Chapter 15)
➤ Yahoo! Stock Quotes (see Chapter 25)
➤ Yahoo! Travel (see Chapter 22)
➤ Yahoo! TV (see Chapter 16)
➤ Yahoo! Weather (see Chapter 15)
➤ Yahoo! Yellow Pages (see Chapter 7)

Click the **More** link to access even more Yahoo! services.

Yahoo! Directory

Yahoo! lists more than a million Web sites in the Yahoo! directory. You can access the Yahoo! directory by searching (via the **Search** box at the top of the Yahoo! home page) or by *browsing*. When you browse, you click through all the different categories in the directory—and you start right on the home page. Yahoo! lists 14 main categories on the home page, including

- ➤ Arts & Humanities
- ➤ Business & Economy
- ➤ Computers & Internet
- ➤ Education
- ➤ Entertainment
- ➤ Government
- ➤ Health
- ➤ News & Media
- ➤ Recreation & Sports
- ➤ Reference
- ➤ Regional
- ➤ Science
- ➤ Social Science
- ➤ Society & Culture

More About Browsing

To learn more about browsing the Yahoo! directory, see Chapter 5, "Search the Web with the Yahoo! Directory."

When you click a category link, Yahoo! displays a page that lists all the *subcategories* within the category. When you click a subcategory link, you may see more subcategories (branching out beneath the selected subcategory) or you may see the Web sites listed within that subcategory. The best advice is to keep clicking—narrowing down your browsing—until you find the site you want.

Yahoo! News

The box on the right side of the Yahoo! home page contains three major sections:

- ➤ **In the News**—Today's top headlines.
- ➤ **Marketplace**—Today's top bargains from Yahoo! merchants.
- ➤ **Inside Yahoo!**—Today's newest or most interesting Yahoo! sites.

Yahoo! Around the Country—and Around the World

You're probably used to accessing the standard U.S. Yahoo! site; you probably didn't know that there were 20 other Yahoo!s, all created for specific countries around the world. If you want to go to another country's Yahoo! (many of which are displayed in their native languages), just scroll to the bottom of the Yahoo! home page and click the World Yahoo! you want to visit. (Figure 1.6 shows Yahoo! Sweden.)

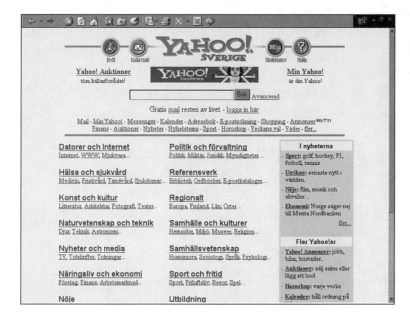

Figure 1.6

It looks just like regular Yahoo!, but that's not English—welcome to Yahoo! Sweden (or Sverige, as the locals call it).

As big as Yahoo! is globally, it's also small enough to target the sites and businesses and events of your local community. Yahoo! includes local Yahoo!s for virtually every community in the U.S.—some of which you can click at the bottom of the Yahoo! home page. (Other Yahoo! Get Local sites can be found at `local.yahoo.com`, or by entering your zip code in the box at the bottom of the Yahoo! home page.)

Other Yahoo!s

There are even *more* Yahoo! sites than those mentioned so far. Several of these other sites are listed at the very bottom of the Yahoo! home page, including

More About Global and Local Yahoo!s

To learn more about the country and community Yahoo! sites, see Chapter 4, "Home and Abroad: Local and Global Yahoo!."

➤ Y! Internet Life (Yahoo!'s joint magazine venture with Ziff-Davis—this link takes you to the *Yahoo! Internet Life* page on the ZDNet site)

➤ Yahoo! Autos (see Chapter 23 for more information)

➤ Yahoo! Bill Pay (see Chapter 25)

➤ Yahoo! Careers (see Chapter 26)

➤ Yahoo! Digital (see Chapter 17)

➤ Yahoo! Entertainment (see Chapter 16)

➤ Yahoo! Finance (see Chapter 25)

➤ Yahoo! Greetings (see Chapter 10)

➤ Yahoo! Health (see Chapter 18)

➤ Yahoo! Local Events (see Chapter 4)

➤ Yahoo! Message Boards (see Chapter 12)

➤ Yahoo! Movies (see Chapter 16)

➤ Yahoo! Music (see Chapter 16)

➤ Yahoo! Net Events (see Chapter 16)

➤ Yahoo! Real Estate (see Chapter 24)

➤ Yahoo! Seniors' Guide (see Chapter 18)

➤ Yahoo! Small Business (see Chapter 27)

➤ Yahoo! Wallet (see Chapter 21)

➤ Yahooligans! (see Chapter 9)

The Yahoo! Fine Print

At the *very* bottom of the Yahoo! home page are links to Yahoo!'s corporate information, including company history and information, privacy policy, terms of service, contributors, and job openings.

Getting Help at Yahoo!

If you're having trouble using any part of Yahoo!—or if you want to learn more about any of Yahoo!'s sites or services—go to Yahoo! Help Central. Unfortunately, there's no link to Help Central from the Yahoo! home page, but you can go there directly at help.yahoo.com.

As you can see in Figure 1.7, Yahoo! Help Central includes links to all the different Help resources for all the sites in the Yahoo! network. Just click a Help topic to read more.

In addition, you can check out Yahoo! How-To, which is a collection of online tutorials for Internet users. Just click the **Help** link at the top of the Yahoo! home page, or go directly to howto.yahoo.com. Another useful page is Yahoo! Resources (howto.yahoo.com/resources/), which includes links to tips and tricks, an index, a glossary, and other Web and HTML guides.

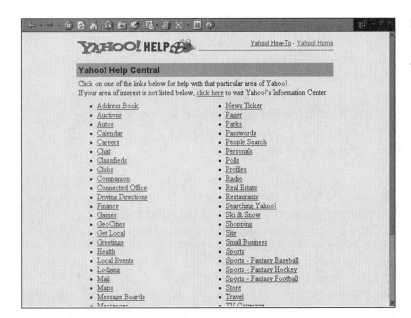

Figure 1.7

Get all the Help you need from Yahoo! Help Central.

Getting Yahoo! in Your Browser

If you're using Internet Explorer 4.0 (or later) or Netscape Navigator 4.0 (or later), you can add a special Yahoo! toolbar—called the Yahoo! Companion—to your Web browser. This toolbar, shown in Figure 1.8, makes Web browsing easier by adding special Yahoo!-specific buttons to your browser.

Go directly to Yahoo!.   Store bookmarks online.   Pull down to go to a specific area on Yahoo!.

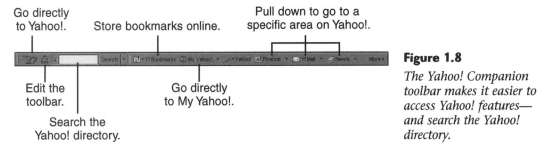

Edit the toolbar.   Go directly to My Yahoo!.   Search the Yahoo! directory.

Figure 1.8

The Yahoo! Companion toolbar makes it easier to access Yahoo! features— and search the Yahoo! directory.

With Yahoo! Companion, you can search the Yahoo! directory directly from you browser, access Yahoo! and Yahoo! sites and services with the click of a button, be alerted when you receive new Yahoo! mail, and store your favorite sites as online bookmarks on the Yahoo! site—accessible from any computer.

To download and install Yahoo! Companion, follow these steps:

1. Click the **Companion** link on the Yahoo! home page, or go directly to companion.yahoo.com.

19

2. When the Yahoo! Companion page appears, click the **Get Yahoo! Companion Now** button.

3. The Companion toolbar is now automatically installed on your browser, and a new browser window is opened.

4. When the Edit Yahoo! Companion page appears, choose which of several pre-configured toolbars you want. (If you click the **Make My Own** link, you can choose which individual buttons are displayed on the toolbar.)

5. Click the **Finished** button when you're done.

After you've installed the Yahoo! Companion, you can edit the toolbar at any time by clicking the **Edit** button and selecting an editing option, such as Add/Edit Buttons or Icons and Colors. For example, if you choose to Add/Edit Buttons, your browser jumps to the Customize Yahoo! Companion page shown in Figure 1.9, where you can select from a variety of different toolbar buttons. If you want to remove the Companion toolbar from your browser, click the **Edit** button and select **Uninstall**.

Figure 1.9

*Click the **Edit** button and select **Add/Edit Buttons** to add extra buttons to the Yahoo! Companion toolbar.*

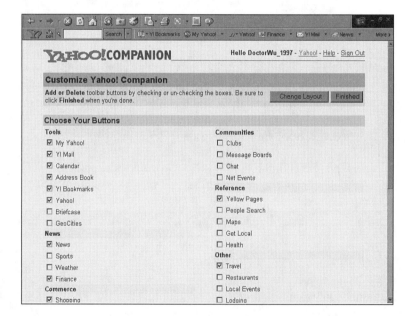

Getting in Touch with Yahoo!

If for whatever reason you ever need to communicate with anyone at Yahoo!, Table 1.1 lists some of the key Yahoo! email addresses or Web-based forms:

Table 1.1 Yahoo! Email and Web Addresses

Purpose	Email Address	Web Page
Advertising	NA	www.yahoo.com/info/advertising/
Changing a listing	NA	add.yahoo.com/fast/change/
Employment	hr@yahoo-inc.com	join.yahoo.com
General feedback	NA	www.yahoo.com/info/support/ contacts/experience.html
Investor relations	investor_relations @yahoo-inc.com	www.yahoo.com/info/investor/
Submit a bug report	NA	www.yahoo.com/info/support/ contacts/bugs.html
Suggestions	NA	www.yahoo.com/info/support/ contacts/experience.html

If you're in the neighborhood, you can drop into the Yahoo! offices at 3420 Central Expressway, Santa Clara, CA, 95051. If so, you might want to call (408) 731-3300 or fax (408) 731-3301 first.

The Least You Need to Know

➤ Yahoo!, founded in 1995, has become the most popular network of sites on the Web.

➤ You access the Yahoo! home page at www.yahoo.com.

➤ Most Yahoo! sites and services can be accessed from the Yahoo! home page.

➤ Yahoo! Companion (companion.yahoo.com) is a special toolbar you add to your Web browser that makes it easier to jump directly to Yahoo! sites and services.

➤ The best place for help about Yahoo! is Yahoo! Help Central, located at help.yahoo.com.

HIYA LIL' BUDDY...

Chapter 2

Create Your Own Personal Yahoo! with My Yahoo!

In This Chapter

➤ Learn how to register for a Yahoo! ID and password

➤ Find out how to create your own personalized My Yahoo! page

➤ Discover how to customize your My Yahoo! content, layout, and colors

Yahoo! is a great site—but it's the *same* site for all 100+ million users. In this age of "mass customization," wouldn't you rather have a version of Yahoo! that is custom-tailored to your own personal tastes?

If you want your own personal Yahoo!, take heart—and check out *My Yahoo!*, where you can pick and choose what you see and what you *don't* see every time you log on!

Getting to My Yahoo!

You can get to My Yahoo! by clicking the **Personalize** link on the Yahoo! home page, or by going directly to my.yahoo.com. The first time you visit My Yahoo! you must register for the service and customize your page. After that, each time you go to My Yahoo! you'll see *your* Yahoo!, exactly as you configured it!

Registering for My Yahoo!—and Other Yahoo! Services

The first time you visit my.yahoo.com, you'll see either a registration page or a generic My Yahoo! page—both of which ask you to either sign in or register.

If you have a Yahoo! ID and password, all you have to do is enter them into the **Yahoo! ID** and **Yahoo! Password** boxes on the My Yahoo! page, and then click the **Sign In** button. You are taken to your personal version of My Yahoo!, ready for customizing.

Sign In Once, and Never Check Out

If you want My Yahoo! to remember your ID and password on future visits, check the **Remember My ID & Password** option on the sign-in page. The next time you go to my.yahoo.com, Yahoo! remembers who you are (thanks to a "cookie" on your hard disk that tracks your site visits) and automatically displays your version of the My Yahoo! page, no sign-in required. (Many Web sites use cookies —small files on your hard disk—to "remember" registered users and streamline signing in on future visits.)

If you don't yet have a Yahoo! ID and password, you need to register. (Don't worry— registration is free!) Just follow these steps:

1. From the Welcome to My Yahoo! page, click the **Sign Me Up** link.
2. When you see the Sign up Now form, shown in Figure 2.1, fill in all the blanks. (You'll need to think up an ID name and password, and supply your real email address, zip code, and other relevant information.)

One ID, Many Uses

Your Yahoo! ID works with all Yahoo! sites and services that require registration, including My Yahoo!, Yahoo! Companion, Yahoo! Mail, Yahoo! Auctions, Yahoo! Messenger, Yahoo! Briefcase, Yahoo! Finance, and Yahoo! Calendar. After you register once, you don't have to register again—just use the same ID and password when you want to access these other sites/services.

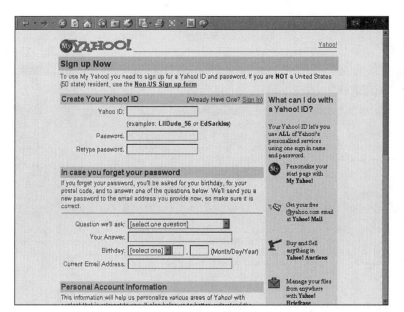

Figure 2.1

Sign up for a Yahoo! ID and password, which you can also use with Yahoo! Mail, Yahoo! Auctions, and other Yahoo! sites and services.

3. Click the **Submit This Form** button.

4. When the Welcome to Yahoo! page appears, you can choose to enter additional information useful at other Yahoo! sites, or to proceed to My Yahoo!. Click the **Continue to My Yahoo!** link to proceed.

Making My Yahoo! *Your* Yahoo!

After you've registered or signed on, you see the generic My Yahoo! page shown in Figure 2.2. This is an okay page—and it gives you an idea of what you can do with My Yahoo!—but the whole point of using My Yahoo! is to create a *customized* page. Read on to learn how to customize your My Yahoo! page.

The Fine Print

If you're concerned about what Yahoo! might do with the information you provide when you sign up, you can check out their posted policy at `http://docs.yahoo.com/info/privacy/`.

Customizing What You See on the My Yahoo! Page

My Yahoo! can display a variety of different types of content, each in its own *module*. It's up to you to choose which content modules you want to display.

Add another page
to your My Yahoo!.

Choose your colors
and personal greeting.

Figure 2.2

*The generic My Yahoo!
page is ready for your
personal touch.*

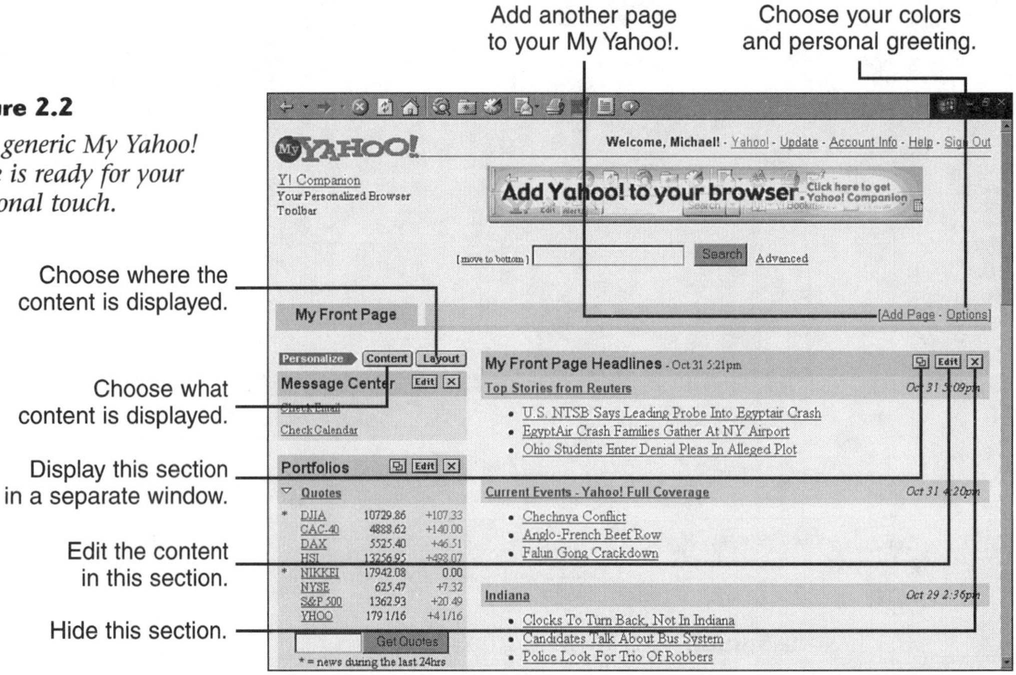

Choose where the
content is displayed.

Choose what
content is displayed.

Display this section
in a separate window.

Edit the content
in this section.

Hide this section.

Welcome, Michael! · Yahoo! · Update · Account Info · Help · Sign Out

YI Companion
Your Personalized Browser
Toolbar

Add Yahoo! to your browser. Click here to get Yahoo! Companion

[move to bottom]   Search Advanced

[Add Page · Options]

My Front Page

Personalize Content Layout

Message Center Edit X
Check Email
Check Calendar

Portfolios Edit X
▽ **Quotes**
      DJIA   10729.86   +107.33
  *   CAC-40   4888.62   +140.00
      DAX   5525.40   +46.51
      HSI   13256.95   +498.07
  *   NIKKEI   17942.08   0.00
      NYSE   625.47   +7.32
      S&P 500   1362.93   +20.49
      YHOO   179 1/16   +4 1/16
                  Get Quotes
  * = news during the last 24hrs

My Front Page Headlines - Oct 31 5:21pm Edit X

Top Stories from Reuters   Oct 31 5:09pm

 • U.S. NTSB Says Leading Probe Into Egyptair Crash
 • EgyptAir Crash Families Gather At NY Airport
 • Ohio Students Enter Denial Pleas In Alleged Plot

Current Events - Yahoo! Full Coverage   Oct 31 4:20pm

 • Chechnya Conflict
 • Anglo-French Beef Row
 • Falun Gong Crackdown

Indiana   Oct 29 2:36pm

 • Clocks To Turn Back, Not In Indiana
 • Candidates Talk About Bus System
 • Police Look For Trio Of Robbers

To select which modules are displayed on your My Yahoo! page, follow these steps:

1. From the My Yahoo! page, click the **Content** button.

2. When the Personalize Page Content page appears (see Figure 2.3), put a check mark next to each module you want to display. *Uncheck* those topics you *don't* want to display. You can choose to display up to 20 different modules.

3. If you want to call your page something other than My Front Page, enter the new name in the **Page Name** box.

4. Click the **Finished** button.

Yahoo! Tip

L for Left, R for Right

My Yahoo! uses a two-column layout, with the left column narrower than the right. Different content modules are different sizes, and thus are assigned to either left or right columns. A module listed on the Personalize Page Content page with an (L) has to go to the left; a module listed with an (R) has to go to the right column.

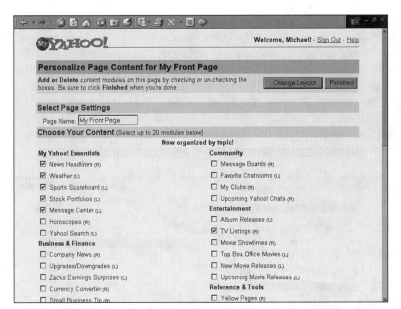

Figure 2.3

Check which content modules you want to display from the Personalize Page Content page.

My Yahoo! now displays your new page, containing all the modules you selected. If you want to change the modules displayed, click the **Content** button again and refine your selection. (You can also click the X button on any module to remove it from your page.) Otherwise, proceed to customize the content *within* each module.

Customizing Content—Module by Module

Most modules let you customize the content that is displayed within the category module. For example, you can create your own list of stocks to display in the Portfolios module and choose what types of news are displayed in the My Front Page Headlines module.

Although the specific customization is different for each module, the general steps are the same:

1. Click the **Edit** button on the module you want to customize.

2. When the next page appears, read the instructions carefully, and then make the appropriate choices. This may include selecting or deselecting topics, choosing how many headlines are displayed, entering stock tickers for your portfolio, and so on.

3. Click the **Finished** button to register your choices.

One Is Never Enough

Can't fit everything you want onto a single page? Then create *additional* My Yahoo! pages by clicking the **Add Page** link. Additional pages appear as tabs on top of your main My Yahoo! page; click a tab to see that page.

Let's look at a few examples. Go to the My Front Page Headlines section and click the **Edit** button. This displays the Choose Your Headlines page, which lists all the available sections—Headline News & Politics, Business & Industry, Community, Entertainment, and so on. You have to configure each of these sections separately, so click the **Headline News & Politics** link to begin. When the Edit Your Headlines page appears, as shown in Figure 2.4, you see all the different news sources that Yahoo! has made available. Check those sources you want to display, and uncheck those you don't want to read. Click **Finished** to return to the Choose Your Headlines page, and perform the same operation on all the other news sections.

Figure 2.4

Choose from a variety of news sources on the Edit Your Headlines page.

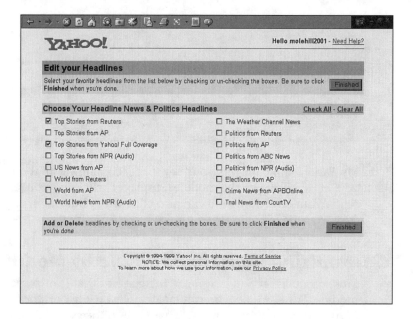

As another example, click the **Edit** button on the Portfolios module. When the Edit Portfolios page appears, you can choose to edit the current portfolio, or (by clicking the **Create a New Portfolio** button) add another portfolio to your My Yahoo! display. To add stocks to the current portfolio, click the **Edit** button; when the Edit Your Portfolio page (shown in Figure 2.5) appears, enter the ticker symbols for your stocks in the **Symbols** box. (If you don't know a symbol, click the **Look Up Symbol** link.) If you want My Yahoo! to track the performance of your portfolio, scroll down to the bottom of the page and check the appropriate options in the **Advanced Features** section; click the **Enter More Info** button to enter the number. of shares you own, original purchase price, and other data. When you click all the **Finished** buttons to return to your My Yahoo! page, your personalized portfolio(s) are displayed as entered.

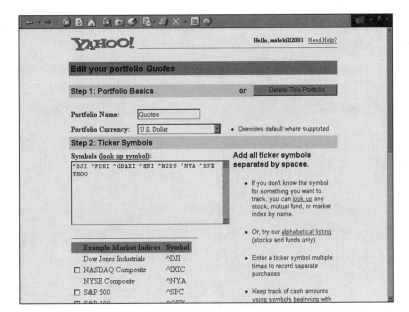

Figure 2.5
Enter the ticker symbols for your stocks on the Edit Your Portfolio page.

Personalizing Your Page Layout

After you've decided on all your content, you need to arrange that content on your page. You can change *where* My Yahoo! displays each module (within each module's left- and right-column parameters) by following these steps:

1. From the My Yahoo! page, click the **Layout** button.
2. When the Personalize Page Layout page appears (shown in Figure 2.6), select a module from either the **Left Side** or **Right Side** lists, and then click the up- or down-arrow buttons to move the module up or down on your page.
3. Click **Finished** to see your new layout..

Group Your Investments

My Yahoo! lets you display multiple portfolios. This lets you create different groupings of investments—by investment account, perhaps, or by investment type—and display the groupings as different portfolios.

Personalizing Your Page Colors—and Other Options

If you don't like the default colors of the My Yahoo! page, you can choose from a variety of other color schemes. Just follow these steps:

1. From the My Yahoo! page, click the **Options** link.

Figure 2.6

Move your modules up and down the page with the up and down arrow buttons.

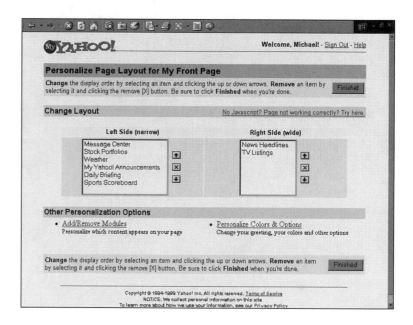

2. When the Personalize My Yahoo! Options page appears (shown in Figure 2.7), choose from one of the seven predefined color schemes, or click **Customize** to display the Personalize Custom Colors page and choose your own colors for each page element.

Figure 2.7

Choose your colors and change your greeting on the Personalize My Yahoo! Options page.

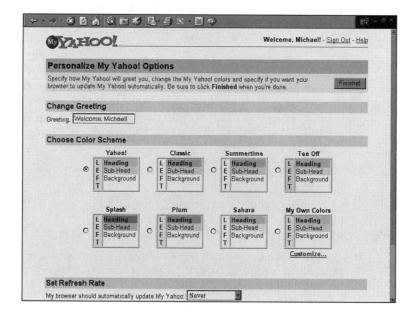

3. If you want to see a greeting other than "Welcome" when you load your My Yahoo! page, enter a new greeting in the **Change Greeting** box.

4. To determine how often My Yahoo! is refreshed, pull down the **Set Refresh Rate** list and choose a time period. (If you're online for long periods of time and want to be updated with current stock prices, you might want to choose the **Every 15 Minutes** option.)

5. Click **Finished** when done.

Your My Yahoo! is now complete—and ready to be changed again whenever you feel like it!

Left and Right Must Remain Seperate

Modules listed in the Left Side list cannot be moved to the Right Side list, and vice versa.

Display a Module in a Separate Window

Some modules—such as the Portfolio and Headlines modules—include a Detach button, which is not found on other modules. When you click the **Detach** button, the contents of that module are displayed in a separate window on your desktop. This is a great way to display constantly updated information (such as stock prices) while freeing up your Web browser for other surfing.

The Least You Need to Know

➤ Before you access any Yahoo! service, you need to register for an ID and password.

➤ My Yahoo! (my.yahoo.com) is a personalized page that displays news headlines, stock quotes, weather forecasts, sports scores, and other information of your choosing.

➤ You can customize My Yahoo! content, layout, and colors—and detach certain modules to display information outside your Web browser.

31

Chapter 3

Surf Safer with Yahoo! Family Accounts

In This Chapter

➤ Find out how to restrict your children's access to inappropriate content and services on the Yahoo! site

➤ Learn how to create a Yahoo! Family Account and child IDs for each of your children

➤ Discover 10 tips for safer surfing for all members of your family

---

The Internet contains an almost limitless supply of information; some of it is good, and some of it is potentially bad. Protecting your children from the bad stuff is a difficult but important task for any parent—it's made somewhat easier by Yahoo!'s Family Accounts.

In a Family Way: Understanding Yahoo! Family Accounts

A Yahoo! Family Account enables you to create separate Yahoo! IDs for each of your children and then control what information your children give to Yahoo!—and what Yahoo! features they can and can't access.

After you've established a Yahoo! Family Account, you can

➤ Create separate Yahoo! IDs for any child in your family.

➤ Add already existing IDs (if your child already has a Yahoo! ID) to your new Family Account.

➤ Modify your child's password and account information.

➤ Modify your child's email blocklists, friend "buddy" lists, and instant message ignore lists—in effect, controlling who they communicate with online.

➤ Sign in to Yahoo! *as your child* to monitor and modify his or her account.

There are two classes of children's IDs available with Yahoo! Family Accounts: Under 13 and 13 to 18. Each age class has its own unique restrictions as part of a Family Account; Table 3.1 details these restrictions.

Table 3.1   Family Account Restrictions

Restricted Features	Under 13	13–18
Add address or phone number to account information	X	
Create a Public Profile	X	
Found their own Yahoo! Club	X	
Participate in Auctions	X	X
Participate in Sweepstakes or Promotions	X	
Post a listing on People Search	X	
Post a Personals Ad	X	
Receive special offers from Yahoo!	X	
See listings for or participate in Adult Auctions Areas	X	X
See listings for or participate in Adult Chat	X	X
See listings for or participate in Adult Clubs	X	X
See listings for or participate in Adult Shopping Areas	X	X

In short, Under 13 IDs are prohibited from entering any personal information online, participating in auctions or personals, or accessing any adult areas. The 13–18 IDs are only prohibited from participating in auctions and accessing adult areas—they *can* leave personal information online.

In addition, the primary ID on a Family Account (meaning *you!*) can log into Yahoo! under any of the other IDs. This enables you to monitor and make changes to your child's account using all of Yahoo!'s various tools—such as blocklists, buddy lists, and so on.

Fill Out the Forms: Setting Up Your Family Account and IDs

Creating a Family account is similar to creating a regular Yahoo! account. The big difference is that—to establish the age of the primary account member—you have to enter a credit card number. (The assumption is that no one under 18 has a credit card.) Yahoo! will not make charges to your card; it only uses the card for age ID purposes.

Family Accounts: Protection on Yahoo! Only

Establishing a child's ID under a Family Account only affects your child's use of the Yahoo! family of sites. It does *not* prohibit them from accessing any adult sites or material outside of Yahoo! on the rest of the Internet. In fact, a child ID does not even protect your child from seeing links to adult sites in the Yahoo! directory—Yahoo! provides no filtering apparatus for its own directory listings!

Create Your Account

If you haven't yet created a Yahoo! account, go to family.yahoo.com. You should see the Welcome to Yahoo! Family Accounts page; click the **Sign Me Up** link and complete the steps listed back in Chapter 2, "Create Your Own Personal Yahoo! with My Yahoo!" The only difference is when you create a new account from the Yahoo! Family Accounts site, you'll need to provide your credit card information. (This information is not asked for when you register from any other Yahoo! services page.)

If you already have a Yahoo! account, enter your Yahoo! ID and Password; Yahoo! deposits you at the main Yahoo! Family Accounts page, shown in Figure 3.1.

No Card, No Account

If you don't have a credit card or prefer not to enter your credit card number, you can't establish a Yahoo! Family Account. You can, however, still create a normal Yahoo! account.

Add a Child ID

Now that you've created an account, you have to add a new child ID for each of your children. Follow these steps:

1. From the Yahoo! Family Accounts page (family.yahoo.com), click the **Add Child Account** button.

2. If you haven't yet registered your credit card number, you'll see the Instant Account Verification page. Click the **Secure Account Verification** button, enter your credit card information, and then click **Finished**.

3. When the Add Child Account page appears, click the **Finish Adding Your Child's Account** link.

4. When the Review Child's Account Information page appears, enter the appropriate information, and then click the **Add Child Account** button.

Figure 3.1

Create a Yahoo! Family Account to restrict and monitor your children's access to certain Yahoo! features.

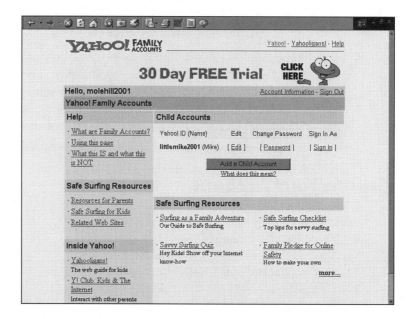

You are returned to the Yahoo! Family Accounts home page.

Yahoo! Tip

Use an Existing Account

If your child already has an existing Yahoo! ID, you can add that ID to your account from the Add Child Account page. Just enter your child's ID and password, and then click the **Add Child** button.

Signing In—As Your Child

After your child's ID is added to your Family Account, you can

➤ Sign in as your child to edit their buddy list, chat settings, email blocklist, and so on.

➤ Edit your child's account information.

➤ Edit your child's public profile or People Search listing (if they are aged 13–18; younger children aren't allowed to create profiles or listings).

➤ Change your child's password (although they can always change it back!).

To sign in as your child and edit his or her account settings, follow these steps:

1. From the Yahoo! Family Accounts home page, click the **Sign In** link next to your child's name.
2. When the Signed In As Child page appears (shown in Figure 3.2), click the service or setting link you want to monitor or edit.
3. Follow the instructions on the linked page, and then return to the Signed In As Child page to monitor/edit additional services and settings.
4. When you're done with your child's account, click the **Sign In as Yourself** link to enter Yahoo! under your own ID.

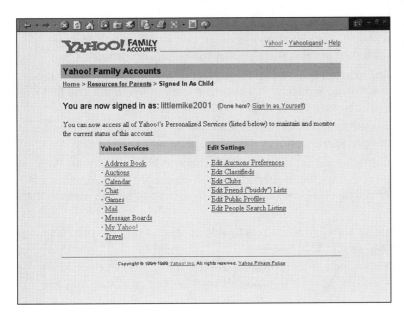

Figure 3.2

Sign in as your child to monitor the use of Yahoo! services and edit important settings.

Change Their Password

For protective purposes—or just to lock your kids out of their accounts—Yahoo! lets you change your children's passwords. To change a password, go to the Yahoo! Family Accounts page and click the **Password** link. When the Change Password page appears, enter a new password in the **Choose New Password** box, confirm the password, and then click the **Finished** button. Note, however, that your child will receive an email confirming the password change—and that your child will be able to change his/her password on their own the next time they log in.

Ten Tips to Make the Internet Safer for Children

Yahoo! Family Accounts only protect your children while they're on the Yahoo! network of sites—and even then, it doesn't protect them from any adult-oriented listings in the Yahoo! directory. The rest of the Internet is still fair game, and filled with inappropriate content.

The best way to help your children avoid the bad stuff on the Internet is to surf the Web with them. Here are 10 tips you can use to make your family's surfing and searching a little safer:

1. Be sure your children know never to give out any identifying information (home address, school name, telephone number, and so on—nothing more specific than city or state) or to send their photos to other users online.

2. Never allow a child to arrange a face-to-face meeting with another user without parental permission and supervision. If a meeting is arranged, make the first one in a public place, and be sure to accompany your child.

3. Set reasonable rules and guidelines for Internet use by your children; consider limiting the number of minutes/hours they can spend online each day.

4. Monitor your children's Internet activities. Ask them to keep a log of all Web sites they visit; oversee any chat sessions they participate in; even consider sharing an email account (especially with younger children) so you can oversee their messages.

5. Make Internet surfing a family activity. Set aside an hour a day for you to surf the Internet *together*, as a family.

6. Make a pact with your kids—you'll provide the Internet access in return for them adhering to certain safe-surfing rules. If they break a rule, you pull the access.

7. Consider giving each of your children an online pseudonym so they don't have to use their real names online.

8. Tell your children never to respond to messages that are suggestive, obscene, belligerent, threatening, or make them feel uncomfortable—and encourage your children to tell you if they receive any such messages.

9. Let your children know that people online might not be who they seem; just because someone says they're a 10-year-old girl doesn't necessarily mean that they're really 10 years old, or a girl.

10. Encourage the use of family-friendly directories and filtered search sites. One of the better directories for children aged 7–12 is Yahooligans!, discussed in Chapter 9, "Search for Kids' Stuff with Yahooligans!."

The bottom line is that you have to take responsibility for your children's online activities. Provide the guidance they need to make the Internet a fun and educational place to visit.

The Least You Need to Know

➤ Yahoo! Family Accounts enable you to create separate IDs for each of your children.

➤ Child IDs for children under 13 prohibit them from entering any personal information on Yahoo!, participating in auctions or personal ads, or accessing adult content.

➤ Child IDs for children 13–18 prohibit them from participating in auctions or accessing adult content—they *can* enter personal information online.

➤ Yahoo! Family Accounts only protect your children while they're on the Yahoo! network of sites—the rest of the Internet is unrestricted by Yahoo!.

➤ The only real protection for your children on the Internet is *you*—and their own common sense!

Chapter 4

Home and Abroad: Local and Global Yahoo!

In This Chapter

➤ Discover Yahoo!'s country-specific sites

➤ Find out how to access local Yahoo! sites

➤ Learn how to locate Yahoo! event listings for your town

You're familiar with the main U.S. Yahoo! site—but did you know that Yahoo! offers regionalized sites for more than twenty different countries, as well as local sites for thousands of communities throughout the United States?

World Yahoo!

If you're a U.S. resident, the main Yahoo! site (www.yahoo.com) is a great site. But if you live outside the U.S., you could get frustrated at the American-centric site listings—and if you don't speak English, you might not be able to use the site at all!

For that reason, Yahoo! has been busy creating a network of World Yahoo!s, complete with country-specific site listings and pages created in the native language. Figure 4.1 shows one of these sites, Yahoo! Mexico.

Figure 4.1

Yahoo! Mexico—the perfect site for Hispanic users!

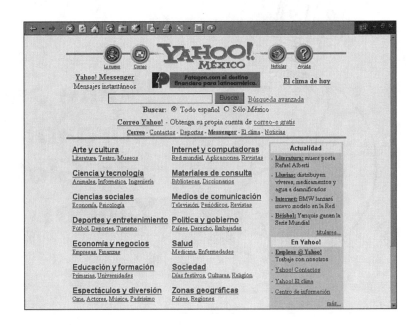

All the World Yahoo!s are listed at the bottom of the U.S. Yahoo! home page, or you can go directly to the sites using the addresses listed in Table 4.1.

Table 4.1   World Yahoo!s

World Yahoo!	Web Address
Asia	asia.yahoo.com
Australia and New Zealand	www.yahoo.com.au
Brazil	br.yahoo.com
Canada	ca.yahoo.com
China	cn.yahoo.com
Chinese	chinese.yahoo.com
Denmark	www.yahoo.dk
France	www.yahoo.fr
Germany	www.yahoo.de
Hong Kong	hk.yahoo.com
Italy	www.yahoo.it
Japan	www.yahoo.co.jp
Korea	www.yahoo.co.kr
Mexico	mx.yahoo.com
Norway	www.yahoo.no
Singapore	sg.yahoo.com

World Yahoo!	Web Address
Spain	www.yahoo.es
Spanish	espanol.yahoo.com
Sweden	www.yahoo.se
Taiwan	tw.yahoo.com
U.K. and Ireland	www.yahoo.co.uk

Get the Language Plug In

Some foreign languages (such as Chinese and Japanese) use a special character set. To properly view these World Yahoo!s, you must install the character set on your computer before you access the site. If you don't have the proper character set installed, the Yahoo! site displays a page informing you, and provides instructions on how to download and install the proper characters. (If you don't see this page, check with your Web browser's manufacturer on how to install the foreign-language characters in your browser.)

Yahoo! Get Local

Yahoo! isn't just a big national site—it's also a network of thousands of local sites customized to the events and listings of local communities across the United States. You can access any local site by entering a zip code in the **Enter Zip Code** box at the bottom of the Yahoo! home page, or by going directly to the Yahoo! Get Local page (local.yahoo.com) shown in Figure 4.2. From the Yahoo! Get Local page you can browse by state, search by city name, or go directly to a zip code-specific site.

Each local site (such as the one shown in Figure 4.3) includes a variety of region-specific features, including

➤ Links to Yahoo! sites for nearby cities
➤ Local lottery results
➤ Local maps and driving directions
➤ Local news headlines
➤ Local sports scores
➤ Local weather forecasts
➤ Local Web Directory (a listing of local Web sites, by category)

43

Figure 4.2

Go to the Yahoo! Get Local page to browse through or search for any local community site.

Search by city.

Go directly to a zip code-specific site.

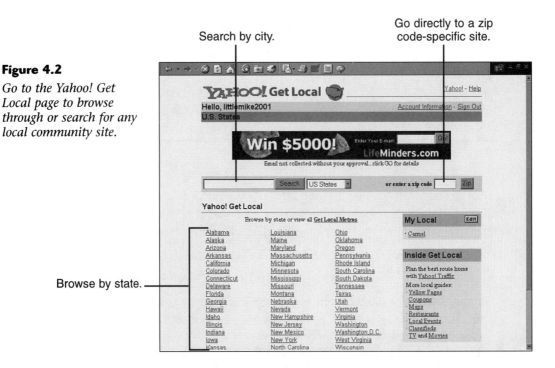

Browse by state.

Figure 4.3

Go to your local site to access area headlines, weather, sports scores, and Web sites.

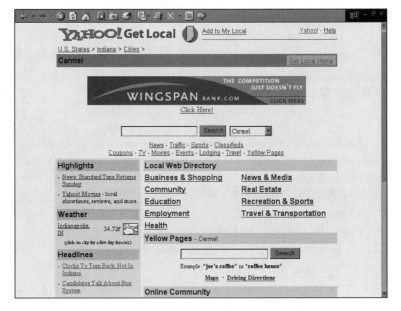

Go Directly to Your Community Site with My Local

If you want to "lock in" your area's local Yahoo! site, Yahoo! lets you create a My Local page, which is linked to both your My Yahoo! page and the Yahoo! Get Local page. To add pages to your My Local list, go to any local community page and click the **Add to My Local** link at the top of the page. Yahoo! now displays the Edit Locations page; verify the location you just visited, and then click the **Add Location** button. Click **Finish** when done.

Find Out What's Happening with Yahoo! Local Events

In addition to the Yahoo! Get Local sites, Yahoo! also provides a comprehensive guide to local events all across the United States. As you can see in Figure 4.4, Yahoo! Local Events (localevents.yahoo.com) provides listings for all kinds of events, from concerts to sporting events to trade shows.

Figure 4.4

Look for hometown happenings on the Yahoo! Local Events page.

You can browse Yahoo! Local Events by type of event (category) or by location (either state or metro area). You can even search for local events by entering a query into the **Search** box and clicking the **Find Events** button.

For some of the listings in Yahoo! Local Events you can even purchase tickets online via Ticketmaster. If you see a Ticketmaster button next to an event, just click the button to purchase your tickets.

These Aren't Really Yahoo!'s Listings...

The listings in Yahoo! Local Events are compiled from outside sources, including Ticketmaster, Culture-Finder, Stagebill, and Trade Show Central. Yahoo! claims no responsibility for the accuracy of the listings.

Even More Local Listings

Yahoo! contains several other areas listing local news and information. These include

➤ **Lottery results**—Go to `features.yahoo.com/lottery/` and select a state.

➤ **Maps**—Go to `maps.yahoo.com` and enter a city, state, or zip code.

➤ **Movie show times**—Go to `movies.yahoo.com` and enter your location.

➤ **News headlines**—Go to `dailynews.yahoo.com/h/lo/` and select an area.

➤ **Restaurant listings**—Go to `restaurants.yahoo.com` and select a metropolitan area.

➤ **Traffic reports**—Go to `traffic.yahoo.com` and select a metropolitan area.

➤ **TV listings**—Go to `tv.yahoo.com` and enter your zip code.

➤ **Weather forecasts**—Go to `weather.yahoo.com` and enter a city or zip code.

The Least You Need to Know

➤ Yahoo! offers country-specific World Yahoo! sites for more than 20 different countries.

➤ Yahoo! Get Local (`local.yahoo.com`) offers locally focused Web sites for thousands of countries across the United States.

➤ Yahoo! Local Events (`localevents.yahoo.com`) offers local listings for concerts, trade shows, and other events.

Part 2

Find Anything and Anyone:
Yahoo! Search

More people use Yahoo! to search the Internet than for any other purpose. Turn the page to learn secrets from the pros to help you perform more effective—and efficient—searches!

HELLOOOOOO...?

Chapter 5

Search the Web with the Yahoo! Directory

In This Chapter

➤ Learn how to browse through the hierarchy of categories in Yahoo!'s Web directory

➤ Find out how to effectively search the Yahoo! Web directory

➤ Discover the secrets of successful searchers

➤ Learn how to submit your own site to the Yahoo! directory

With more than 100 million users per month, Yahoo! is the most popular of all the search sites on the Web. Chances are you use Yahoo! to search for sites on the Web—and are probably dissatisfied with both the searching process and the results you generated. Would you like to become a better Yahoo! searcher? Then read this chapter—and improve your search results *immediately!*

The Difference Between Search Engines and Directories—and Why You Should Care

You may look at sites like Yahoo! and Excite and AltaVista as serving similar functions, which they do. The reality, however, is that there are some very real differences in *how* they go about organizing the Web.

Web Directories Pick 'Em by Hand

One approach to organizing the Web is to physically look at each Web page and stick each one into a hand-picked category. After you collect enough Web pages, you have something called a *directory*. A directory doesn't search the Web—in fact, it only catalogs a small part of the Web. But a directory is organized and easy to use, and lots and lots of people use Web directories every day.

In terms of directories, Yahoo! is both the oldest and the largest. The Yahoo! Web directory catalogs more than 1 million individual Web sites in a well-organized fashion.

Search Engines Pick 'Em with Robots

It's important to note that a directory is *not* a search engine. A *search engine* is not powered by human hands; instead, it uses a special type of software program (called a *spider* or *crawler*) to roam the Web automatically, feeding what it finds back to a massive bank of computers. These computers hold *indexes* of the Web—in some cases entire Web pages are indexed, in other cases only the titles and important words on a page are indexed. (Different search engines operate differently, you see.)

In any case, as the spiders and crawlers operate like little robot Web surfers, the computers back at home base create a huge index (or database) of what the robots find. Some search engines' indexes contain up to 150 million entries—which means, of course, that even the best search engine still leaves more than half the Web untouched and unavailable to searchers.

The Biggest Search Engines

If you want to venture outside the comfort of the Yahoo! directory, the biggest search engines on the Internet are Northern Light (www.northernlight.com), AltaVista (www.altavista.com), and HotBot (www.hotbot.com).

How Do You Pick 'Em?

So, which is better, a directory or a search engine? It all depends on what you want:

➤ If you want the *most* results, use a search engine.

➤ If you want the most *current* results, use a search engine.

➤ If you want *hand-picked* results, use a directory.

➤ If you want the *best-organized* results, use a directory.

Why More People Pick 'Em with Yahoo!

Although the largest search engines index more than 150 million Web pages, the Yahoo! directory only holds about a million pages. So if you want *quantity* in your search results, you should go elsewhere. However, if you stick with Yahoo!, you'll generate a higher *quality* of results—fewer "bad" and duplicative pages are present on Yahoo! than on any other search site.

In addition, Yahoo! offers what is arguably the easiest-to-use search site on the Web. What makes Yahoo! so easy to use? First, unlike the indexes at the big search engine sites, the Web sites listed in the Yahoo! directory aren't automatically grabbed off the Web by spider software, they're added by hand. Second, the same human beings who add the sites to the directory also arrange them in a logical series of topics and subtopics.

The bottom line is that Yahoo!'s human dimension makes it easy to use and guarantees high quality results.

How Yahoo! Picks 'Em

Did you ever wonder how a particular page ended up at the top of the search results list? Yahoo! uses three criteria to rank its results:

➤ **Keywords**—If you've entered multiple keywords, those Web pages that match more of your keywords rank higher than those pages that match fewer keywords.

➤ **Inclusion in title**—If your keywords are included in the Web page's title, that page is ranked higher than one in which your keywords are found only in the Body or URL of the page.

➤ **Category**—Remember that Yahoo! is a directory composed of multiple categories and subcategories arranged in hierarchies. Those categories that are higher up in the Yahoo! tree hierarchy are ranked higher than those lower in the hierarchy.

Yahoo! does a fairly good job of listing the best sites first. In fact, if you're fed up with getting hundreds or thousands of irrelevant results from other search engines, Yahoo!'s shorter but better qualified lists of matches can be a breath of fresh air!

Finding Web Pages with Yahoo!—The Easy Ways

There are two ways to find things on Yahoo!: *browsing* and *searching*. Let's look a little at each.

Browsing Yahoo! Categories

The first way to find things on Yahoo! is to navigate through the topic classifications on the Yahoo! home page, shown in Figure 5.1. You do this by clicking a category on the Yahoo! home page, which displays a listing of subcategories within the main category. Then you click a subcategory to display subcategories of that subcategory, and so on, until you get to actual Web page links. (In other words, you browse from the general to the specific.)

Figure 5.1

Click a category to browse through the Yahoo! directory.

Yahoo! directory categories

@Yahoo!

You'll notice that some categories end with the "@" sign, such as Dinosaurs@. This means that the particular category is listed in more than one location within the Yahoo! directory.

As an example, suppose you're looking for information on crocodiles. You start by clicking the **Science** link on Yahoo!'s home page. When the Science listings appear, you look at all the subtopics available (from Acoustics to Web Directories) and decide to click **Animals, Insects, and Pets**. After deciding that crocs are neither insects nor pets, you need to choose yet another subtopic from the next page displayed (that in this case, runs the gamut from Animal Behavior to Xenotransplantation, which has to do with the use of live animal cells in human patients). If you know your species, you know that crocodiles are reptiles, so you click **Reptiles and Amphibians**. When the next page appears, you click **Reptiles**, and when the next page appears, you click **Crocodiles and Alligators**. Finally, you see the Crocodiles and Alligators page (shown in Figure 5.2), which has about a dozen links to sites that have something to do with crocs.

This searching by browsing is certainly a no-brainer way to navigate the Yahoo! directory, but it's time-consuming, and, if you're like me, you often don't know what things go in which categories. I much prefer the second way of finding things on Yahoo!—by searching.

Keep Your Place

As you navigate through the various subtopics in the Yahoo! directory, it's easy to forget just where you are. To help you remember where you are and where you've been, a simple navigation line is shown at the top of every Yahoo! category page. For example, the Crocodiles and Alligators page is at the end of the following category tree: Home>Science>Biology>Zoology>Animals, Insects, and Pets>Reptiles and Amphibians>Reptiles>Crocodiles and Alligators. Note that this category tree includes two branches that you didn't visit: Biology and Zoology. Clicking links in a Yahoo! listing sometimes jumps you to subcategories not in a direct path from where you currently are. However, the nice thing about Yahoo!'s navigation tree is that you can click any subtopic within the tree and jump there directly. In our current example, clicking **Reptiles and Amphibians** takes you directly to the Reptiles and Amphibians page you visited earlier, and clicking **Home** takes you back to the Yahoo! home page.

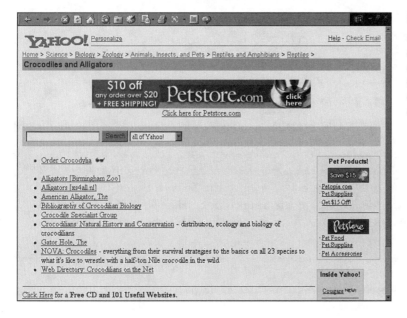

Figure 5.2

Click through enough categories and subcategories and you'll generate a list of matching Web sites—click any link to jump directly to that site.

This searching by browsing is certainly a no-brainer way to navigate the Yahoo! directory, but it's time-consuming, and, if you're like me, you often don't know what things go in which categories. I much prefer the second way of finding things on Yahoo!—by searching.

Simple Searches Simplified

Even though Yahoo! is a directory—not a search engine—Yahoo! still employs a search engine that enables you to locate subjects in its directory. Try to keep that clear—you can't search the Web from Yahoo!, but you *can* search Yahoo! itself!

I find searching Yahoo! preferable to browsing Yahoo!; even though the Yahoo! directory only holds a million pages, that's still too many pages to browse through expediently. So if you use Yahoo! a lot, you should learn how to search the directory.

The Yahoo! Search box, shown in Figure 5.3, is at the top of Yahoo!'s main page. Searching Yahoo! is as simple as entering your keyword or words and then clicking the **Search** button.

Figure 5.3

Search the Yahoo! directory from the Search box at the top of the Yahoo! home page.

Search Within a Browse

You can actually search while you're browsing—which is a great way to find specific information within some of the larger, less manageable categories. After you've browsed to a category, type a query into the **Search** box at the top of the page, pull down the list next to the **Search** box, select **Just This Category**, and then click the **Search** button. Yahoo! searches within the current category for the keywords you entered.

When you initiate a search, Yahoo! returns three types of results (shown in Figure 5.4)—in the following order:

➤ **Yahoo! Category Matches**—This first cut of the data lists those Yahoo! categories that match your search parameters (such as the Home>Science>Biology> Zoology>Animals, Insects, and Pets>Reptiles and Amphibians>Reptiles> Crocodiles and Alligators categories mentioned earlier). Click any category match to display Yahoo!'s complete site listings for that category. This is typically a short list of categories; if your search doesn't directly match any Yahoo! categories, nothing is listed here.

➤ **Yahoo! Site Matches**—The second type of result lists sites in the Yahoo! directory that match your search parameters. The results do not list individual pages within a site—only the main page of the site itself. Yahoo! displays these results grouped within large Yahoo! categories. Typically this list is larger than the category matches.

➤ **Web Pages**—This final type of result goes *outside* of the Yahoo! directory (using the Inktomi search engine, which also is used by HotBot and several other search sites) to list individual Web pages that meet your search criteria. Note that these Web page listings are not available when you're browsing through Yahoo!'s category lists,.

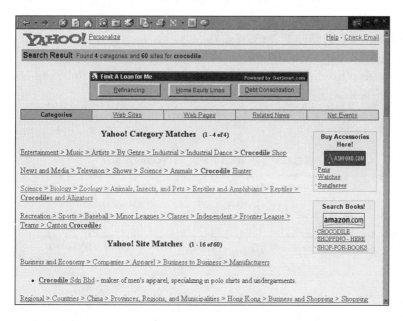

Figure 5.4

Yahoo! search results, with the closest matches listed first—just click a link to go to the matching page.

You can scroll to the bottom of any Yahoo! results page and click the **Categories**, **Web Sites**, or **Web Pages** links to go directly to those types of listings. You can also click the **Related News** links to find news headlines about your search topic or click the **Net Events** link to find any online chat events concerning the topic at hand.

Search Other Search Sites from Yahoo!

At the very bottom of every Yahoo! search results page are links to other Web search sites, such as AltaVista, GoTo.com, HotBot, Infoseek, and Deja.com. If you click any of these links, you're taken directly to that search page, with your current search criteria automatically plugged into the new search engine and the results already displayed. If you don't find what you're looking for at Yahoo!, you can use the bottom-of-the-page links to automatically launch the same search in a different search engine. (By the way, if you click the **More** link at the bottom of the page, you display Yahoo!'s Searching the Web category, which lists a variety of other search sites and resources.)

Fine-tuning Your Yahoo! Search

Yahoo! lets you fine-tune your search with a number of wildcards and operators. These auxiliary commands refine your query by excluding or including certain keywords—or by directing the search to just a part of the Web page.

Table 5.1 lists the commands you can use to fine-tune your Yahoo! search results:

Table 5.1   Yahoo! Search Parameters

To Do This:	Use This Command:	Example:
Search for part of a word	*	mon*
Must *include* a word	+	monty +python
Must *exclude* a word	–	monty –python
Search for a complete phrase	" "	"monty python"
Only search in the title of the page	t:	t:monty python
Only search in the URL of the page	u:	u:monty python!

Note that if you enter more than one word in a query with no operator between them, Yahoo! assumes you want to look for either word—in a way, inserting an "OR" between the words. In other words, Yahoo! automatically searches for pages that contain *any* of your keywords. As a result, if you're looking for a specific title or phrase, consider enclosing it in quotes or using plus signs to indicate required keywords.

Find More Stuff with Yahoo!'s Advanced Search Options

Not satisfied with the quality of results from a standard Yahoo! search? Then click the **Advanced Search** link on Yahoo!'s home page to access Yahoo!'s Advanced Search Options, shown in Figure 5.5.

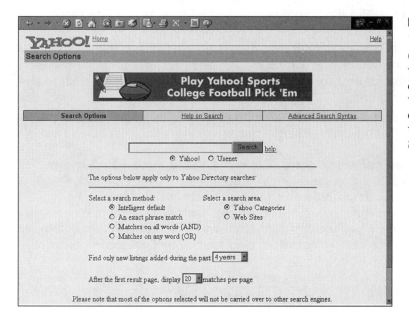

Figure 5.5

Yahoo!'s Advanced Search Options—tell Yahoo! whether you want an exact phrase match, whether to imply AND or OR operations, and whether to limit results to newer listings.

Most of what you can do on the Advanced Search Options page you can do with normal commands and operators from the standard Yahoo! search. However, a few additional parameters are available from this page, including

➤ **Search the Web or Usenet**—Instead of searching the Web, you can search Usenet newsgroups by clicking the **Usenet** option. This is the only way to search Usenet on the Yahoo! site.

➤ **Intelligent default**—This is the standard Yahoo! search mode.

➤ **An exact phrase match**—This has the effect of putting quotation marks around your keywords to search for an exact phrase.

No Boolean

Unlike many of the large Internet search engines, Yahoo! search does not let you use Boolean operators—such as AND, OR or NOT—within your query.

➤ **Matches on all words (AND)**—This changes the default OR operator to AND, enabling you to search for pages that include all the words in your query.

➤ **Matches on any word (OR)**—This returns you to the default OR mode to search for any of the words in your query.

➤ **Search Yahoo! categories**—This limits your search to Yahoo! categories only—it doesn't search for individual Web pages.

➤ **Search Web sites**—This limits your search to sites in the Yahoo! directory only—it doesn't search for matching Yahoo! categories.

➤ **Find only new listings**—You can elect to search for sites listed in the Yahoo! directory only within the past day, three days, one week, one month, three months, six months, or three years. This helps you to narrow your search to relatively newer sites.

➤ **After the first page, display XX matches per page**—This customizes the number of results listed per page—after the initial page, that is.

Should you use Yahoo!'s Advanced Search Options? If you're annoyed by an overlarge quantity of matching sites generated by a normal search, the Advanced Search Options will refine your search and generate fewer, better-qualified results. Know, however, that sometimes the *best* information comes from sites that appear to be only peripherally related to your query; I'll always choose to receive *more* results and count on serendipity (and my natural curiosity!) to help me find that one perfect page!

More Directories

Yahoo! offers several additional directories for more specialized searching. These include Yahoo! People Search (discussed in Chapter 6, "Search for People with Yahoo! People Search"), Yahoo! Yellow Pages (discussed in Chapter 7, "Search for Businesses with Yahoo! Yellow Pages"), Yahoo! Image Surfer (discussed in Chapter 8, "Search for Pictures with Yahoo! Image Surfer"), and Yahooligan! for kids (discussed in Chapter 9, "Search for Kids' Stuff with Yahooligans!"). You access these directories separately from the main Yahoo! Web directory.

Super-Secret Search Strategies That *Always* Work

If you've spent any time at all searching the Yahoo! directory, you know that searching is easy—it's getting good results that's hard.

To get good results—results that zero in precisely on the information you want without throwing in pages and pages of irrelevant data—you need to know the right way to search. And the right way to search is all about asking the right questions.

Imagine you're a detective questioning a suspect, and you only have a limited number of questions you can ask. Do you waste a question by asking "Where were you on the night of the crime?" The suspect can answer that question many different ways, most of them vague: "California." "Home." "Out." "Someplace better than here."

A better question is one that is more precise and allows less latitude in how it is answered. "Were you at 1234 Berrywood Lane on the night of the crime?" For this question, there are only two acceptable answers: "Yes" or "No." Either of these answers gives you the information you're looking for, with no chance for evasion or misinterpretation.

Searching the Web is like playing detective. Ask the right questions, and you get useful answers. Ask vague questions, and you get useless answers.

It's that simple.

Super-Secret Search Strategies Revealed!

If you want to learn all the secrets of successful Internet searchers, check out my book, *The Complete Idiot's Guide to Online Search Secrets*. It contains almost 400 pages of instructions and advice for improving your searching—on hundreds of different sites across the Internet! This book is available wherever computer books are sold, or online at www.molehillgroup.com/cig-oss.htm.

Five Steps to Better Searching

Is there one correct way to perform an online search? No, of course not; every searcher has his or her preferred style and approach.

However, there are some general guidelines that I recommend you follow:

1. Start by thinking about what you want to find. What words best describe the information or concept you're looking for? What alternate words might others use instead? Are there any words you can *exclude* from your search to better define your query?

2. Construct your query. Use as many keywords as you need—the more the better. If appropriate, use Yahoo!'s Advanced Search Options page.

3. Evaluate the matches on the search results page. If the initial results are not to your liking, refine your query and search again.

4. Select the matching pages that you want to view, and begin clicking through to those pages.

5. Save the information that best meets your needs.

Sounds logical, doesn't it? I'm going to bet, however, that you regularly skip over at least half of the steps in this list. Pay particular attention to the first step (thinking about how to search) and step 3 (evaluating your results and refining your search). The keys to better searching are better planning and learning from your mistakes.

The bottom line? Think more *before* you search, and spend more time learning from your results afterwards.

Use the Right Words to Talk About the Right Words

The individual words that you enter into a Search box are called *keywords*. Collectively, all your keywords (and the operators and modifiers in-between the words) combine to form a *query*. Just remember that a query is composed of keywords, not the other way around, and you'll have it straight.

Use the Right Words

When you construct your query, you do so by using one or more *keywords*. Keywords are what Yahoo!'s search engine looks for when it processes your query. Your keywords are compared to pages listed in the Yahoo! directory; the more keywords found on a Web page, the better the match.

You should choose keywords that best describe the information you're looking for—using as many keywords as you need. Don't be afraid of using too many keywords; in fact, using too *few* keywords is a common fault of many novice searchers. The more words you use, the better idea the search engine has of what you're looking for. Think of it as describing something to a friend—the more descriptive you are (that is, the more words you use), the better picture your friend has of what you're talking about.

It's exactly the same way when you "talk" to the Yahoo! search engine.

If you're looking for a thing or place, choose keywords that describe that thing or place in as much detail as possible. For example, if you're looking for a car, one of your first keywords would, of course, be **car**. But you probably know what general type of car you're looking for—let's say its a *sports* car—, so you might enhance your query to read **sports car**. You may even know that you want to find a *foreign* sports car, so you change your query to read **foreign sports car**. And if you're looking for a classic model, your query could be expanded to **classic foreign sports car**. As you can see, the better your description (using more keywords), the better the search engine can "understand" what you're searching for.

If you're looking for a concept or idea, you should choose keywords that best help people understand that concept or idea. This often means using additional keywords that help impart the meaning of the concept. Let's say you want to search for information about senior citizens, so your initial query would be **senior citizens**. What other words could you use to describe the concept of senior citizens? How about words like *elderly, old,* or *retired*? If these words help describe your concept, add them to your search: **senior citizens elderly old retired**. Trust me—adding keywords like these will result in more targeted searches and higher-quality results.

One other thing to keep in mind—think about alternative ways to say what you're looking for. (In other words, think about *synonyms*!) If you're looking for a *car*, you could also be looking for a *vehicle* or an *automobile* or an *auto* or for *transportation*. It doesn't take a search guru to realize that searching for **car vehicle automobile auto transportation** will generate better results than simply searching for **car**.

When You Don't Know the Right Words, Use Wildcards

What if you're not quite sure of which word form to use? For example, would the best results come from looking for *auto, automobile,* or *automotive*? Yahoo! lets you use *wildcards* to "stand in" for parts of a word that you're not quite sure about. For Yahoo! searches, the "asterisk" character (*****) is used as a wildcard to match any character or group of characters, from its particular position in the word to the end of that word. So, in our previous example, **auto*** would return all three words—auto, automobile, *and* automotive.

Wildcards are powerful tools to use in your Internet searches. I like to use them when searching for people when I'm not totally sure of their names. For example, if I'm searching for someone whose name might be Sherry or Sheryl or Sherylyn, I search for **sher*** and I'll get all three names back in my results. To take it even further, if all I know is that the person's name starts with an "s," I'll search for **s***—and get back Sherry and Susan and Samantha as matches.

Wildcards can also return unpredictable results. Let's say I'm looking for Monty Python, but I'm not sure whether Monty is spelled "Monty" or "Montey," so I search for **mon***. Unfortunately, this wildcard matches a whole bunch of "mon" words, including Monty—and money, monsters, and Mongolia. In other words, if your wildcards are too broad, you'll find a lot more than you were initially looking for.

Modify Your Words with +, –, and " "

A *modifier* is a symbol that causes a search engine to do something special with the word directly following the symbol. Yahoo! lets you use these three modifiers in your queries:

> ➤ **+ (always include the following keyword)**—Use the + modifier when a keyword *must* be included for a match. As an example, searching for **+monty +python** returns Monty Python pages or pages about pythons owned by guys

named Monty—because any matching page must include both the words, but not necessarily in any order.

➤ **– (always *exclude* the following keyword)**—Use the – modifier when a keyword must *never* be part of a match. For example, searching for **+monty –python** returns pages about guys named Monty but does *not* return pages about Monty Python—because you're *excluding* "python" pages from your results.

➤ **" " (always search for the exact phrase within the quotation marks)**—Use the " " modifier to search for the precise keywords in the prescribed order. As an example, searching for **"monty python"** only returns pages about the British comedy troupe Monty Python—you're searching for both the words, in order, right next to each other.

One More Tip: Save Your Searches!

If you actually manage to execute a search that results in a perfect set of matches, you probably want to save your results so you can access them again in the future. Learn how to save specific results pages as Bookmarks or Favorites within your Web browser—this way you can click the bookmark/favorite and return to that ideal page of results without replicating the query from scratch.

Be a Part of Yahoo!—How to Add *Your* Site to the Yahoo! Directory

Where do you think Yahoo! gets all the sites and pages listed in its directory? Although it does have a team of people out scouring the Web for new sites, Yahoo! also accepts submissions from site owners and Web surfers—just like you.

To submit a site to the Yahoo! directory, follow these steps:

1. Within the Yahoo! directory, go to the specific category where you want your site to be listed.
2. Click the **Suggest a Site** link at the bottom of that category's page.

3. When the Suggest a Site page appears, read the instructions and then click the **Proceed to Step One** button.

4. From the step 1 page (shown in Figure 5.6), enter the site's title, Web address (URL), and a brief description, and then click the **Proceed to Step Two** button.

5. When the step 2 page appears, enter any additional categories you want your site to be listed in, and then click the **Proceed to Step Three** button.

6. When the step 3 page appears, enter the contact information for your page, and then click the **Proceed to Step Four** button.

7. When the step 4 page appears, enter any time-sensitive information about your site, as well as any final comments, and then click the **Submit** button.

Narrow It Down!

If you try to submit your site from a top-level Yahoo! category you'll receive a "Please Be More Specific" message stating that your suggestion is too broad. If you receive this message, you need to drill down to a more specific category before you make the submission.

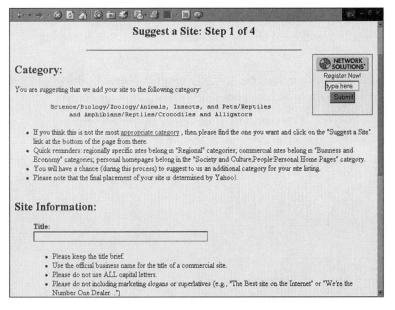

Figure 5.6

Adding your site to the Yahoo! directory—read the instructions and fill in all the blanks, and then wait for a human Yahoo! to approve your submission.

After you've submitted your site, get ready for a long wait. Given the facts that the Yahoo! directory is created by human beings, that there are only 24 hours in a day, and that thousands of sites are submitted each day, it could be several weeks or months until your site is added to the directory—if it's added at all. Every site submit-

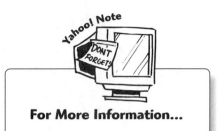

ted must be hand-checked and hand-approved by one of the Yahoo! staff, and not every site meets Yahoo!'s demanding standards. (Remember—there are over 300 million pages on the Web, and the Yahoo! directory lists only about 1 million of these pages.)

For More Information...

For more detailed information on submitting a site, go to Yahoo!'s Suggestion Tips page at www.yahoo. com/info/suggest/.

The Least You Need to Know

➤ Yahoo! is a directory, not a search engine, and contains links to more than a million different Web pages.

➤ You can find Web pages at Yahoo! either by browsing through categories or by using Yahoo!'s search capabilities.

➤ You can fine tune your searches of the Yahoo! directory with the following operators: *, +, –, and " ".

➤ When you click the **Advanced Search** link you jump to Yahoo!'s Advanced Search Options page, which offers enhanced fine-tuning of your queries.

➤ You can submit your own site to the Yahoo! directory by clicking the **Suggest a Site** link found on the bottom of any Yahoo! category page.

Chapter 6

Search for People with Yahoo! People Search

In This Chapter

➤ Learn how to look up people's street addresses and phone numbers with Yahoo! People Search

➤ Find out why it's more difficult to find an email address than a street address

➤ Discover how to search for Yahoo! users and people with their own personal Web pages

---

It's no surprise that one of the more popular types of Web searches involves looking for people—specifically, for people's street addresses, phone numbers, and email addresses.

Although you can search for people in the main Yahoo! Web directory, chances are you'll find them only if they have their own Web page or are mentioned on someone else's Web page. A much better way to search for people and businesses on the Internet is to use a directory specifically designed for this purpose—such as Yahoo! People Search.

Better Than a Phone Book: Looking Up Addresses and Phone Numbers

When you want to search for someone's street address or phone number, use the Yahoo! People Search directory, located at people.yahoo.com. From this page, shown in Figure 6.1, you can search for people anywhere in the United States.

Figure 6.1

Search for long lost friends and deadbeat relatives (or vice versa!) with Yahoo! People Search.

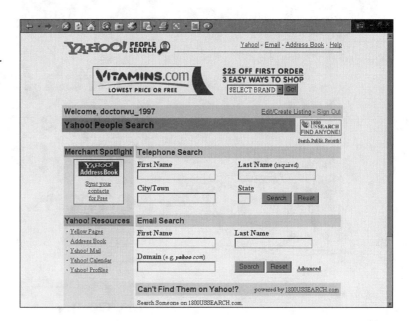

Where Do All These Names Come From?

The telephone and address data in the Yahoo! People Search directory is compiled by a third party, Experian, from the listings published by your local telephone company. If you want to provide new or updated information to Experian, contact them directly at (800) 407-1088.

How to Search with People Search

To search for someone via Yahoo! People Search, follow these steps:

1. From the Yahoo! People Search page (people.yahoo.com), go to the Telephone Search section.

2. Enter as much information as you know of the following: last name, first name, city, and state. The only *required* information is the person's last name, although the more information you can provide, the more targeted the search—and the results—will be.

3. Click the **Search** button.

Yahoo! now displays the Phone Search Results list, shown in Figure 6.2. This page lists all names matching your query, and for each listing includes the full name, street address, city, state, zip code, and phone number.

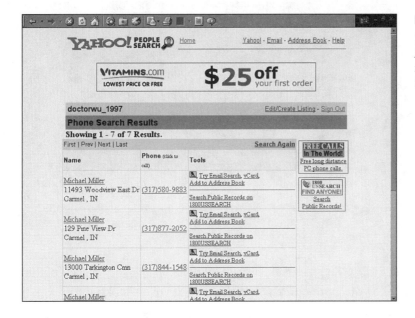

Figure 6.2

The results of a Yahoo! People Search—click any name to display more information.

To display more information about any person listed in the Phone Search Results list, click the person's name. This displays the Detailed Information page, shown in Figure 6.3. From here you can

➤ Display a list of nearby businesses (click the **Neighborhood** link).

➤ Display a map of this person's neighborhood (click the **Map** link).

➤ Search for this person's email address (click the **Try Email Search** link).

➤ Find the cheapest long-distance rates to phone this person (click the phone number link).

➤ Add this person to your Yahoo! Address book (click the **Add to Address Book** link).

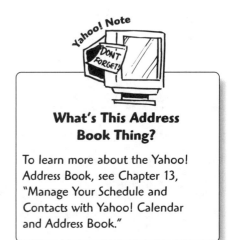

What's This Address Book Thing?

To learn more about the Yahoo! Address Book, see Chapter 13, "Manage Your Schedule and Contacts with Yahoo! Calendar and Address Book."

Figure 6.3

Use the Detailed Information to display a map of this person's neighborhood, list nearby businesses, or add this person to your Yahoo! Address Book.

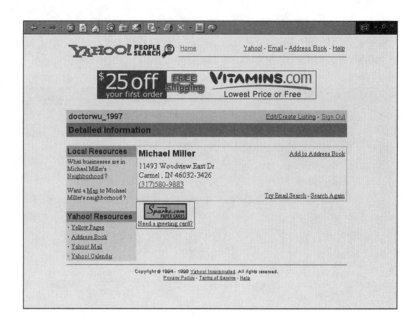

Tips for Better Searching

Here are some tips to help you more quickly find the person you're looking for:

➤ The more information you enter, the better the results. At the very least, enter a last name and a state (two-letter abbreviation, please). Follow this strategy if you know exactly who you're looking for and have a good idea where they live.

➤ Conversely, the less information you enter, the broader your results. Follow this strategy if you don't have a clue about who you're really looking for.

Protecting Privacy

To protect personal privacy, unlisted numbers are not accessible in the Yahoo! People Search directory.

➤ If you can't find the person you're looking for, it's either because you entered their information incorrectly, they don't live where you think they live, they've moved, or they have an unlisted number.

➤ If you know only part of an item, enter that part. For example, if you're looking for someone named Sherry, search for **sherry**. If you're not sure whether she goes by Sherry or Sheryl, search for **sher**. If you're not sure of her first name at all—but you know it begins with an "s"—search for **s**. If you don't remember her first name at all, leave the First Name box blank.

➤ Remember, many women don't list their phone numbers using their full first name—try searching by their first initial, instead.

➤ Many married women don't list their phone numbers with their own name, preferring either to list their husband's name only—or to list *both* their names, husband first. So if you're looking for a married woman and can't find her, try looking for her husband.

➤ If you're not sure precisely where someone lives, enlarge your search area. If you can't find someone in Madison, then look in all of Wisconsin.

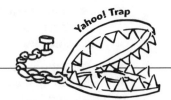

Just Because It's on the Web Doesn't Mean It's Up-to-Date

Because most Web white pages directories—including Yahoo! People Search—get their information from telephone company listings and traditional white pages phone books, the online listings are only as good and as current as their old-fashioned brethren. That means that some listings might be three to six months out-of-date—not the kind of instantaneous updating you might expect from Web-based resources—and particularly troublesome if you're looking for the new address of someone who has recently moved.

Finding a needle@haystack.com: Looking Up Email Addresses

In addition to searching for someone's street address and phone number, you can also use Yahoo! People Search to look for someone's email address. This is a trickier—and often less successful—process.

Why It's Harder to Find an Email Address Than a Street Address

Looking up names, street addresses, and phone numbers online is relatively easy because the practice is well established—the huge database of names, addresses, and numbers already exists in the offline world. (It's called a telephone directory!) Looking up email addresses, however, is not quite as easy—because no central directory of email addresses exists.

What, you say? Surely a universal directory of email addresses must be available!

Wrong. Sorry.

The One Sure-fire Way to Find Someone's Email Address

Ask them for it!

Every Internet service provider, every commercial online service, and every major corporation with its own Internet domain issues and controls its own email addresses. Think about that—that's hundreds of thousands of different "gatekeepers," each assigning its own addresses, each keeping its own individual directories. To date, no effort has been successful in getting every assignor of email addresses to cooperate with every other service or server, thus no central repository of email addresses exists.

Although Yahoo! People Search maintains a large directory of email addresses, it lists only those email addresses that Yahoo! knows about—which means addresses provided by major Internet service providers and commercial online services, as well as email addresses of Yahoo! Mail users and addresses volunteered by Yahoo! users (via the registration process). This ends up being a small subset of all the available email addresses on the Internet—but at least it's a place to start!

Searching for Email Addresses

To look up an email address with People Finder, follow these steps:

1. From the Yahoo! People Search page (people.yahoo.com), go to the Email Search section.
2. Enter as much of the following information as you know: first name, last name, and domain of the person's email address (that's the part *after* the @).
3. Click the **Search** button.

If Yahoo! finds a match to your query, it displays the Email Basic Search Results page, shown in Figure 6.4. You can click an email address to send this person an email message, or click the person's name to display any additional information (when available), such as city, state, or street address.

If Yahoo! *doesn't* find a match, it displays a No Matches page, and advises you to either search again or use the Advanced Search.

Performing an Advanced Email Search

To fine-tune an email search, click the **Advanced** link on the Yahoo! People Finder page. This displays the Advanced Email Search page, shown in Figure 6.5, which includes additional search criteria, such as city, state, country, and old email address. (Using the Old Email Address option is a great way to track someone who has changed addresses recently.) Fill in as much information as you know, and then click the **Search** button.

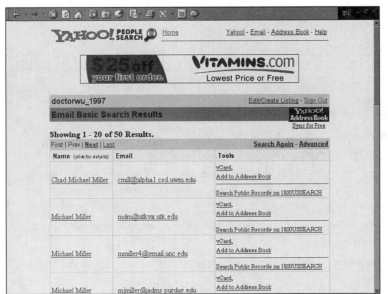

Figure 6.4

Yahoo!'s email search results—click an email address to send an email message, or click a name to display any other available information about this person.

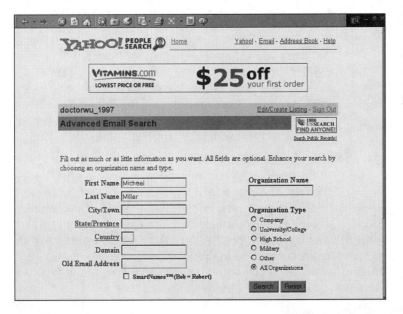

Figure 6.5

Use the Advanced Email Search to expand your search criteria—including looking for someone via a previous email address.

Adding Your Email Address to the Yahoo! Directory

If you want to help others find *your* email address online, you can always manually add your email address(es) to the Yahoo! People Search directory. Click the **Edit/Create Listing** link at the top of the Yahoo! People Search page to display the Create Your Yahoo! People Search Listing page; enter as much (or as little) information as you want, and then click the **Finished** button.

When All Else Fails...

If you can't find who you're looking for in the Yahoo! People Search directory, you can use the 1800USSearch.com service to look for them. This is a pay service (typical charges: $19.95–$39.95) available from the Yahoo! People Search page. Just scroll down to the Can't Find Them on Yahoo!? section, enter the appropriate information, and click the **Submit** button. You are taken to the 1800USSearch.com site, where you can choose the type of report you want, and enter your payment information.

Remember—It's a *Public Profile!*

Any information you enter into your Yahoo! public profile is visible to anyone scanning the profiles—so if you don't want it to be public, don't enter it into your profile!

Maybe They're on Yahoo!: Searching the Yahoo! Profiles

Yahoo! includes profiles of many of its registered users. You can search these public profiles from the Yahoo! Profiles page (search.profiles.yahoo.com). Yahoo! lets you search by Yahoo! ID, person's name, or person's interests. You can also click the **Power Search** link to expand the search criteria—adding fields for email address, gender, age range, marital status, and location.

To create or edit your own Yahoo! public profile, click the **Edit My Profile** link on the Yahoo! Profiles page to display your own Public Profiles page. If you want to create a new profile, click the **Create New Public Profile** button; if you want to edit an existing profile, click the **Edit** link next to your profile name. Your public profile can contain your Yahoo! ID, real name, email address, location, age, marital status, sex, occupation, photo, home page, and favorite cool links.

Figure 6.6 shows a typical Yahoo! profile.

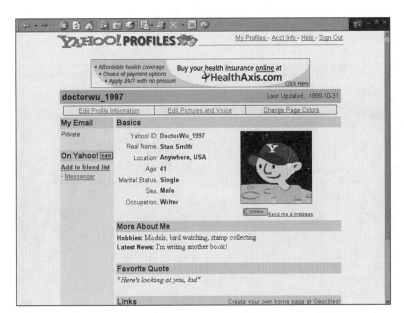

Figure 6.6

Let other users know all about you via your Yahoo! public profile.

Maybe They Have a Web Page: Searching for Personal Home Pages

Another way to find someone online is if they've created their own personal Web page. The Yahoo! Web directory includes a huge section listing personal Web pages created by users all across the Internet—at last count nearly 50,000 individual pages were listed.

To look for personal Web pages in the Yahoo! directory, go to the Yahoo! home page and browse to the Society and Culture>People>Personal Home Pages category. From this page, shown in Figure 6.7, you can browse through pages by the first letter of the person's last name, or choose to search for a person within this category. When you find the listing for the person you want, click their name to go to their personal Web page.

Figure 6.7

Search for personal home pages via the Yahoo! Web directory.

Search for a person's name.

Pull down to search within this category.

Click to display all pages by last name.

Click to display *all* personal Web pages (WARNING: This takes a long time to load!).

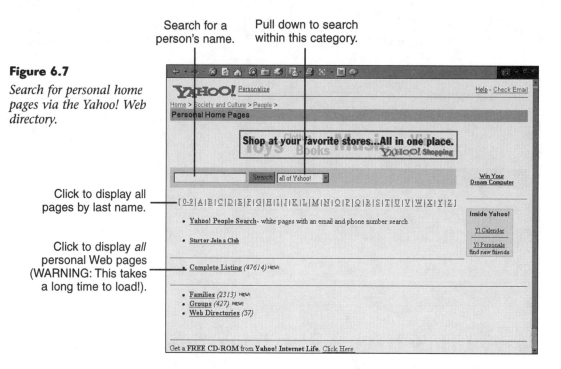

The Least You Need to Know

➤ Yahoo! People Search lets you search for people's street addresses and phone numbers.

➤ You can also use People Search to search for email addresses, but with less likelihood of success.

➤ Search for other Yahoo! users via their Yahoo! public profiles.

➤ Use the Yahoo! Web directory to search for people with their own personal Web pages.

Chapter 7

Search for Businesses with Yahoo! Yellow Pages

In This Chapter

➤ Learn how to search for businesses in the Yahoo! Yellow Pages directory

➤ Discover how to find businesses closest to your current address

➤ Find out how to display a map of the business' neighborhood—and generate step-by-step driving directions

---

Just as you have both white pages and yellow pages directories sitting by your telephone, Yahoo! offers both "white pages" (Yahoo! People Search) and yellow pages directories online. You use Yahoo! People Search when you want to find people; you use Yahoo! Yellow Pages when you want to find businesses.

Let Your Fingers Do the Searching...

The Yahoo! Yellow Pages directory works much like the regular Yahoo! Web directory. You can browse through different categories of businesses, or search for specific businesses or types of businesses. When you first access the Yellow Pages, you input your zip code, so Yahoo! can direct you to businesses in your area; you can also change your location at any time to search for businesses anywhere in the United States.

You access Yahoo! Yellow Pages (shown in Figure 7.1) by either clicking the **Yellow Pages** link on the Yahoo! home page or by jumping directly to yp.yahoo.com.

Figure 7.1

Yahoo! Yellow Pages lets you either browse through business categories or search directly for any U.S. business.

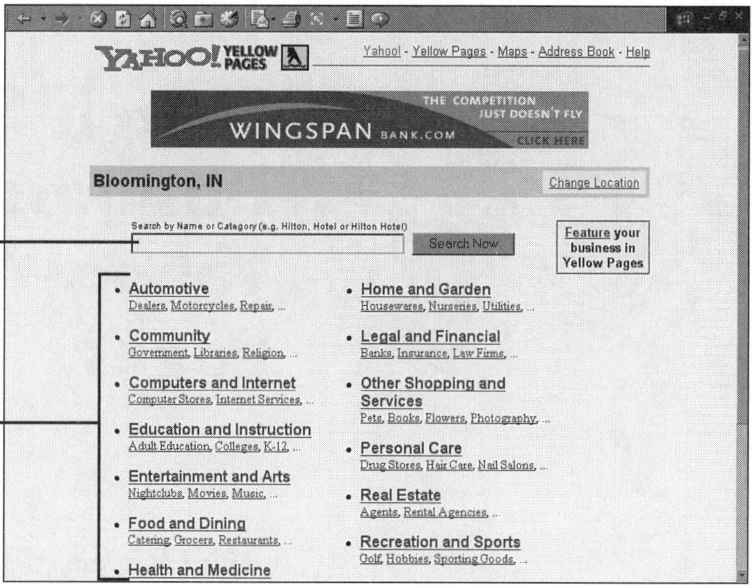

Search for a business here.

Browse through business categories.

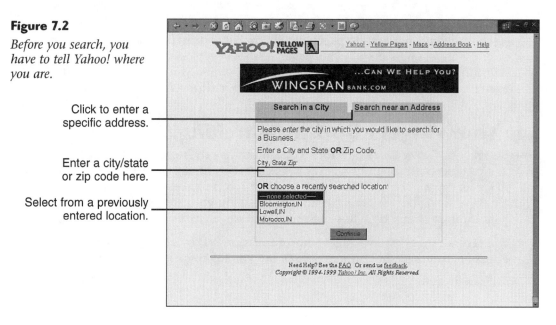

Tell Them Where You Are

The first time you try to browse or search the Yahoo! Yellow Pages, you'll see the page shown in Figure 7.2. This page lets you tell Yahoo! where you are (or where you're looking). You can enter your location in one of a number of ways:

Figure 7.2

Before you search, you have to tell Yahoo! where you are.

Click to enter a specific address.

Enter a city/state or zip code here.

Select from a previously entered location.

➤ Enter your city and state in the **City**, **State Zip** box.

➤ Enter your zip code in the **City**, **State Zip** box.

➤ If you've previously entered a location for a Yellow Pages search, choose from the list of recently searched locations.

➤ Click the **Search Near an Address** link to enter a specific address; Yahoo! then finds the closest businesses to that address.

After you've entered a location, Yahoo! keeps that location on file for future searches. If, at any time, you want to search in a different location, click the **Change Location** link on the Yahoo! Yellow Pages page and select a new location.

Browsing the Listings

You browse through the Yellow Pages categories the same way you browse through categories in the Yahoo! Web directory. Click first on one of the 14 major categories on the Yahoo! Yellow Pages page; when subcategories for that category are displayed, click the appropriate subcategory. Keep clicking through the subcategories until you find the exact type of business, with individual businesses listed.

Searching the Listings

Searching the Yellow Pages is like any other Yahoo! search. Enter either the name (or partial name) or category of a business in the Search box, and then click the **Search Now** button. You can use the same search commands you use in a Yahoo! Web search; remember that entering a partial name is better than entering no name at all.

How to Add Your Business to the Yellow Pages

Yahoo! licenses the content of the Yellow Pages directory from infoUSA.com. To add or modify your listing in the directory, go directly to infoUSA.com's Add or Change Your Business Listing page, at `kickapoo.infousa.com/data_col/`.

Yahoo! now searches the directory and returns a list of businesses that match your query. Click a business name for more details.

Using the Listings

When Yahoo! displays a page of business listings, like the one shown in Figure 7.3, you actually see *two* groups of listings. At the top of the page are any *Featured Businesses*, and underneath is a complete listing of businesses. Featured Businesses are simply businesses who've paid for the privilege (and don't appear in every category); there's nothing inherently special about them, other than their willingness to spend more money than their competitors.

Don't Forget Yahoo!'s *Other* Directory

The Yahoo! Yellow Pages list *all* businesses in an area, whether they're on the Internet or not. Many businesses have their own Web sites, of course, and many of these sites are listed in the regular Yahoo! Web directory. If you think a business has a Web site, try searching the regular directory for that business, or browse through the Yahoo! categories until you find the business you're looking for.

Businesses
with Web sites

Figure 7.3

A typical page of business listings; click the business name for more information and a map.

Featured businesses (and they pay for that privilege!)

General listings

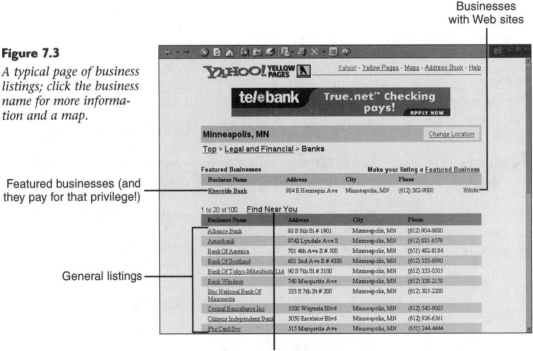

Click here to list businesses in
order of distance from a specified address.

The general business listing includes the name, address, city, state, and phone number for each business listed. If a business has a Web site, a **Website** link appears next to the listing; click this link to jump to that site.

If you want to see businesses in order of their proximity to a specific address, click the **Find Near You** link. This lists businesses in order of distance to your address, closest first. Each listing includes the approximate distance (in miles) from your address.

To learn more about any listed business, click that business' name in the listings. Yahoo! now displays a page similar to that in Figure 7.4, listing complete business information, links to related categories, and a map of the business' location. To generate driving directions from your location to their location, click the **Driving Directions** link.

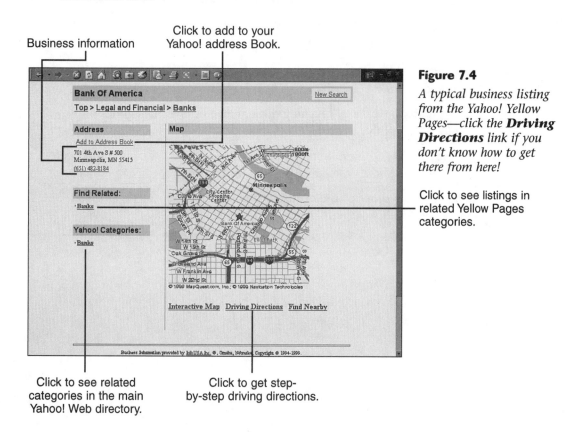

Business information

Click to add to your Yahoo! address Book.

Click to see related categories in the main Yahoo! Web directory.

Click to get step-by-step driving directions.

Figure 7.4

*A typical business listing from the Yahoo! Yellow Pages—click the **Driving Directions** link if you don't know how to get there from here!*

Click to see listings in related Yellow Pages categories.

Add This Business to Your Address Book

If you want to add this business to your Yahoo! Address Book, click the **Add to Address Book** link on the business' listing page. To learn more about the Address Book, see Chapter 13, "Manage Your Schedule and Contacts with Yahoo! Calendar and Address Book."

The Least You Need to Know

➤ The Yahoo! Yellow Pages (yp.yahoo.com) includes listings for businesses across the United States.

➤ You can find a business by browsing through the business categories or by searching through the directory.

➤ When you click a business listing, you display a detailed list of information for that business, including a map with a link to step-by-step driving directions.

➤ List businesses in order of their proximity to your location by clicking the **Find Near You** link.

I GOT 'EM OFF WITH YAHOO!!

YEP! THAT'S A LOTTA PICTURES OF CATS.

Chapter 8

Search for Pictures with Yahoo! Image Surfer

In This Chapter

➤ Learn how to use Yahoo! Image Surfer to search the Web for pictures

➤ Find out how to display pictures that are similar to a selected picture

➤ Discover all the different graphic formats available on the Web

Have you ever needed or wanted to find a picture of a red sports car? Or of a particular supermodel or celebrity? What about a digital copy of a painting by Rembrandt?

You can try to search for pictures and graphics in the normal Yahoo! Web directory, but your results will be hit-and-miss. (Just try entering your topic plus the keywords **picture** or **graphic**.) A somewhat better—and infinitely more enjoyable—way to search for picture files is by using the Yahoo! Image Surfer.

Image Surfer is located at ipix.yahoo.com. It works much the same as the regular Yahoo! directory—you can either browse through categories of pictures or search for specific types of pictures. The results pages display up to six different "thumbnails"; click a thumbnail to go to the page where that picture is displayed.

What Kinds of Images Are Available on the Web?

Before we get going, it helps to know what you're looking for. Table 8.1 lists the various image and movie file formats you're likely to find on the Web.

Table 8.1   Image and Movie File Formats

File Format	Description
.bmp	A simple graphics format (abbreviation for "bitmap") that is the default format for Windows desktop backgrounds.
.gif	A popular Web-based graphics format (pronounced "jif"). GIF files can include transparent backgrounds (so that a Web page background can show through) and can include multiple images for a simple animated effect.
.jpe	An alternate file extension for JPG graphics files.
.jpg	Another popular Web-based graphics format (pronounced "jay-peg"). JPG files are often slightly smaller in size than comparable GIF files.
.mov	A video format (for "QuickTime Movie") used for video clips.
.mpg	A video format (pronounced "em-peg") used for video clips.
.pcx	An older graphics format (pronounced "pee-see-ex") not normally used on Web pages. PCX files can be used as desktop backgrounds for more recent versions of Windows.
.pdf	A file type from Adobe that lets you view pages on your screen exactly as you would see them on paper. (PDF stands for Page Definition Format.)
.png	A newer graphics format (pronounced "ping") designed to ultimately replace the GIF format—although it's not yet widely used.
.qt	An alternate file extension for QuickTime Movie (.mov) files.
.ram	A video format (for "RealMovie") designed for real-time streaming video feeds.
.rm	An alternate file extension for either RealAudio or RealMovie files.
.tif	A graphics format (pronounced "tif") not widely used on Web pages. TIF files are popular with professional desktop publishers.

Don't Steal the Art!

Many image files on the Web are copyrighted and cannot legally be used without permission (or, in some cases, payment). Although it's probably okay to download a graphics file for use on your personal computer (assuming the Feds aren't going to raid your house looking for illegal pictures), using graphics without permission for commercial use—for a newsletter or a personal Web page, for example—is definitely a legal no-no.

Searching for Pictures with Image Surfer

When you access the Yahoo! Image Surfer page (located at ipix.yahoo.com), you can choose to search for particular images, or to browse through preselected image categories. If you choose to search, you follow the same procedures you do with any other Yahoo! search; enter your query in the search box, and then click the **Search** button.

The results of your search are displayed on a separate page, like the one shown in Figure 8.1. You'll see *thumbnails* of the images found by Image Surfer, six. to a page. Click an image to go to the Web page where that image was found.

Figure 8.1

This is what you get when you search for "yasmine bleeth" with the Yahoo! Image Surfer—just click the image to go to the host site.

It's *Not* a Directory

Unlike most sites on the Yahoo! network, Image Surfer is *not* a directory—it's a search engine, using the Visual RetrievalWare™ "visual search" technology provided by Excalibur Technologies.

Browsing the Image Surfer Categories

If you choose to browse through the Image Surfer categories, Image Surfer displays a slightly different results screen than if you perform a search—complete with some additional features.

As you can see in Figure 8.2, the category results page includes these additional features:

➤ **Visual search**—Click this link to display more pictures that look similar to the one you selected.

➤ **Image info**—Displays detailed information about the selected image, including the URL of the page containing the image.

➤ **Random**—Click this link to display a random selection of images in this particular category.

Figure 8.2

Browse by category and get more functionality from Yahoo! Image Surfer.

Display images similar to this one.

Display a random selection of images from this category.

Display information about this image.

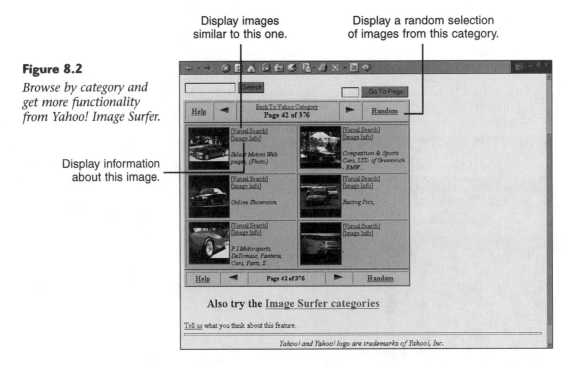

As with the search results page, click any image to jump to the page containing that image.

Now You Found It; How Do You Keep It?

If you want to download a picture you found on the Web onto your hard disk, right-click anywhere on the picture and select the **Save Picture** option from the pop-up menu in your Web browser. Remember to go to the host page *first* and save that picture—the thumbnail displayed by Image Surfer is generally too small and low-resolution to be of much good to you.

You can also turn any image your Web browser displays—even a page's background—into Windows desktop wallpaper by right-clicking and choosing the **Set As Wallpaper** command.

The Least You Need to Know

➤ Yahoo! Image Surfer is a search engine that finds pictures on the Web.

➤ You can search for images or browse for images by category.

➤ Click an image thumbnail to go to the Web page containing that image.

➤ When you browse for images, Image Surfer offers additional features—including a Visual Search for similar images and a link to random images within the selected category.

POKEMON!

Chapter 9

Search for Kids' Stuff with Yahooligans!

In This Chapter

➤ Learn how to browse and search for kids' sites in the Yahooligans! directory

➤ Discover all the other kid-friendly features of Yahooligans!, including online games, downloadable pictures and sounds, and news and sports stories

➤ Find out what resources Yahooligans! offers to parents and teachers

With 300+ million pages on the World Wide Web, how do you know which are best—and safest—for your kids to visit? Which sites are the most fun, the most educational, and the most safe—and how do you find these perfect kids' sites?

The best route to the best kids' sites on the Web is through Yahoo!—in particular, through Yahoo!'s Yahooligans! directory.

What's Different About Yahooligans!

Yahooligans! (found at www.yahooligans.com, or by clicking the **Yahooligans!** link on the Yahoo! home page) is a kids-oriented directory that is part of the Yahoo! network of sites. Each site listed in the Yahooligans! directory has been carefully checked by an experienced educator to ensure that the site's content is appropriate for children aged 7–12.

As you can see in Figure 9.1, Yahooligans! works just like the main Yahoo! Web directory, which means you can find sites by either browsing through categories or directly searching. The difference is that this directory includes categories and sites of particular interest to children and teenagers—as well as additional features and services.

Club Yahoo!   Online games   Cool site of the day

Figure 9.1

Browse or search the Yahooligans! directory for the best kids' sites on the Web.

Search Yahooligans! here. ——

Click any category to browse the Yahooligans! directory.

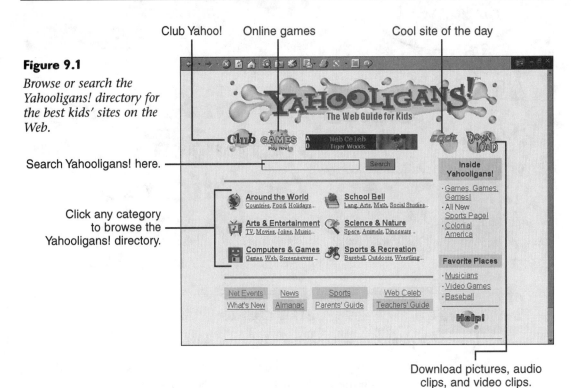

Download pictures, audio clips, and video clips.

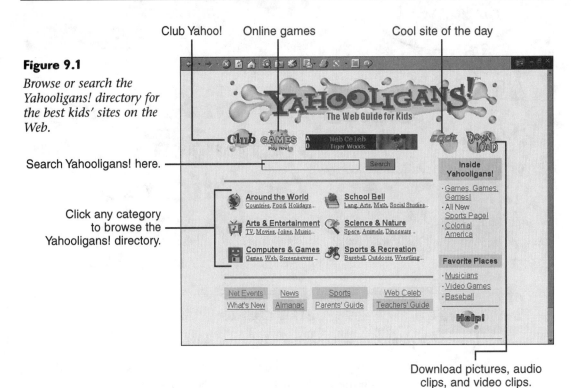

Just in Case...

If you happen to find a site in the Yahooligans! directory that you feel contains inappropriate content, notify the Yahooligans! staff at safety@yahooligans.com.

A few other differences exist in how Yahooligans! works, including

➤ Yahooligans! lists a maximum of only 100 matches per query.

➤ Yahooligans! search does not head back out to the Web for Web Page matches (as the Yahoo! search does, after it exhausts matches within the Yahoo! Web directory).

➤ The Yahooligans! directory does not include sites with any content inappropriate for younger Web surfers.

➤ Yahooligans! includes some additional services designed especially for children, including a link to Cool Web sites, a What's New page, and Club Yahooligans!, complete with a newsletter, hats, t-shirts, and other goodies.

Browsing and Searching the Yahooligans! Directory

You browse and search the Yahooligans! directory as you do the main Yahoo! Web directory. To search the directory, enter your query in the **Search** box on the Yahooligans! home page (www.yahooligans.com) and click the **Search** button. To browse through the categories, just click a major category to see related subcategories; keep clicking until you find the sites you're looking for.

Checking Out the Rest of Yahooligans!

Yahooligans! is more than just a directory of family-friendly Web sites. Yahooligans! also includes a variety of fun and informational services, from downloadable pictures to interactive online games.

Lots of Fun Stuff in One Cool Place: Club Yahooligans!

Click the **Club** link on the Yahooligans! home page to go to Club Yahooligans!, shown in Figure 9.2. Club Yahooligans! includes links to all sorts of fun features, including

Figure 9.2

Loads of fun at Club Yahooligans!

➤ **Yahooligans! Games**—A half-dozen games you can play online with other users. (See the "Play to Win at Yahooligans! Games" section, later in this chapter, for more information.)

More Opinions with Yahooligans! Polls

You'll see our Polls throughout the directory in a variety of categories—just look for them on the right-hand side of the page and share your opinion with the world!

➤ **Shout Out!**—A weekly survey about something important—or just something fun. Cast your vote, then see how everybody else voted.

➤ **Hyper Site**—The best site of the week, as picked by the Yahooligans! staff.

➤ **This Day in History**—Where you can find out what happened on the day you were born—or any other date you enter.

➤ **Web-Celeb**—With an in-depth profile of Yahooligans!' celebrity of the month.

➤ **Random Link**—Where you can jump to *any-where* on the Internet with a single click—as long as you don't mind not knowing where you're going!

➤ **Jokes**—With a joke of the day chosen from all the jokes sent in by Yahooligans! users.

➤ **Daily Trivia**—Interesting and fun trivia for sports fans.

➤ **News**—With links to Big Picture stories; each story includes links to related stories and Web sites, audio and video clips, and pictures.

➤ **Sports**—Where you can find the latest news and statistics for your favorite teams and players.

➤ **Downloader**—Which lets you download pictures, sound clips, and video clips of your favorite musicians, celebrities, and other famous people, places, and things. (See the "Pictures and Sounds to Keep at Yahooligans! Downloader" section, later in this section.)

➤ **Cam for Kids!**—With links to kid-friendly Webcams all around the world.

Play to Win at Yahooligans! Games

Yahooligans! Games is a collection of free online games you can play on your own computer with other Yahooligans! users, over the Internet. Click the **Games** link to see the Yahooligans! Games page, shown in Figure 9.3. From there you can choose to play any of the following games:

➤ Checkers

➤ Chess

➤ Go Fish

➤ Reversi

➤ Tic Tac Toe

➤ Word Search

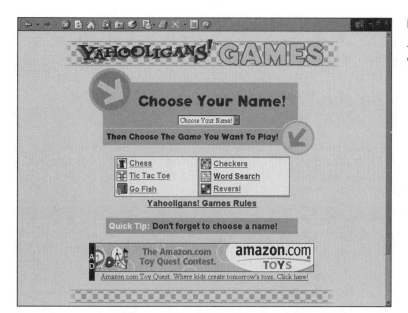

Figure 9.3
Play games online—with other users—at Yahooligans! Games.

Here's What You Need to Play...

To play Yahooligans! Games, you need (in addition to an Internet connection!) a Java-enabled browser, such as the 4.0 and higher versions of Internet Explorer or Netscape Navigator. Note that earlier versions of Windows (prior to Windows 95) and WebTV do not support Java technology and can't be used to play Yahooligans! Games.

After you choose a game, you have to create an *identity* to use while you're playing. You'll have to select which *game room* you want to join, and then join a *game table* in progress or start a new game table. Any table that has a Join button needs players, and you should feel free to jump right in and join the games at that table. If you create your own table you can invite other players to join you by clicking the **Invite** button.

Before you begin play, you may want to brush up on the rules for that particular game. You find the rules by going to that game's room-list page and then clicking the **Rules** link.

Most Yahooligans! games work in pretty much the same way. You make a move by either double-clicking a game element or by dragging and dropping an element to a new position. Other actions are accomplished by clicking the appropriate button.

The Coolest Sites on the Web at Yahooligans! Cool Page

When you click the **Cool** link you see the Yahooligans! Cool Page, shown in Figure 9.4. This is a list of five Web sites that Yahooligans! staff finds neat or fun or interesting or even educational. Click any link to jump directly to the cool site.

Figure 9.4

The coolest sites on the Web, per the Yahooligans! Cool Page.

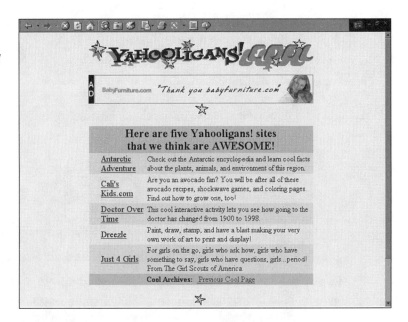

Pictures and Sounds to Keep at Yahooligans! Downloader

Click the **Download** link to go to Yahooligans! Downloader, shown in Figure 9.5. Here you can search for or browse through pictures, sounds, and videos that you then download directly to your PC. These downloadable files have been specially chosen to be interesting to kids—and safe from inappropriate content.

What kind of items can you find at Yahooligans! Downloader? The Downloader Pictures section contains these categories:

➤ Animals & Nature

➤ Clip Art

➤ Entertainment

➤ Holidays

➤ People

➤ Photo Galleries

➤ Places

➤ School Bell

➤ Screensavers and Wallpaper

➤ Space

➤ Sports

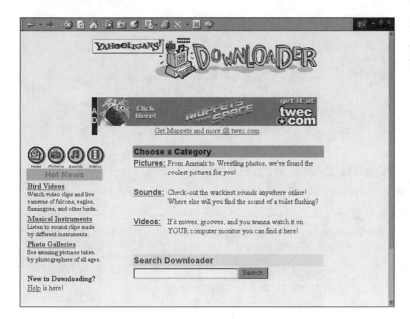

Figure 9.5

Find kids-safe pictures, sounds, and videos at Yahooligans! Downloader.

For example, if you want to find a picture of the Back Street Boys or Brittany Spears, click the **Pictures** link on the Downloader page, then click the **People** link, and then navigate to all the pictures of your favorite celebrity.

Find Out What's Happening Online with Yahooligans! Net Events

To find out what kid-centric events are happening on the Internet, click the **Net Events** link on the Yahooligans! home page. When the Net Events page appears (shown in Figure 9.6), you'll find listings for online chats, interviews, and other Internet-based events.

Figure 9.6

Look for chats, Netcasts, and other online events on the Yahooligans! Net Events page.

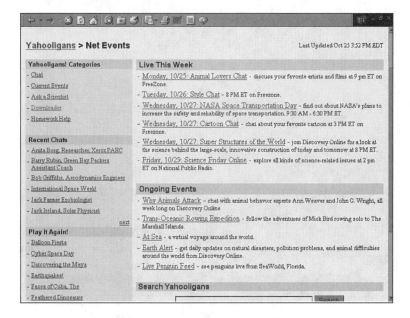

Yahooligans! for Parents and Teachers

Yahooligans! isn't just for kids; the site also includes resources for parents and teachers.

Click the **Parents' Guide** link to jump to the Yahooligans! Parents' Guide. This page includes lists of sites related to safety and privacy, guides to family surfing and safe online communication, and a Savvy Surfing Quiz.

Click the **Teachers' Guide** link to see the Yahooligans! Teachers' Guide. This page includes a wealth of information for educators, including online tutorials and lesson plans, newsletters, and links to professional organizations and educational sites.

The Least You Need to Know

➤ Yahooligans! is a directory of Web sites of interest to and safe for children aged 7–12.

➤ Yahooligans! also contains a variety of kid-friendly content, including downloadable pictures, online games, jokes, trivia, and age-appropriate news and sports.

➤ For adults, Yahooligans! includes resources for both parents and teachers.

Part 3

Make Yahoo! Work for You: Yahoo! Services

Want free email? How about chat or instant messaging? Or online scheduling and contact management? Look here to learn all about the cool—and free—services offered by Yahoo!

Chapter 10

Free Email, Anywhere, with Yahoo! Mail

In This Chapter

➤ Learn how to send and receive email messages with Yahoo! Mail

➤ Discover how to configure Yahoo! Mail for your own personal needs

➤ Find out how to combine Yahoo! Mail with your other POP email accounts

➤ Discover how to send electronic greeting cards with Yahoo! Greetings

---

Chances are you already have one or more email accounts through your Internet service provider, commercial online service (such as America Online), or place of employment. Why in the world would you want yet another email account?

To answer that question, think about how you use email today. Traditional email accounts require the use of a separate email program (such as Outlook Express, Netscape Messenger, or Eudora) to send and receive messages, and you can only access your account through a specific PC (unless you want to go through a lot of technical gyrations to configure a new machine for your particular email account). Wouldn't it be nice to have email you can access with your Web browser, no other software necessary, from any PC anywhere in the world?

If you want universal email, accessible from any Web browser on any PC, you want Yahoo! Mail. Yahoo! Mail is a Web-based email service, totally free of charge, that you can use to replace or supplement your existing email account(s).

Signing Up For and Accessing Yahoo! Mail

If you've already signed up for a Yahoo! service (such as My Yahoo!, discussed back in Chapter 2, "Create Your Own Personal Yahoo! with My Yahoo!"), you already have a Yahoo! ID and password. If so, you're only a few more clicks away from creating a Yahoo! Mail account and receiving a new email address.

From the Yahoo! home page, click the **Mail** link or go directly to mail.yahoo.com. If you already have a Yahoo! ID, enter it and your password in the appropriate boxes, and then click **Sign In**. If you don't yet have an ID, click the **Sign Me Up!** link and follow the onscreen instructions (discussed back in Chapter 2) to create a Yahoo! account.

When you see the Welcome to Yahoo! Mail screen, either accept the email address provided in the Email Name box (which is your Yahoo! ID added to @yahoo.com) or click the **Create a New Identity** link to create a new public profile under a different name—and thus create a different email address. You'll also want to enter a first name and last name (which don't have to be your real names, by the way) that will be displayed alongside your email address whenever you send Yahoo! Mail messages. Click the **Sign Me Up** button to continue.

Your Email Home

After you register—and anytime afterward—click the **Check Email** link on the Yahoo! home page or go directly to mail.yahoo.com—you see the Yahoo! Mail home page shown in Figure 10.1. While most of this page is totally unrelated to email, the column at the left of the page contains all the links you need to manage your Yahoo! Mail. In addition, any new messages in your inbox are noted in the Unread Messages section at the top of the page.

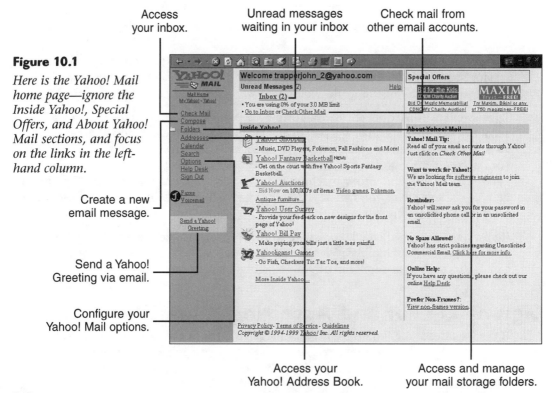

Access your inbox.

Unread messages waiting in your inbox

Check mail from other email accounts.

Figure 10.1

Here is the Yahoo! Mail home page—ignore the Inside Yahoo!, Special Offers, and About Yahoo! Mail sections, and focus on the links in the left-hand column.

Create a new email message.

Send a Yahoo! Greeting via email.

Configure your Yahoo! Mail options.

Access your Yahoo! Address Book.

Access and manage your mail storage folders.

Make It Your Own: Customizing Yahoo! Mail

Before you start sending and receiving Yahoo! Mail, you might want to configure some of your email options. You get to all your options by clicking the **Options** link on the Yahoo! Mail page.

When the Options page appears (shown in Figure 10.2), you can configure the following options:

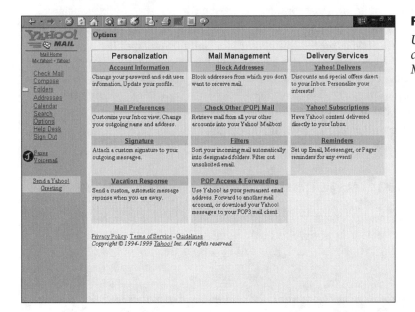

Figure 10.2

Use the Options page to customize your Yahoo! Mail account.

➤ **Account Information**—Use this to edit your Yahoo! member information including name, address, and other information.

➤ **Mail Preferences**—Use this to configure the way Yahoo! Mail appears on your screen. You can edit your From name, Reply-To address, whether you save sent messages, how new messages are listed in your inbox, how your messages are displayed onscreen (font size, screen width, and so on), and how much of the original message is "quoted" when you reply to a message.

➤ **Signature**—Create a custom signature (up to seven lines long) that is automatically inserted at the bottom of every email message you send.

➤ **Vacation Response**—This turns on an automatic response (with a message of your choosing) when you're away on vacation.

➤ **Block Addresses**—Use this to list email addresses you don't want to receive messages from—a great way to block spam and junk email.

➤ **Check Other (POP) Mail**—Click this link to check email in your other non-Yahoo! email accounts. (See the "Check Email from Another Account with Your Yahoo! Mail" section later in this chapter for more information.)

➤ **Filters**—Use this to send an incoming message that meets specified criteria to a specific folder—also includes a special SpamGuard function you can use to cut down on the amount of spam and junk email you receive.

➤ **POP Access and Forwarding**—Click here to enable your other email software to check email in your Yahoo! Mail account. (See the "Check Your Yahoo! Mail from Another Account" section later in this chapter for more information.)

➤ **Yahoo! Delivers**—Click here to sign up for "discounts and special offers" (re: email advertising) from Yahoo!'s advertising partners.

➤ **Yahoo! Subscriptions**—Click here to subscribe to one of three different free Yahoo! email newsletters. *Yahoo! Daily Wire* is a daily newsletter listing new Web sites, important Net events, and the latest news headlines. *Yahoo! Weekly Picks* is a weekly selection of favorite sites and online news. *Yahoo! Weekly Live Wire* is a weekly list of upcoming live Net events. After you subscribe, these newsletters are delivered via email directly to your Yahoo! Mail inbox.

➤ **Reminders**—Use this to set up lists of important dates and events, and then receive reminders via Yahoo! Mail, Messenger, or Pager.

Anything for Me? Checking Your Inbox for New Mail

Checking your Yahoo! Mail is as simple as clicking the **Check Mail** link on the Yahoo! Mail home page. When you click this link, you see the Yahoo! Mail Inbox, shown in Figure 10.3.

Figure 10.3

All your new email is waiting for you in the Yahoo! Mail Inbox.

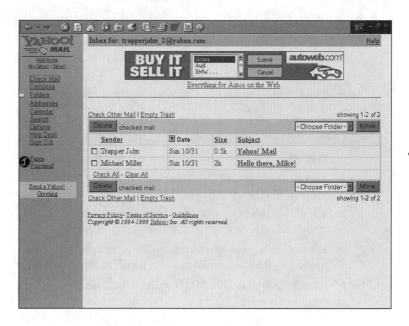

All your recent messages are listed in your inbox. You can now perform the following operations:

➤ To **read** a message, click the subject link for that message.

➤ To **check for new messages** in your non-Yahoo! email accounts, click the **Check Other Mail** link.

➤ To **delete** a message without reading it, check the box next to the message and then click the **Delete** button.

➤ To **move** a message to another email storage folder, check the box next to the message, select the folder from the message's **Choose Folder** list, and then click the **Move** button.

➤ To **re-sort** your messages by Sender, Size, or Subject, click the links above the selected column. (By default, Inbox messages are sorted by date received.)

It's in the Trash

When you delete a Yahoo! Mail message, that message is sent to a special Trash folder. Yahoo! automatically dumps the contents of this folder on a periodic basis; you can manually empty the Trash folder (to keep other users from looking at your trash) by clicking the **Empty Trash** link on the Inbox page. You can also *undelete* a message from the Trash folder; just go to the **Trash** folder page, check the message you want to keep, select a new folder from the **Choose Folder** list, and then click the **Move** button.

Reading the Mail

When you click a message in your Inbox, that message opened onscreen, as shown in Figure 10.4. With a message opened on your desktop, you can perform the following actions (in addition to just reading it, of course):

➤ To **close** the message and return to the inbox (without deleting or replying to the message), click the **Inbox** link.

➤ To **delete** the message, click the **Delete** button.

➤ To **reply** to the sender of this message, click the **Reply** button.

➤ To **reply** to both the sender of this message and all other recipients, click the **Reply All** button.

➤ To **forward** this message to another recipient, click the **Forward** button and then pull down the adjoining list to determine how the forwarded message should appear (either inline with the text of your accompanying message, or as an attachment to your new message).

➤ To **download** any files attached to this message, click the **Download** link (not visible if no files are attached).

➤ To **move** this message to a storage folder, select a folder from the **Choose Folder** list and click the **Move** button.

Figure 10.4

Read a Yahoo! Mail message.

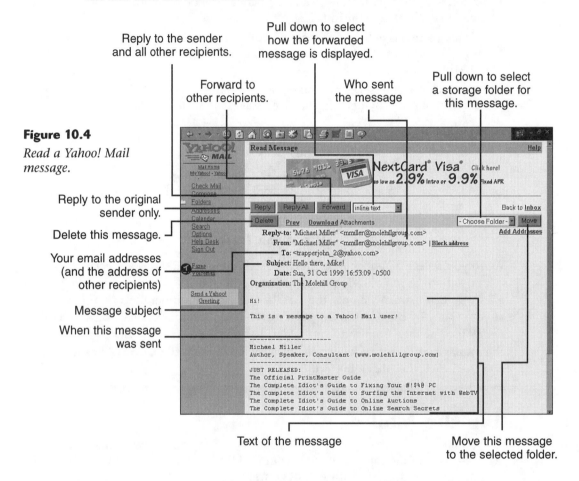

Replying to a message is similar to creating a new message (discussed next), except that the text from the original message is automatically "quoted" in the reply, and the To: and Subject: boxes are already filled in for you.

The Lost Art of Writing: Sending Email to Friends and Family

To create and send a new email message, follow these steps:

1. From the Yahoo! Mail page, click the **Compose** link.

2. When the Compose Mail page appears, shown in Figure 10.5, enter the recipient's email address in the To: box. If you're sending to more than one recipient, separate the addresses with commas.

Enter carbon copy recipients.

Check to save a copy of this message.

Enter recipients' email addresses.

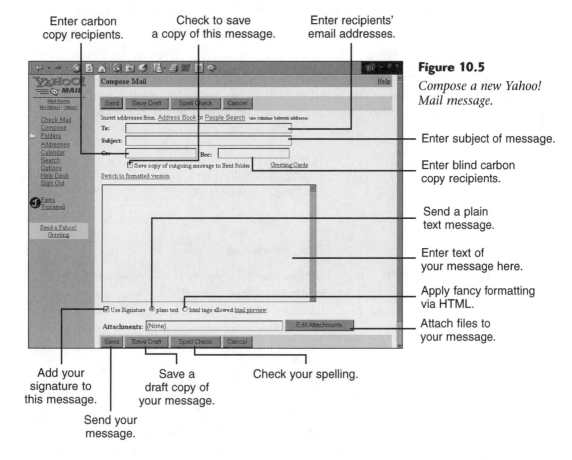

Figure 10.5

Compose a new Yahoo! Mail message.

Enter subject of message.

Enter blind carbon copy recipients.

Send a plain text message.

Enter text of your message here.

Apply fancy formatting via HTML.

Attach files to your message.

Add your signature to this message.

Save a draft copy of your message.

Check your spelling.

Send your message.

3. If you want to Cc: (carbon copy) or Bcc: (blind carbon copy) additional recipients, enter their email addresses in the respective boxes.

4. Enter the subject of your message in the Subject box.

5. Enter the text of your message in the large text box.

103

Use Your Address Book

You can insert email addresses directly from your Yahoo! Address Book into the To: box by clicking the **Address Book** link. See Chapter 13, "Manage Your Schedule and Contacts with Yahoo! Calendar and Address Book," for more information.

6. If you want to add your signature at the end of the message, check the **Use Signature** option.

7. If you want to format this message with HTML coding, check the **html tags allowed** option; otherwise, make sure the **plain text** option is checked.

HTML Allowed

If you check the HTML option, you can manually insert HTML codes within your text; see Chapter 30, "Create Sophisticated Pages with HTML" for more information about HTML coding. Note, however, that not all email programs can receive HTML-encoded email. It's much safer to send your email as plain-text messages.

8. If you want to save a draft of this message and return to it at a later time, click the **Save Draft** button.

9. If you want to save a copy of this message in your Sent folder (when you send it, of course!), check the **Save Copy of Outgoing Message** option.

10. If you want to attach a file to this message, click the **Edit Attachments** button; when the Attachments window appears, click the **Browse** button to locate the file(s), click the **Attach File** button, and then click the **Done** button when finished.

11. Before you send your message, click the **Spell Check** button to check the spelling in your text.

12. Click the **Send** button to send your completed message.

Store Your Messages—in Folders

Yahoo! Mail uses *folders* to store all your email messages. Your Inbox is one such folder; the Trash folder is another.

You can create your own folders to store read or unread messages by following these steps:

1. From the Yahoo! Mail page, click the **Folders** link.
2. When the Folders page (shown in Figure 10.6) appears, enter the name of your new folder in the **Folder name** box.
3. Click the **Create new folder** button to create the folder.

View the number
of read and unread
messages in each folder.

Enter the name
for a new folder here.

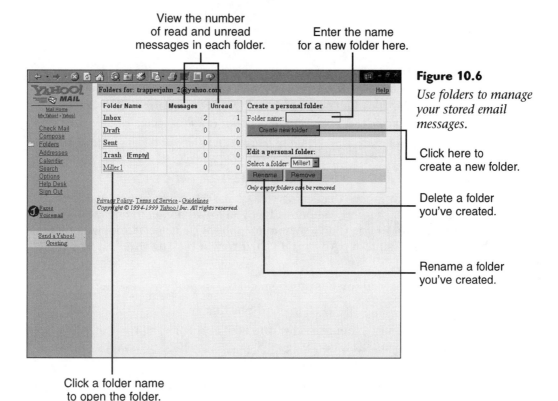

Figure 10.6

Use folders to manage your stored email messages.

Click here to
create a new folder.

Delete a folder
you've created.

Rename a folder
you've created.

Click a folder name
to open the folder.

You can open any folder and view its contents by navigating to the **Folders** page and clicking the name of the folder in the **Folder Name** list.

Share Your Mail: Using Yahoo! Mail to Check Your Other Mail Accounts, and Vice Versa

Yahoo! Mail is designed to interact with any other email accounts you might already have. You can configure Yahoo! Mail to check the mail in your other accounts, or even to send your Yahoo! Mail to the inboxes of another email account.

POP Goes the Email

In order to share email between Yahoo! Mail and another email account, your other account must be what is called a *POP* account. Most ISP-based email is POP-compatible; America Online email is not POP-compatible. If in doubt, ask your current email provider if your current account is a POP account.

Forward Your Yahoo! Mail to Another Account

If you signed up for the Yahoo! Delivers service (that's the targeted junk mail service, discussed earlier in this chapter), Yahoo! will let you forward your Yahoo! Mail to another email account. (If you didn't sign up for Yahoo! Delivers, Yahoo! won't let you share your email—kind of petty, but it's their way of making their advertisers happy.)

To redirect your Yahoo! Mail to your other email account, follow these steps:

1. From the Yahoo! Mail page, click the **Options** link.

2. When the Options page appears, click the **POP and Forwarding** link.

3. If you haven't yet signed up for Yahoo! Delivers, you'll see a signup page. Fill it out, then click the **Finish** button.

4. When the Mail Delivery Status page appears, go to the Step 1 section, check the **Forwarding** option, and enter your other email address (not your Yahoo! Mail address) in the box.

5. Go to the Step 2 section and choose whether your other email account can receive HTML messages or text messages only.

6. Click the **Submit** button.

7. When the next page appears, click the **Send Verification Now** button; Yahoo! will send a message to your Yahoo! Mail address via your other email address.

8. Launch your other email program and check your inbox. You should have a message there regarding your Yahoo! Mail account. Open that message and click the enclosed link (or enter that link into your Web browser) .

9. When your browser displays the Verify Account page, enter the **Confirmation Code** included with the email message, along with your Yahoo! password, and then click the **Verify Account** button.

Your email forwarding should now be activated. To turn off email forwarding, return to the **Mail and Delivery Status** page, check the **Web and POP Access** option, and then click **OK**.

Check Your Yahoo! Mail at Yahoo!—and at Your Other Account

The option we just discussed turned off your Yahoo! Mail inbox and forwarded all your Yahoo! Mail to another account. If you want to receive your Yahoo! Mail at another account and still have access via your Yahoo! Mail inbox (and your Web browser), you have to select a different option—and reconfigure your email software for a new POP mail account.

Follow these steps:

1. From the Yahoo! Mail page, click the **Options** link.

2. When the Options page appears, click the **POP and Forwarding** link.

3. If you haven't yet signed up for Yahoo! Delivers, you'll see a signup page. Fill it out and then click the **Finish** button.

4. When the Mail Delivery Status page appears, go to the Step 1 section and check the **Web and POP Access** option.

5. Go to the Step 2 section and choose whether your other email software can receive HTML messages or text messages only.

6. Click the **Submit** button.

7. Yahoo! now displays a page of instructions and settings. Read this page carefully and then proceed.

8. Open your email program (Outlook Express, Netscape Messenger, Eudora, or whatever).

9. From within your email program, add a new POP mail account. (Check the Help system with your email program for exact instructions on how to do this.)

10. For the Incoming Mail (POP3) Server settings, use the address pop.mail.yahoo.com.

11. For the Outgoing mail (SMTP) Server settings, use the address smtp.mail.yahoo.com.

12. For the Account Name or Login Name settings, use your Yahoo! Mail address, but without the @yahoo.com.

13. For the Email Address settings, use your full Yahoo! Mail address (including the @yahoo.com).

14. For Password settings, use your Yahoo! Mail password.

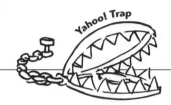

Additional Account—or Replacement?

Most email programs let you set up multiple mail servers. Some, however, don't. If your email program lets you send and receive email only from a single account, know that setting up that software to receive Yahoo! Mail will delete the settings you need to access your current email account.

When you configure Yahoo! Mail in this fashion, you can still access your Yahoo! Mail account from Yahoo!

Check Email from Another Account with Your Yahoo! Mail

Just as you can configure your existing email program to send and receive Yahoo! Mail, you can also configure Yahoo! Mail to receive messages from your existing email account—as long as it's a POP-compatible email account.

To configure Yahoo! Mail to receive email from another account, follow these steps:

Three at a Time

Yahoo! Mail can be configured to receive email from up to three POP accounts.

1. From the Yahoo! Mail page, click the **Options** link.

2. When the Options page appears, click the **Check Other (POP) Mail** link.

3. When the Check Other Mail page appears, click the **Add Mail Server** button.

4. When the **Create Other Mail Account** page appears, enter the following information about your other email account: Mail Account Server, Mail Account Username (typically the first part of your email address, before the @), Mail Account Password, and Port Number (typically 110).

5. To automatically send the email messages retrieved from the other service to a specific Yahoo! Mail folder, pull down the **Download to Folder** list and select a folder.

6. To leave mail messages on the other email server, even if you downloaded those messages to your Yahoo! Mail inbox, check the **Leave Mail on POP Server** option. (This option allows you to see your messages on both Yahoo! Mail and your other email service.)

7. To have Yahoo! Mail retrieve only new messages from your other account, check the **Retrieve New Message Only** option.

8. If you use filters on your Yahoo! Mail, check the **Use Filters** option to run all messages received from the other service through your Yahoo! Mail filters.

9. Check a color in the **Indicator** section to display all messages from this account in a specific color. (If you receive messages from multiple accounts, using a different color for each account helps keep things organized.)

10. Click the **OK** button to activate this function.

Once you've configured Yahoo! Mail to retrieve your messages from another account, you can check that other account for new mail by clicking the **Check Other Mail** link on either the Yahoo! Mail page or the Inbox page.

Say I Love You or Just Hello: Sending Yahoo! Greetings

Here's another valuable use of email—to send electronic greeting cards to friends and family.

An electronic greeting card is actually a Web page that contains a graphical message. You pick the greeting you want to relay, and then Yahoo! Greetings sends the recipient an email informing them of their new online card. Your friends and

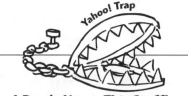

I Don't Know This Stuff!

If you don't know any of this information, check the options settings for your current email software or contact your email service provider.

No Web-Based Email

Yahoo! Mail cannot be configured to receive email from other Web-based email services, such as Hotmail.

You Only Get It When You Want It

Yahoo! Mail retrieves messages from other accounts only when you request them. It does not check these accounts for new email automatically.

family use their Web browsers to access the special greeting card page, and then become overwhelmed at your sensitivity and depth of feeling. (Well, *maybe* on the sensitivity and feeling thing....)

Choosing and Sending a Yahoo! Greeting

When you access the Yahoo! Greetings page (greetings.yahoo.com) shown in Figure 10.7, you can choose from one of the featured greetings, or you can browse through the various greeting categories. After you've found the greeting you want to send, click on the greeting to personalize it.

Figure 10.7

Browse through the categories and choose a card from Yahoo! Greetings.

When the Personalize This Greeting page appears, scroll down and fill out all the appropriate boxes. You can send the same card to multiple recipients (up to 10 at a time) by entering multiple addresses in the To: field, separated by commas. You can also choose to receive notification when the card has been received by checking the **Please notify me when the recipient views this card** option.

Click the **Preview Your Greeting** button to see what your card looks like before you send it. If you like what you see, click the **Send This Greeting** button to send the card. (If you don't like what you see, click the **Make More Changes** button to return to the previous screen.)

Picking Up a Yahoo! Greeting

As soon as you click the **Send This Greeting** button, Yahoo! Greetings sends your recipient an email notifying him or her that they have a greeting waiting on the

Yahoo! Greetings site. This email will include a link to the page containing the greeting; when they click this link, they jump directly to your greeting, as shown in Figure 10.8.

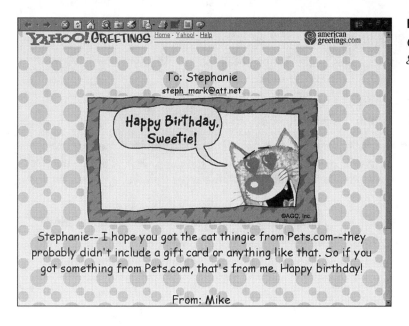

Figure 10.8

Oh boy—an online greeting card!

No Link, Then Paste

If your recipient for some reason can't access the link to their greeting card, they can instead cut the link URL from the email message, paste it into the Address box in their Web browser, and access the page manually.

The Least You Need to Know

➤ Yahoo! Mail (mail.yahoo.com) lets you send and receive email from any computer with an Internet connection and a Web browser—all you have to do is log on with your Yahoo! ID and password.

➤ You check your messages in the Yahoo! Mail Inbox folder; you can save read or unread messages in other folders you create.

➤ Yahoo! Mail enables you to attach files to your email messages and to automatically include a signature line with all your messages.

➤ For maximum flexibility, you can forward all your Yahoo! Mail messages to another email account; read your Yahoo! Mail messages with your normal email software; and check your other email messages from your Yahoo! Mail Inbox.

➤ Yahoo! Greetings (greetings.yahoo.com) lets you send electronic greeting cards to anyone on the Internet.

Chapter 11

Talk Until Your Fingers Fall Off with Yahoo! Chat and Messenger

In This Chapter

➤ Learn how to talk with other users in Yahoo! Chat rooms

➤ Discover how to use your computer's microphone to participate in Yahoo! Voice Chat

➤ Find out how to send and receive instant messages with Yahoo! Messenger

People like to talk to one another. Communication is the foundation of our society, and the Internet has helped foster communication among hundreds of millions of computer users around the world.

Yahoo! is doing its part to encourage communication with two tools you can use for real-time online communication. These two tools are Yahoo! Chat and Yahoo! Messenger

There's Room for Everyone in Yahoo! Chat

Yahoo! Chat is a *group* communications tool. Once you load the Yahoo! Chat software, you enter a topic-specific *chat room,* where you join other users in a group conversation. You send messages to the room using your keyboard and read everyone else's messages on your computer screen. You can even send *Private Messages* to other users in a chat room, so you can keep your personal conversations out of the public eye.

Yahoo! also features *chat events*, special chat sessions featuring celebrity or expert guests; these events take place in an *Event Auditorium* and often have hundreds or thousands of users in attendance. In addition, if you have a microphone and a speaker hooked up to your computer, you can participate in Yahoo! Voice Chat, a chat room where you can talk instead of type.

Choose a Room, Load the Software, and Start Chatting

Yahoo! Chat is accessible by clicking the **Chat** link on the Yahoo! home page or by going directly to chat.yahoo.com. The first time you visit you'll be prompted for your Yahoo! ID and password; if you don't yet have a Yahoo! ID, take this opportunity to register.

The Yahoo! Chat page, shown in Figure 11.1, is your home page for all of Yahoo!'s chat activities. From here you can access featured chat rooms and chat events, or click the **Complete Room List** link for a list of all available Yahoo! Chat rooms.

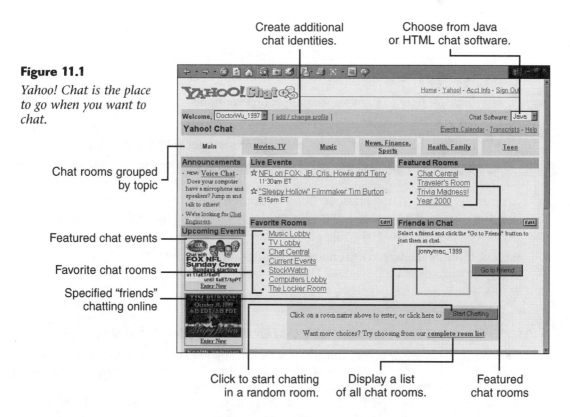

Figure 11.1

Yahoo! Chat is the place to go when you want to chat.

Create additional chat identities.

Choose from Java or HTML chat software.

Chat rooms grouped by topic

Featured chat events

Favorite chat rooms

Specified "friends" chatting online

Click to start chatting in a random room.

Display a list of all chat rooms.

Featured chat rooms

After you select a chat room, Yahoo! has to load special chat software into your Web browser. This is done automatically, using Java technology.

No Java? Use HTML!

If you have a newer browser (Netscape 2.0 or higher or Internet Explorer 3.01 or higher running on Windows 95, Windows 98, Windows NT, or Windows 2000—which should cover most of you), Yahoo! will automatically load the Java chat software into your browser—assuming your browser is Java-enabled. (Check your browser's Help screens to find out how to enable Java in your browser.) If you have an older browser or Java-incompatible system (such as WebTV), Yahoo! will load an HTML version of its chat software. This HTML chat software functions similarly to the Java version, but with fewer bells and whistles. (You can manually select either the Java or HTML chat software from the Chat Software list at the top of the Yahoo! Chat page.)

Chatting—with Your Fingertips!

When you enter a chat room, you see the screen shown in Figure 11.2. All messages are displayed in the Chat pane; everyone chatting in the room is listed in the Chatters pane.

You enter your message in the **Chat** box and then click the **Send** button or press **Enter** to send the message to the room. After you send a message, it appears in the Chat pane, listed in-line with all the other messages. If you want your messages to stand out amidst the visual cacophony of a busy chat room, consider changing the color or style of your text. To change the color of your messages, select a different color from the Color list. To change the style of your message text, click the **B** (bold), **I** (italic), or **U** (underline) buttons.

In addition to sending text messages, you can send *emotions* to the chat room. Clicking the **Emotions** button displays an Emotions window. Click any emotion from this list and that emotion will be sent (as a message) to the chat room.

Everybody else in your chat room is listed in the Chatters list. In addition, you can display a list of all the participants in every Yahoo! Chat room by clicking the **Who's Chatting** button in the **Tools** section.

If you want to change chat rooms, click the **Change Room** button in the **Tools** section. When you click this button, Yahoo! displays the chat room list; click a room name to change to that room.

115

Figure 11.2

*A typical chat room—enter a message in the **Chat** box, hit **Send**, and then chat away!*

Click to send an emotion.

Send a Private Message.

Other people in the chat room

Messages

Use these controls to spice up your message.

Enter your message here.

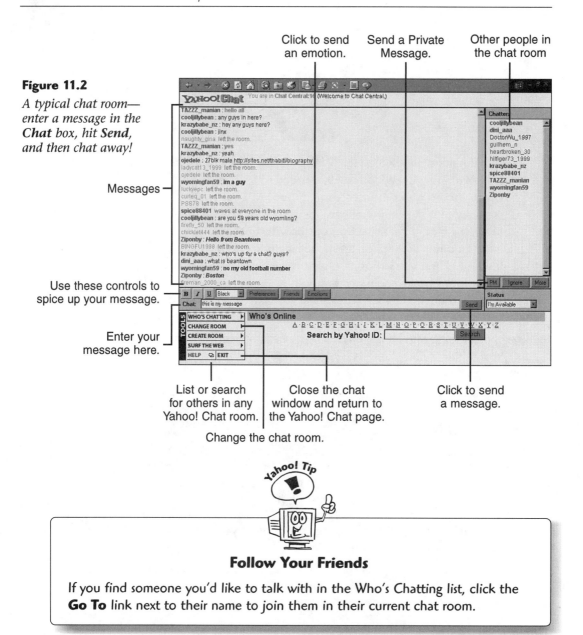

List or search for others in any Yahoo! Chat room.

Close the chat window and return to the Yahoo! Chat page.

Click to send a message.

Change the chat room.

Follow Your Friends

If you find someone you'd like to talk with in the Who's Chatting list, click the **Go To** link next to their name to join them in their current chat room.

Taking Your Chat Private

If you find someone in the chat room you'd like to talk to one-on-one—outside the prying eyes of everyone else in the chat room—you can send them a Private Message. This sends a message directly to the selected chatter; that person can then reply privately to your Private Message and thus carry on a private conversation.

To send a Private Message to someone in your chat room, select that person's name in the **Chatters** list and then click the **PM** button. When Yahoo! displays the PM window, enter your private message and click the **Send** button. Keep the PM window open to continue your private conversation.

You can also send Private Messages to Yahoo! users who aren't in your chat room. Just click the **PM** button without first selecting another user; when the PM window appears, enter the other person's Yahoo! ID in the **To:** box, enter your message, and then click the **Send** button.

Making Friends in Chat

Yahoo! lets you create a Friends List of all your favorite chat buddies. When someone on your Friends List is online and chatting, you'll see their Yahoo! ID displayed in the Friends in Chat list on the Yahoo! Chat page and in the info pane just above the Chat pane in any chat room. You can join the chat room your friends are in by selecting their names in the **Friends in Chat** list and then clicking the **Go To Friend** button.

Friends for All Occasions

The Friends List you create in Yahoo! Chat is also used by Yahoo! Messenger (discussed later in this chapter) and Yahoo! Games (discussed in Chapter 16, "Movies, Music, and More with Yahoo! Entertainment").

To add someone to an existing Friends List, follow these steps:

1. From any chat room, click the **Modify List** link at the top of the page—or click the **Edit** button in the Friends in Chat section of the Yahoo! Chat page.
2. When the Create and Edit Your Groups page appears, select a group of friends from the **Edit Your Existing Groups** list and click the corresponding **Edit** link.
3. From the **Add New Friends** page, enter the Yahoo! ID of your friend in the Friend's **Identity** box.
4. In the **Message** box, enter a brief message to notify your friends that you've added them to your Friends List.
5. Click the **Add Friend** button.

Repeat this procedure to add additional friends to your list.

Chat with the Stars

Yahoo!'s chat events provide a forum for you to ask questions of celebrity and expert guests. When it's time for the chat event to start, enter that event's Event Auditorium by clicking the event name on the Yahoo! Chat page.

After you're in the Event Auditorium, you can sit back and read the questions posed by other users, along with the guest's replies. Ask your own question by entering the question in the **Ask a Question** box and then click the **Ask** button to send that question to the event's moderator. The moderator will determine the appropriateness of your questions and then (if accepted) put it in line with all the other questions being asked.

You can also chat with other users in an Event Auditorium, using the standard chat operations and commands. This makes things a little confusing; look for the Y! icon to identify questions being asked, and the "star" icon to identify the guest's answers.

Throw Away the Keyboard—Yahoo! Voice Chat Is Here!

If you have a microphone and speakers connected to your PC system, you can participate in Yahoo! Voice Chat, an audio version of normal Yahoo! Chat.

To use Yahoo! Voice Chat, all you have to do is click the **Voice Chat** link on the Yahoo! Chat page and then log into one of the Voice Chat rooms. From the Voice Chat screen, click and hold the **Talk** button, then speak into your microphone. The name of whichever user is currently talking is displayed in the box next to the Talk button.

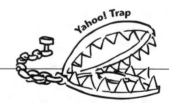

Are You Really Chatting If No One Can Hear You?

If you can't hear anyone talking in a Voice Chat room, check to make sure your computer speakers are properly connected and turned on, that their volume is set at an audible level, and that you haven't muted all your Windows system sounds. If no one can hear you talk, make sure your microphone is plugged in and working properly and that the microphone's input level is set correctly. (To set your microphone's input level, open the Windows **Control Panel** and select the **Multimedia** icon; when the Multimedia Properties dialog box opens, select the **Audio** tab, and then click the **Recording Control** button in the Recording section. When the Recording Control dialog box appears, increase the Microphone Balance setting.)

Open a Person-to-Person Chat with Yahoo! Messenger

Yahoo! Messenger is both software and service, designed to let you communicate instantly—and privately—with other Yahoo! members. When the Yahoo! Messenger software is running, you can send instant messages to any other Yahoo! user currently online, as well as receive up-to-the-minute stock prices, news headlines, sports scores, weather forecasts, and notification of any waiting Yahoo! Mail.

Before You Message—Download the Software

Before you can use Yahoo! Messenger, you have to download and install the Yahoo! Messenger software. You do that by following these steps:

1. Go to the Yahoo! Messenger page by clicking the **Messenger** link on the Yahoo! home page, or by going directly to messenger.yahoo.com.

2. Click the **Download** link for your particular operating system. (Yahoo! Messenger is available for Windows 95/98/NT, Macintosh, Palm OS, and in a Java version to run within any Java-enabled Web browser.)

3. When the File Download dialog box appears, check the **Run this program from its current location** option, and then click **OK**.

4. Yahoo! will now download the file to your hard disk and then automatically launch the setup program. Follow the onscreen instructions to complete the installation.

5. When the installation is complete, Yahoo! Messenger will automatically start and prompt you to log in. Enter your Yahoo! ID and password, and then click **OK**.

After Yahoo! Messenger is installed, there are several ways to launch the program, including:

➤ Double-click the **Y!** icon in the Windows tray.

➤ Select the **Y!** icon on the Windows desktop.

➤ Click the **Start** button and select **Yahoo! Messenger**.

To have Yahoo! Messenger launch automatically whenever you start your computer, launch Yahoo! Messenger, pull down the **Edit** menu, and then select **Preferences**. When the Preferences dialog box appears, select the **General** tab, check the **Automatically Launch Yahoo! Messenger** option, and then click **OK**.

Chatting with Yahoo! Messenger

After Yahoo! Messenger is running you see the Yahoo! Messenger window shown in Figure 11.3. When you click the **Friends** tab, all the members of your Friends List are displayed in the main Messenger window; friends online are displayed in bold.

View the profile of
the person you're
chatting with or edit
your Yahoo! Profile.

Add people to
your Friends List.

Search for someone
to talk with or
invite a friend to
download the Yahoo!
Messenger software.

Send messages and
conference requests.

Figure 11.3

*Use Yahoo! Messenger to
chat with other users, in
real time, privately.*

Messenger window—
displays your Friends
List, news headlines,
and so on.

Your availability sta-
tus (click the Status
button to change).

Display alerts.

Display your Friends List.

Hide tools and tabs
and shrink the
Messenger window.

Display stock prices.

Display news headlines.

Toggles Yahoo!
Search box on or off.

Display sports scores.

Display weather
forecasts and
conditions.

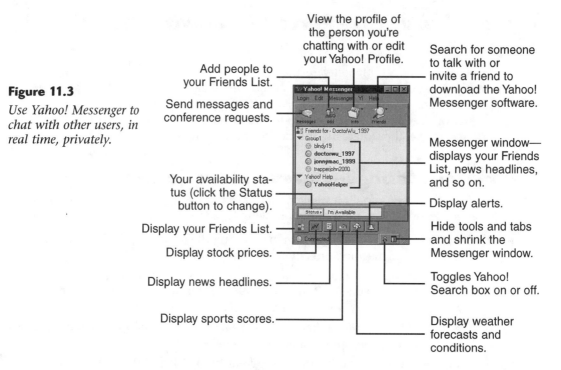

To send an instant message, double-click any name in your Friends List. When the
Send Instant Message window appears (shown in Figure 11.4), enter your message
and click the **Send** button. (You can spice up your text with bold, italic, underline, or
color, if you want.)

Figure 11.4

*Enter your message and
click the **Send** button.*

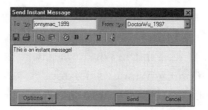

Other Message-Like Things You Can Do with Instant Messenger

Yahoo! Messenger lets you perform several other message-related functions (all from
the main Yahoo! Messenger window), including the following:

➤ Add a friend to your Friends List by clicking the **Friends** button and selecting
Add a Yahoo! Friend. When the Add a Yahoo! Friend/Group dialog box appears,
enter your friend's Yahoo! ID in the Step 1 box, enter a message to your friend in
the Step 4 box, and then click the **Add** button.

➤ Search for other (non-Friend) users to talk to by clicking the **Friends** button and selecting **Search for New Friends**. When you jump to the Search Public Profiles page in your Web browser, enter your search criteria and click one of the **Search** buttons.

➤ If you want to send instant messages to someone who hasn't yet downloaded and installed the Yahoo! Messenger software, click the **Friends** button and select **Invite a Friend to Get Messenger**. When you jump to the Invite a Friend to Use Yahoo! Messenger page in your Web browser, enter the appropriate information and click the **Invite a Friend** button.

➤ You can also use Yahoo! Messenger to create pseudo-chat rooms called *conferences*. A conference is essentially an instant message exchange among multiple users. To start a conference, click the **Messages** button and select **Start a Conference**. When the Invite Friends to a Conference dialog box appears, select names from the **Friend List** and then click the **Add** button to add them to your Chat Invitation List. Click the **Invite** button to send invitations to and initiate your conference.

➤ Yahoo! Messenger also offers its own version of Yahoo! Voice Chat. Assuming your computer system is equipped with microphone and speakers, click the **Messages** button and select **Start a Voice Chat**. When the Invite Friends to a Voice Chat dialog box appears, select names from the Friend List and click the **Add** button to add them to your Chat Invitation List. Click the **Invite** button to send invitations to and initiate your voice chat.

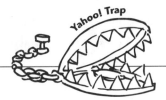

You Can Only Talk to People Who Are Signed Up and Online

You can only send instant messages to other users who have Yahoo! Messenger installed on their system, who have a Yahoo! ID, are currently online, and are currently connected to or running Yahoo! Messenger, Yahoo! Chat, or Yahoo! Games.

Getting News, Sports, and Stock Information with Yahoo! Messenger

When connected to the Internet, Yahoo! Messenger also displays news headlines, sports scores, weather forecasts and conditions, and stock prices. Click the **Stocks** tab to display prices for your portfolio; the **News** tab to display news headlines; the **Sports** tab to display sports scores; or the **Weather** tab to display weather forecasts.

No Tab? Then Edit Your Preferences

If any of these tabs aren't visible in your version of Yahoo! Messenger, pull down the **Edit** menu and select **Preferences**. When the Preferences dialog box appears, click the **Appearances** tab, check those tabs you want displayed and click **OK**.

Yahoo! Messenger picks up the selections you made back on your My Yahoo! page to display on these information tabs. For example, when you click the **Stocks** tab, Yahoo! Messenger displays current pricing for the portfolio you created in My Yahoo!. See Chapter 2, "Create Your Own Personal Yahoo! with My Yahoo!," for more information on changing these settings.

Receiving Alerts with Yahoo! Messenger

You can also configure Yahoo! Messenger to alert you when any of the following occurs:

➤ Someone in your Friends List comes online

➤ You receive a response to a Yahoo! Personals ad

➤ You receive new Yahoo! Mail

➤ Your stocks hit an upper or lower limit or reach a certain volume limit

➤ You're ready to start a meeting recorded in Yahoo! Calendar

Select the **Alerts** tab to see any current alerts.

Customize Yahoo! Messenger

To configure Yahoo! Messenger's look and feel—along with its various alert options—pull down the **Edit** menu and select **Preferences**. When the Preferences dialog box appears, select the appropriate tab and then make your choices from the available settings. Click **OK** to register your new settings.

The Least You Need to Know

➤ Yahoo! Chat enables you to chat (via your keyboard) with other users in public topic-specific chat rooms.

➤ You access Yahoo! Chat rooms and chat events from the Yahoo! Chat page at `chat.yahoo.com`.

➤ Yahoo! Voice Chat works just like regular Yahoo! Chat, except you use your computer's microphone to send voice messages to the chat room.

➤ Yahoo! Messenger (found at `messenger.yahoo.com`) is a self-running software program that lets you send instant text messages to other Yahoo! users, as well as receive alerts when you receive new Yahoo! Mail.

Chapter 12

Join the Discussions at Yahoo! Clubs and Message Boards

In This Chapter

➤ Learn all about Yahoo! Clubs—what they are, and what you can do in one

➤ Find out how to create your own Yahoo! Club

➤ Discover where and how to leave public messages on Yahoo!, about any topic

---

The Internet is a great way for people with special interests to gather and exchange ideas. Whether you're into model trains, European soccer, or soap operas, you can find a legion of similar fans online.

Yahoo! makes it easy for you to hang out with people who share your special interests, via Yahoo! Clubs and Yahoo! Message Boards. When you gather via Yahoo!, it doesn't matter where you live—you can meet with friends around the globe in the Yahoo! community!

Join the Club—the Yahoo! Club, That Is

A Yahoo! Club is like a mini-Yahoo!, run by you and other Yahoo! users, focusing on a specific topic or area. You can create a Yahoo! Club yourself, centered on any topic you like, and then invite your friends, family, and other Yahoo! users to visit and participate in Club activities.

What's in a Club?

Any Yahoo! Club can have the following sections:

➤ **Address Book**—Use a club Address Book to share names, addresses, and other contact information.

➤ **Calendar**—Create your own club calendar to schedule group chats, special events, and meetings.

➤ **Chat**—Each club can have its own private Yahoo! Chat room chat area where club members can meet informally or for scheduled group chats.

➤ **Contacts**—The Contacts list displays Yahoo! ID and profile information on all club members.

➤ **Custom Web Address**—Each club gets its own unique Web address that members can access directly from their browsers.

➤ **Email**—Yahoo! makes it easy for the club founder to send email messages to all club members.

➤ **Message Boards**—This is a place for you and other club members to post and read electronic messages.

➤ **News**—The club founder can post selected news headlines and stock portfolios on the club page.

➤ **Photos**—You and other club members can post and share your favorite photos and images.

➤ **Web Links Directory**—Create and post a list of favorite or related Web pages.

Figure 12.1 shows a typical club page.

Figure 12.1

Join the club—and have access to a message board, chat room, photos, and other cool stuff.

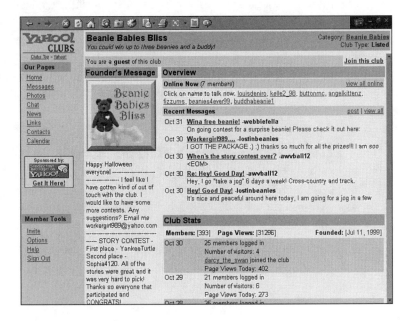

Find a Club, Join a Club

To find a specific Yahoo! Club, or just browse through the list of clubs, click the **Clubs** link on the Yahoo! home page, or go directly to clubs.yahoo.com. From the Yahoo! Clubs page displayed in Figure 12.2, you can browse through clubs in various categories, or search the Yahoo! Club directory.

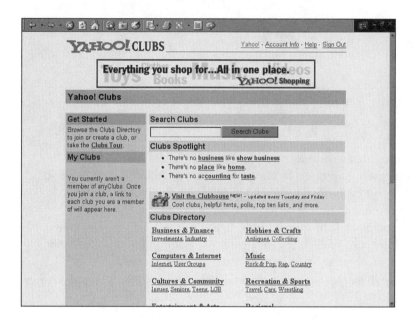

Figure 12.2

Find a club for you on the Yahoo! Clubs page.

If you've joined any clubs, those clubs are listed on the left side of the Yahoo! Clubs page. To join a club, access that club's home page, and then click the **Join This Club** link.

Make Your Own Club

Creating a club doesn't cost anything except your time. Just follow these steps:

1. From the Yahoo! Clubs page (clubs.yahoo.com), browse through the categories until you find the right category for your club.

2. From the appropriate category page, click the **Create a Club** button.

3. After you sign in with your Yahoo! ID and password, you'll see the Create a Club page. Read and verify the information on this page, and then click the **Email Instructions** button.

4. Yahoo! now sends you an email verifying your interest in creating a new club. Included in the email is a link to a Web page; click the URL (or paste it into your Web browser) to jump to that Web page.

127

5. After you jump to the new Create a Club page, enter the name of your club in the **Name** box and your zip code in the **Zip Code** box. Then select whether you want a listed or unlisted club, and click the **Yes! I Accept** button.

Yahoo! now creates a club for you, and provides you with information regarding the location and management of your club.

It's Unlisted

Yahoo! includes both *listed* and *unlisted* clubs. Listed clubs are listed in the Yahoo! Club directory, and are open to the public. Unlisted clubs aren't listed in the directory (duh!) and can only be joined by invitation. To join an unlisted club, you must first receive an invitation to join; follow the instructions in the email invitation to complete your membership. If you're creating a new club, you can make it either listed or unlisted; unlisted clubs are good if you want to limit access to private groups of family members, friends, and co-workers.

Post an Electronic Message on a Yahoo! Message Board

Yahoo! Message Boards are the electronic equivalent of old-fashioned bulletin boards. Each message board is devoted to a specific topic; users can read the messages posted on the board, and then reply or post their own new messages. All messages are visible to the entire public.

Yahoo! offers hundreds of different message boards, each dedicated to a specific topic. At any given time, each board contains dozens or hundreds of messages; messages that reply to other messages (or other replies) are said to comprise a message *thread*.

To access Yahoo! Message Boards, click the **Message Boards** link on the Yahoo! home page, or go directly to messages.yahoo.com. When the Yahoo! Message Boards page appears (shown in Figure 12.3), you can choose to browse for boards by category, or search for a specific board.

After you've selected a specific message board, you'll see the message board's main page, like the one shown in Figure 12.4. The theme of the board (in the form of a "starter" message) is sometimes displayed at the top of the page; all the message threads are listed (by topic) below the Topic heading. Click a topic to read the first message in a thread.

Figure 12.3

Search or browse for specific message boards by topic.

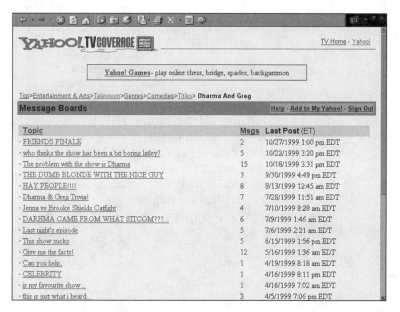

Figure 12.4

A typical Yahoo! Message Board; click a topic to read the messages in that thread.

Each message in the thread appears in its own page, like the one shown in Figure 12.5. Click the **Next** link to read the next message in the thread; click the **Previous** link to back up and read the previous message. To reply publicly to a message, click the **Reply** link; to send a private email to the author of the message, click the author's name.

Figure 12.5

Read a message, post a reply.

View all replies to this message.

Reply publicly to this message.

Read next message.

Read previous message.

Send a private email to the author of the message.

Go to the first message in this thread.

Go to the latest message in this thread.

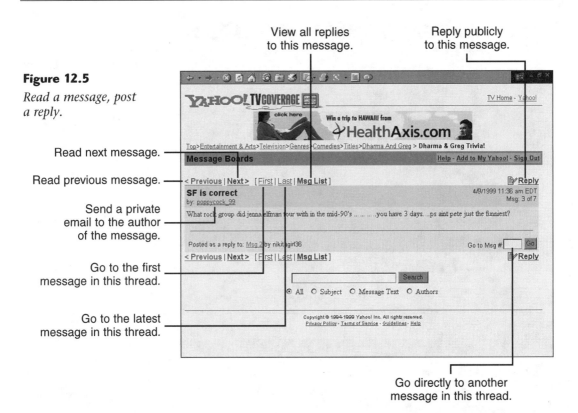

Go directly to another message in this thread.

Sign In to Post

To post messages, you first have to sign in with your Yahoo! ID and password. If you don't have an ID yet, you can read—but you can't post.

To post a new message in a new thread, click the **Create a Topic** link on the main message board page. When the page shown in Figure 12.6 appears, enter a subject for your message in the **Type Message Subject** box, and then enter the text of your message in the **Type Message** box. When you're ready to send your message, click the **Post Message** button; remember, any message you post will be visible to anyone visiting this message board!

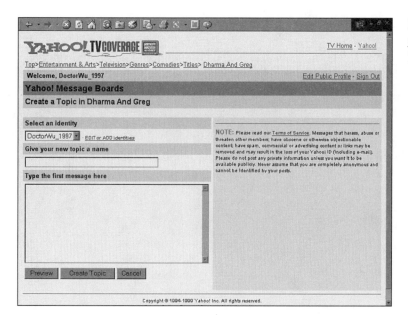

Figure 12.6

Post a new message to a Yahoo! Message Board.

The Least You Need to Know

➤ A Yahoo! Club brings together a message board, chat room, contacts, photos, and other information about a particular subject.

➤ Any Yahoo! member can create his or her own Yahoo! club, on any topic.

➤ Yahoo! Message Boards function like electronic bulletin boards, allowing users to read and post public messages on a specific topic.

Chapter 13

Manage Your Schedule and Contacts with Yahoo! Calendar and Address Book

In This Chapter

➤ Learn how to create an electronic schedule that can be accessed from any Internet-connected PC

➤ Discover how to store your address book contacts on the Web

➤ Find out how to use Yahoo! Address Book with Yahoo! Mail

Most computer users have an electronic calendar of some sort as well as an electronic address book. You use your calendar to keep your private schedule, and your address book to hold the names and addresses of friends, family, and business contacts.

The only problem is, you have your calendar on your work PC, so you can't access it from home. Or you have your address book on your home PC, and you can't access it from work or when you're on the road.

Yahoo! solves this problem with a Web-based calendar and address book—that you can access from *any* PC, anytime, anywhere in the world!

Get Organized with Yahoo! Calendar

Yahoo! Calendar is a scheduling and calendar utility that houses your information on Yahoo!'s Web servers. Because the information is stored on Yahoo!'s computers, not yours, you can access your schedule from any PC with an Internet connection and a Web browser. All you have to do is enter your Yahoo! ID and password, and you have universal access to your appointments and events.

Access Yahoo! Calendar by clicking the **Calendar** link on the Yahoo! home page or directly at calendar.yahoo.com. The default Yahoo! Calendar page, shown in Figure 13.1, displays your schedule for today; click any event or appointment to display more details.

Figure 13.1

Track your schedule— from any PC—with Yahoo! Calendar.

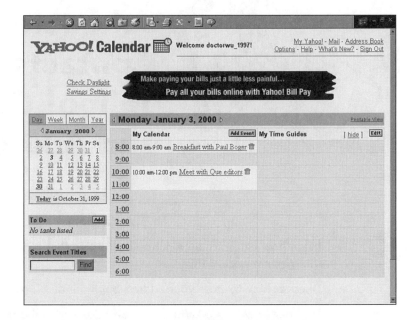

You can also display your Yahoo! Calendar in weekly, monthly, or yearly views. Just click the **Week**, **Month**, or **Year** links above the monthly calendar in the top-left corner of the Yahoo! Calendar page.

How to Fill Up Your Schedule, in 10 Easy Steps

To add a new appointment or event (as shown in Figure 13.2) to your Yahoo! Calendar, follow these steps:

1. From the Yahoo! Calendar page, click the **Add Event** button (at the top of the current schedule).

2. When the New Event page appears, enter the name of the event in the **Title** box.

3. Select the **Date** and **Time** the event starts.

4. If the event lasts all day, check the **All Day Event** option. Otherwise, check the **Timed Event** option and enter either an ending time or the duration of the event.

5. Pull down the **Type** list and select what type of event this is.

6. Enter any comments about this event in the **Notes** box.

134

7. If this is a repeating event (every week, for example), click the **Repeating** button and select the appropriate option.

8. If you want to be reminded of this event via email, click the **Reminders** button and select the appropriate option.

9. If you want to invite other users to this event, click the **Invitations** button and enter the appropriate information.

10. Click the **Save** button to add this event to your calendar; click the **Save and Add Another** button to add this event and then return to this page to add another event.

Select when the event will end...   ...or how long the event will last.

Select the starting time.   Enter the event's title.

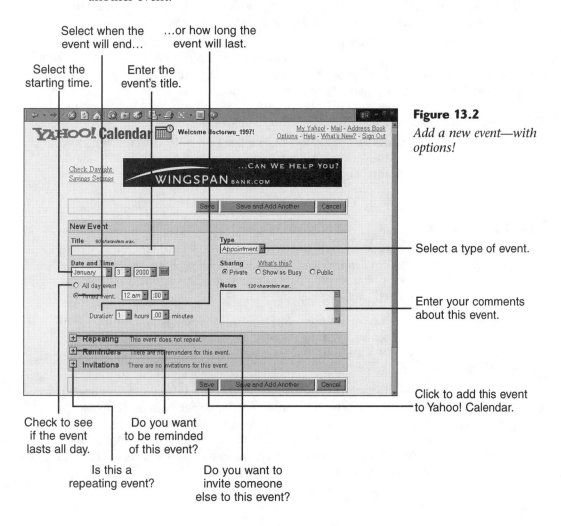

Figure 13.2

Add a new event—with options!

Select a type of event.

Enter your comments about this event.

Click to add this event to Yahoo! Calendar.

Check to see if the event lasts all day.

Do you want to be reminded of this event?

Is this a repeating event?

Do you want to invite someone else to this event?

135

Other Things You Can Do with Yahoo! Calendar

Yahoo! Calendar lets you do more than just track simple appointments and events. Take a look at the other options available:

➤ **Manage a To Do list**—Click the **Add** button in the To Do section of the Yahoo! Calendar page to add tasks to your personal To Do list.

➤ **Share your calendar, publicly**—You can make your calendar visible to friends, family, co-workers, or anyone else with your Yahoo! Calendar address. Click the **Options** link to display the Options page, and then click the **Calendar Sharing** link. When the Calendar Sharing page appears, check the **Activate Sharing** option, note the URL of your public calendar, and then click the **Save** button.

➤ **Synchronize with other calendar programs and organizers**—Do you have another calendar program or a Palm Pilot? You can synchronize your Yahoo! Calendar with another program or organizer using TrueSync software. Click the **Options** link to display the Options page, and then click the **Synchronize** link. When the Synchronization Options page appears, follow the onscreen instructions to download, install, and run the TrueSync software.

➤ **Track public events and holidays**—Click the **Edit** button in the My Time Guides section of the Yahoo! Calendar page to automatically add holidays, sports schedules, and other public events to your calendar.

Address Book

If you want universal access to your contacts, no matter where you are or what PC you're using, use Yahoo! Address Book. The Yahoo! Address Book stores your contact information on Yahoo!'s Web servers, so you can access the information from any PC with an Internet connection and a Web browser.

You access your own personal Yahoo! Address Book by clicking the **Address Book** link on the Yahoo! home page, or by going directly to address.yahoo.com. You are prompted to supply your Yahoo! ID and password, and then you'll see the page shown in Figure 13.3.

All your contacts are listed—sorted by last name—on the Yahoo! Address Book page. If you have a number of contacts, you can search for a specific name, display names by the first letter of the last name, re-sort the contacts by first name, company, or email address, or pull down the View Category list to display only those contacts assigned to a specific category. Yahoo! displays icons next to each name indicating whether that person is online or offline at the moment.

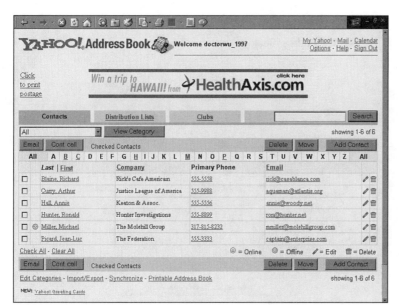

Figure 13.3

Access your contact list from any PC, anywhere in the world, with Yahoo! Address Book.

Use Your Address Book with Yahoo! Mail

The names you enter in Yahoo! Address Book are accessible when you create a new message in Yahoo! Mail. Click the **Address Book** link when you're composing a new email message to display and choose from the list of names from your Yahoo! Address Book. To add a name to your Yahoo! Address Book from an email message, or to add an email address directly from a message someone has sent you, click the **Add to Address Book** link in the email message. (See Chapter 10, "Free Email, Anywhere, with Yahoo! Mail," for more information about sending and receiving email messages.) You can also send email directly from Yahoo! Address Book; just select a person's name and then click the **Email** button.

To add a contact to your address book, click the **Add Contact** button. When the Add Contact page appears (shown in Figure 13.4), enter as much information as possible for your new contact. You can add even more details by clicking the **Add More Details** button; click the **Save** button to add this new contact to your Yahoo! Address Book.

137

Figure 13.4

Add a new contact to your Yahoo! Address Book from the Add New Contact page.

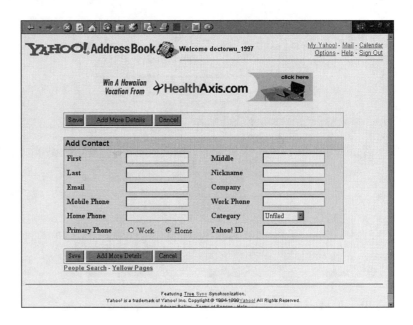

Import, Export, and Synchronize

To import data from another address book to your Yahoo! Address Book—or to export Yahoo! Address Book data to another address book program—click the **Import/Export** link on the Yahoo! Address Book page. To synchronize the data in your Yahoo! Address Book with a contact management program or Palm Pilot organizer, click the **Synchronize** link.

The Least You Need to Know

➤ Yahoo! Calendar lets you track your schedule from any PC connected to the Internet.

➤ Yahoo! Address Book lets you access your contact information from any Internet-enabled PC.

➤ Both Yahoo! Calendar and Yahoo! Address Book can be synchronized with other scheduling/contact management programs, or with Palm Pilot and other electronic organizers.

Chapter 14

Share Files and Photos with Yahoo! Briefcase

In This Chapter

➤ Find out how to share files and photos with other users via Yahoo! Briefcase

➤ Discover how to use Yahoo! Briefcase to transfer files from one PC to another

➤ Learn how to upload files to your Yahoo! Briefcase—and set different access levels for your briefcase folders

Have you ever wanted to share a computer file with a friend or colleague? Did you ever wish you had a way to display your favorite pictures on the Web so that family and friends could view them at their leisure? Do you long for an easy way to transfer files from one PC to another?

Wishes do come true, dear reader—because Yahoo! Briefcase will do all the above, and more!

Your Own Briefcase, on the Web

Yahoo! Briefcase is a way to store files online—on Yahoo!'s Web servers—and then access them from any PC with an Internet connection and a Web browser. You can even set selective access to your Briefcase files, so your friends, family, and co-workers can view, access, and download selected files.

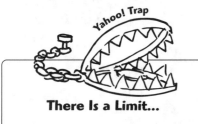

There Is a Limit...

Yahoo! Briefcase can store files with a maximum file size of 5MB. The total amount of space available for storage is 10MB.

Browse Your Briefcase

You access Yahoo! Briefcase directly at briefcase.yahoo.com. You must sign in with your Yahoo! ID and password, and then you'll see the Yahoo! Briefcase page shown in Figure 14.1.

If you want others to access your Yahoo! Briefcase page, they access a Web address that looks like this: briefcase.yahoo.com/bc/*yahooid*. Replace *yahooid* with your own Yahoo! ID to complete the URL.

By default, there are two folders within your briefcase. Click the **My Folder** link to view all the files stored online; click the **My Photo Album** link to display all the pictures and graphic files you've uploaded. You can create additional files and photo albums by clicking either the Create **Folder** or **Album** links.

Figure 14.1

Store files and pictures on your Yahoo! Briefcase page.

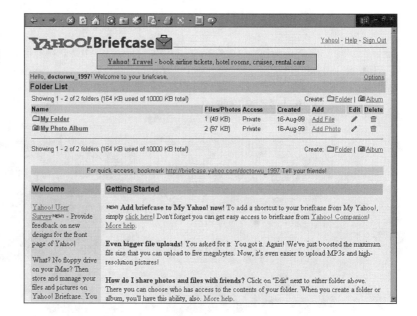

Fill Up Your Briefcase

To add a file to your briefcase, follow these steps.

1. From the Yahoo! Briefcase page, click either the **Add File** or **Add Photo** link.
2. When the Uploading a File or Uploading a Photo page appears (see Figure 14.2 for a peek at the Uploading File option), click the **Browse** button to locate the file on your computer and enter its location and filename in the **On your computer** box.

A Rose Is Still a Rose...

A photo album is just a folder that holds picture or graphic files. Files within a photo album can be viewed as thumbnails by clicking the **View Thumbnails** link. Besides not having access to the thumbnail option, there's no reason why you can't store picture files in a Yahoo! Briefcase folder.

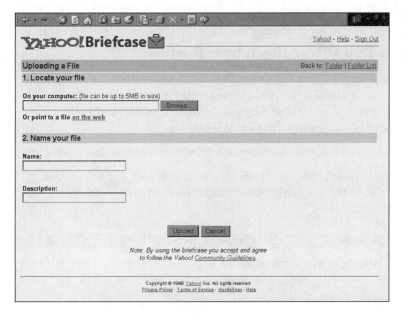

Figure 14.2

Upload a file or photo to your Yahoo! Briefcase.

3. If, instead of uploading your own file, you're pointing to a file elsewhere on the Internet, click the **on the web** link and enter the URL of the selected file.

4. Enter a **Name** and **Description** for the file or photo.

5. Click the **Upload** button.

Share Your Briefcase

You share the files or photos in your briefcase by setting *access levels* for folders within your Yahoo! Briefcase. To change the access level for a folder within your briefcase, click the **Edit** icon next to the folder on your Yahoo! Briefcase page, and then select from one of the following:

➤ **Private**—Only you can access this level; no other user can view or download files in this folder.

➤ **Friends**—Only users whose Yahoo! IDS you've added to your access list can access this level.

➤ **Everyone**—Any Internet user can access this level, even if they don't have a Yahoo! ID.

No Disk Drive? Use Yahoo! Briefcase!

If you own an Apple iMac or other computer that lacks a disk drive, you already know how difficult it is to transfer files from your computer to another machine. You can use Yahoo! Briefcase to upload files you want to transfer, and then access them and download them from the other computer.

Anyone accessing a folder in your Yahoo! Briefcase can download any of the files in the folder. Figure 14.3 shows the contents of a typical folder; to download a file, click the filename.

Figure 14.3

After you open a folder in your briefcase, click the filename to download a file.

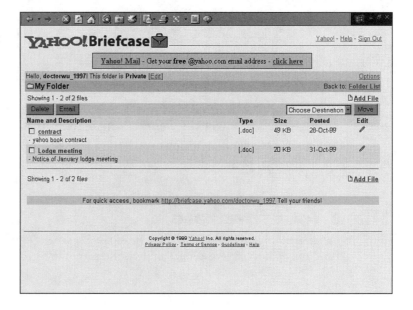

144

Store Your Auction Photos

If you list items at eBay or other non-Yahoo! online auction sites, your item listing can include links to pictures of your item, as long as those picture files are stored on another Web site. You can upload your auction photos to a Yahoo! Briefcase photo album, set the access level for Everyone, and then add the files' URLs to your online auction listing.

The Least You Need to Know

➤ Yahoo! Briefcase is a way to store files and photos on Yahoo!'s Web server— and then access them from any PC.

➤ You can store up to 10MB of files on Yahoo! Briefcase—with each file up to 5MB in size.

➤ By setting different access levels for your briefcase folders, you can allow other users (or all users) to view and download files from your Yahoo! Briefcase.

Part 4

Get Smart, Have Fun: Yahoo! News, Information, and Entertainment

Get news you can use—plus TV listings and MP3 digital music—at Yahoo's topic-specific information sites! (And go directly to Chapter 17, "Listen to Internet Music with Yahoo! Radio, Broadcast, and Digital," to learn all about Yahoo! Radio, Broadcast, and Digital!)

Chapter 15

Headlines, Forecasts, and Scores with Yahoo! News, Weather, and Sports

In This Chapter

➤ Learn about all of Yahoo!'s news sources, including Yahoo! News, Yahoo! News Alerts, and the My Yahoo! News Ticker

➤ Discover all the sports resources available at Yahoo! Sports

➤ Find out how to display local weather conditions and forecasts at Yahoo! Weather

Yahoo! is all about information—and the latest, most important information is called *news*. Yahoo! offers a variety of ways for you to get the latest news—and weather and sports—from simple news headlines to hand-picked news alerts to Internet feeds of television and radio news. Read on to learn the many ways to read the news on the Yahoo! network of sites.

All the News That's Fit to Click

When you want all the latest news, Yahoo! is the place to go. Just about any combination of up-to-the-minute headlines and in-depth reporting is available on Yahoo!'s many news pages, and they're all just a few clicks away! (And when I say up-to-the-minute, I mean *up-to-the-minute*—news headlines at Yahoo! News are updated so fast they often beat the TV news guys on developing stories!)

Get the News *Your* Way with My Yahoo!

The absolute best way to customize the news, sports, and weather you get online is with My Yahoo! (my.yahoo.com). With My Yahoo! you can select *which* news stories, sports scores, and weather forecasts you display on your personalized page—and create a totally customized news page, if that's what you want. To learn more about My Yahoo!, go to Chapter 2, "Create Your Own Personal Yahoo! with My Yahoo!."

Read the Daily News with Yahoo! News

Yahoo!'s main news page is Yahoo! News, shown in Figure 15.1. You get to Yahoo! News by clicking the **News** link on the Yahoo! home page, or by going directly to dailynews.yahoo.com.

Figure 15.1

Your home for news on the Net—Yahoo! News.

At Yahoo! News you'll find the following:

➤ Audio news from ABCNews and National Public Radio

➤ Business news from Associated Press, Motley Fool, TheStreet.com, and US Markets

➤ Entertainment news from Associated Press, E! Online, and Variety

➤ Full coverage reports on major topics

➤ Health news from Associated Press

➤ Links to news for other countries

➤ Links to news photos

➤ Local news for communities across the United States

➤ Oddly Enough(off-beat news stories from around the world)

➤ Political news from ABCNews and Associated Press

➤ Science news from Associated Press

➤ Sports news from Reuters

➤ Technology news from Associated Press, CNET, Internet Report, and ZDNet

➤ Top stories from ABCNews and Associated Press

➤ Video highlights of important news stories

➤ Weather conditions and forecasts

➤ World news from Associated Press and regional news sources

In addition, Yahoo! News includes a Search News feature that lets you look for specific stories, photos, or full coverage reports. Just enter your query in the **Search News** box and click the **Go!** button.

See the News in Photos with the Yahoo! News Image Gallery

If a picture is worth a thousand words, save some syllables and go directly to the Yahoo! News Image Gallery (dailynews.yahoo.com/headlines/g/ts/). Here you can find today's best news photos in four different photo galleries: Top Stories, International, Sports, and Entertainment. Click on a photo to view it at full size.

Have Your News Delivered Directly to Your Inbox with Yahoo! News Alerts

Why wait for the morning (or evening news)—wouldn't you rather be notified immediately when something of interest to you occurs? If you want instant notification of important news, use Yahoo! News Alerts to send you email about breaking news events.

To set up your Yahoo! News Alerts, go to alerts.yahoo.com and click the **Create Alert** button. When the Yahoo! News Alerts Page appears, enter a name for your alert, and then enter words or phrases you want Yahoo! to search for. (You can choose to have Yahoo! search for news that contains—or *doesn't* contain—specific words or phrases.) Select which news sources you want Yahoo! to scan, and then select how you want to be notified—via Yahoo! Mail or Yahoo! Messenger (or both). Tell Yahoo! whether you want to receive daily alerts or have immediate delivery of any alerts. Click the **Finished** button when you're done.

You can set up multiple alerts, of course. Create separate alerts for each type of news story you're interested in—then sit back and let Yahoo! notify *you* when something important happens!

All the News, All the Time, with My Yahoo! News Ticker

If you're connected to the Internet for long periods at a time, why not put a scrolling "ticker" on your desktop so the latest headlines, sports scores, weather conditions, and stock prices are always available? If you're using My Yahoo! (described back in Chapter 2), you can download and install the My Yahoo! News Ticker, which displays information from your My Yahoo! page directly on your desktop.

As you can see in Figure 15.2, the My Yahoo! News Ticker sits on your desktop and scrolls through the information you selected back on your My Yahoo! page. The News Ticker even flashes an alert when you have new email in your Yahoo! Mail inbox!

Figure 15.2

Watch the news scroll by when you install the My Yahoo! News Ticker on your desktop.

Debut In November · Allianz Buys 70 Pct Of Pimco · Citigroup's Weill Upbeat On U.S. Economy · Tech

To install the My Yahoo! News Ticker, go to my.yahoo.com/ticker.html and download the version for your particular operating system. You can use My Yahoo! News Ticker with all versions of Windows and Windows NT, Macintosh, OS/2, and UNIX. (If you connect to the Internet via America Online, use the Java version of the News Ticker.)

It Only Works When You're Connected

Obviously, the My Yahoo! News Ticker can only receive news while your computer is connected to the Internet.

Hear and Watch the News—Online—with Yahoo! Broadcast News

If you're more of a TV or radio person than you are a newspaper person, don't fret—Yahoo! provides access to television and radio news from around the world. When you go to the Yahoo! Broadcast News page (www.broadcast.com/news/), you can choose to watch or listen to news from the BBC World Service, CNBC/Dow Jones, CNN Audioselect, the Legal Channel, Newstrack, Medialink.com, and other sources. You'll need to have the appropriate media player installed on your machine, and a fairly fast and clean Internet connection, but then you can watch and listen to these news broadcasts on your own PC.

Be a Good Sport—with Yahoo! Sports

Yahoo!'s source for sports news, scores, and statistics is Yahoo! Sports, shown in Figure 15.3. You can access Yahoo! Sports by clicking the **Sports** link on the Yahoo! home page, or by going directly to sports.yahoo.com.

Internet Radio and Television—On Your Own PC

To learn more about receiving Internet broadcasts on your own computer, turn to Chapter 17, "Listen to Internet Music with Yahoo! Radio, Broadcast, and Digital."

Yahoo! Sports offers all the latest sports headlines, both concise scores and detailed box scores, and in-depth features on important sports topics. You'll even find links to separate pages for all major sports and leagues—including the NFL, NHL, NBA, MLB, NCAA football and basketball, NASCAR, world soccer, rugby, golf, and tennis.

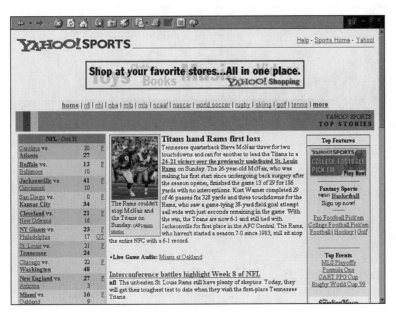

Figure 15.3

Sports scores, stats, and news—at Yahoo! Sports.

Yahoo! Tip

Life Is a Fantasy with Yahoo! Fantasy Sports

If you want to participate in a fantasy sports league, Yahoo! is the place to go. Yahoo! has fantasy leagues for basketball, hockey, football, college football, golf, baseball, soccer, and more. For more information—and to get signed up!—go to the Fantasy Sports section of the Yahoo! Sports page.

Today's Forecast: Always Clear with Yahoo! Weather

If you want to know whether to break out the rain gear, sun block, or snowshoes, go to Yahoo! Weather. Accessible by clicking the **Weather** link on the Yahoo! home page (or by going directly to `weather.yahoo.com`), Yahoo! Weather lets you enter a zip code or city name, and then displays the full-featured weather page shown in Figure 15.4. Yahoo! Weather displays current conditions, a five-day forecast, and links to additional weather resources—including numerous weather maps, weather news, and weatherplanner®, a for-pay service providing long-range weather predictions.

Figure 15.4

Rain or shine, get the latest forecasts at Yahoo! Weather.

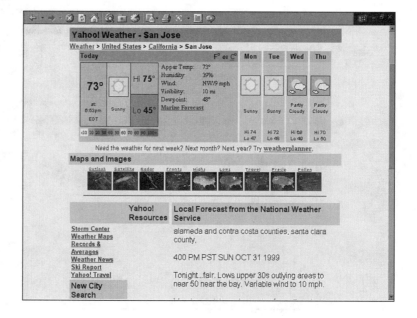

The Least You Need to Know

➤ Go to Yahoo! News (dailynews.yahoo.com) for the latest news headlines and links to other news sources.

➤ My Yahoo! News Ticker (my.yahoo.com/ticker.html) installs on your desktop and provides a scrolling display of the latest headlines, scores, weather conditions, and stock prices.

➤ Scores, stats, and sports news can be found at Yahoo! Sports (sports.yahoo.com).

➤ Weather conditions, forecasts, and maps for your community are displayed at Yahoo! Weather (weather.yahoo.com).

HURRAY FOR HOLLYWOOD

Chapter 16

Movies, Music, and More with Yahoo! Entertainment

In This Chapter

➤ Discover Yahoo! Entertainment, the home base for all of Yahoo!'s entertainment sites

➤ Find out what movies are showing where (and when!) in your area

➤ Display today's TV schedule on your computer screen—even if you watch via cable or a satellite dish

➤ Learn how to play games online, with other Yahoo! users

It's Friday night, you're home from work, and you're looking for something to do. Where do you go?

The place to go for all entertainment news and information—including movie show-times and TV schedules—is Yahoo! Entertainment. Whether your idea of a fun time is going out to a movie, staying in and watching TV, listening to a new CD, or playing a videogame, Yahoo! Entertainment tells you what's new, what's hot, and what's happening—when and where.

A Very Entertaining Place to Start: Yahoo! Entertainment

The home base for all of Yahoo!'s entertainment offerings is Yahoo! Entertainment, shown in Figure 16.1. You can get to Yahoo! Entertainment by clicking the **Entertainment** link on the Yahoo! home page, or by going directly to entertainment.yahoo.com.

Figure 16.1

Think of Yahoo! Entertainment as the Internet's best entertainment portal.

Yahoo! Entertainment includes links to Yahoo!'s more specific entertainment sites—Movies, Music, TV, Games, and Astrology—as well as the latest entertainment news, top ten lists, new releases, and listings and schedules. If you only go to one entertainment page on the Web, make it Yahoo! Entertainment!

Film News, Reviews, and Showtimes at Yahoo! Movies

What new movies are playing in theaters this week? What were last week's top box office draws? What's happening in the world of Hollywood?

For the answers to all these questions—and more—go to Yahoo! Movies (movies.yahoo.com), shown in Figure 16.2. In addition to all the industry news and reviews, you'll also find the latest videotape and DVD releases, and a detailed list of showtimes at your local theaters.

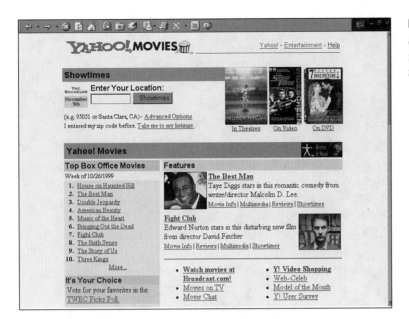

Figure 16.2

Go to Yahoo! Movies for the latest film news and reviews.

Cool Tunes at Yahoo! Music

Whether you listen to country, rap, rock, jazz, or classical, you'll find a wealth of musical resources at Yahoo! Music (music.yahoo.com) . As you can see in Figure 16.3, Yahoo! Music includes major sections for Rock & Pop, Country, Jazz & Blues, and Urban & Electronic genres—as well as links to the latest music news, new CD releases, and CD reviews.

Figure 16.3

Read about—and listen to—the latest releases at Yahoo! Music.

Even More Music at Yahoo!

If you want to listen to music online through your computer speakers, go to Yahoo! Radio (`radio.yahoo.com`), Yahoo! Broadcast (`www.broadcast.com`), and Yahoo! Digital (`digital.yahoo.com`). Yahoo! Digital also lets you download the latest tunes (in MP3 format) to your hard disk. You can go directly to these sites or link to them from the Yahoo! Music page; see Chapter 17, "Listen to Internet with Yahoo! Radio, Broadcast, and Digital," for more information.

Television News, Gossip, and Schedules at Yahoo! TV

Anything good on the tube tonight? You can find out quickly at Yahoo! TV (`tv.yahoo.com`). As you can see in Figure 16.4, Yahoo! TV includes TV news, gossip, reviews, ratings, and listings for your local area. (When you first log into Yahoo! TV, you'll be asked some questions about how you receive your TV signals, so Yahoo! TV can display customized listings for your broadcast stations, cable system, or satellite television provider.)

Figure 16.4

If you can watch it, Yahoo! TV will tell you about it—good or bad!

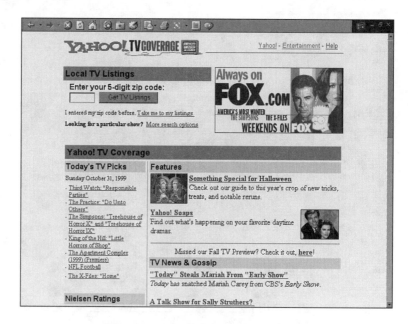

Computer Games, Videogames, and Online Games at Yahoo! Games

Are you a game player? If so, turn to Yahoo! Games (games.yahoo.com). The main Yahoo! Games page (shown in Figure 16.5) has three tabs that take you to the following sections:

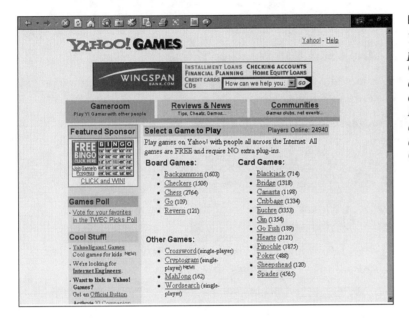

Figure 16.5

Yahoo! Games lets you play online games in the Gameroom, keep up-to-date on videogames and computer games in the Reviews & News section, and share your own tips and rumors in the game Communities.

➤ **Gameroom**—This is where to go if you want to play a game online. From this page you can choose from *board games* (Backgammon, Chess, Checkers, and so on), *card games* (Blackjack, Euchre, Poker, and so on), and *other games* (Crossword Puzzles, MahJong, Wordsearch, and so on). After you select a game to play, you'll need to select a specific gameroom, choose a table, find an online partner, and start playing!

➤ **Reviews & News**—Whether you play PC games, Sony Playstation, or Nintendo N64, this page provides news, tips, and cheats for all the most popular games.

➤ **Communities**—Sometimes the best source of tips and rumors is the gaming community. Learn what your fellow gamers are saying in Yahoo!'s game-related clubs—and check out Net Events of interest to serious gamers.

It's in the Stars at Yahoo! Astrology

Get your daily horoscope—and link to biorhythm, numerology, and tarot sites—at Yahoo! Astrology (entertainment.yahoo.com/astrology/). Just click your sign to see what the stars have to say today!

If It's Happening Online, It's at Yahoo! Net Events

There's a lot happening online these days, from celebrity chats to star-studded Netcast concerts. Get today's online program guide at Yahoo! Net Events (events.yahoo.com)—or just browse through the categories until you find something interesting.

> ### The Least You Need to Know
>
> ➤ Use Yahoo! Entertainment (entertainment.yahoo.com) as your home page for all of Yahoo!'s entertainment offerings.
>
> ➤ Yahoo! Movies (movies.yahoo.com) includes movie news and reviews, and showtimes for movie theaters in your area.
>
> ➤ Yahoo! Music (music.yahoo.com) showcases the latest CD releases and links to Yahoo!'s other music resources.
>
> ➤ Yahoo! TV (tv.yahoo.com) features reviews of the newest shows, plus a detailed TV schedule for your area.
>
> ➤ Yahoo! Games (games.yahoo.com) contains games you can play online, plus news and cheats for the hottest PC games and videogames.

Chapter 17

Listen to Internet Music with Yahoo! Radio, Broadcast, and Digital

In This Chapter

➤ Learn how to listen to Internet radio stations on your PC, using Yahoo! Radio

➤ Discover Yahoo! Broadcast, the comprehensive source of audio and video programming over the Internet

➤ Find out how to download CD-quality music files from Yahoo! Digital

Did you know the Internet can carry more than just text and still pictures? You can also use your PC to listen to audio broadcasts over the Internet—and if you have enough bandwidth, you can even watch video "Netcasts" online. In fact, millions of younger users have discovered how to download CD-quality music—in the burgeoning MP3 format—to create their own custom music collections.

To turn your PC into a full-fledged music machine, all you need is a fast Internet connection, a Web browser, the right music player software—and Yahoo!

All About Streaming Audio and Video

Audio and video signals are "broadcast" on the Internet via what is called *streaming audio and video*. With streaming media, you can start listening to (or watching) media files before an entire file is downloaded, because the streaming media player starts playing while the rest of the download (or live broadcast) continues in the background. Think of it as holding a bowl underneath a running faucet of water, with a second bowl underneath that. You can start filling the bottom bowl from the top bowl even though the top bowl isn't completely filled—and the water from the faucet keeps streaming into the top bowl, even as you pour. What you *don't* want to do is to completely empty the top bowl, which can happen if you pour faster than water streams out of the faucet.

Something similar can happen with streaming media when the stream isn't fast enough to keep up with the part of the program already "buffered" in your media player. In our faucet example, you would simply twist the knob to increase the flow of water; in the Internet world, the only way to increase the stream is to increase the bandwidth of your Internet connection.

Download the RealPlayer

To download the free RealPlayer G2 software, go to the Yahoo! Radio page and click the **Download Real G2 Player** link. Alternately, you can download the player directly from the RealNetworks site, at www.real.com.

Living Up and Down the Dial at Yahoo! Radio

Yahoo! Radio is the simplest way to listen to audio over the Internet. To use Yahoo! Radio, you need to have RealPlayer G2 installed on your system; after this software is installed, using Yahoo! Radio is as easy as pushing buttons on a car radio.

When you go to Yahoo! Radio (radio.yahoo.com) you'll see a big Click Here link. Assuming you already have the Real G2 Player installed, click the **Click Here** link, and Yahoo! loads the Yahoo! Radio window onto your desktop, as shown in Figure 17.1.

Adjust the volume.

Select a channel.

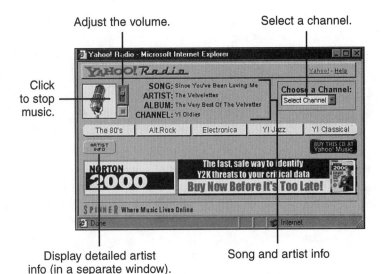

Click to stop music.

Figure 17.1

Listen to Internet radio stations with Yahoo! Radio.

Display detailed artist info (in a separate window).

Song and artist info

To listen to music with Yahoo! Radio, pull down the **Choose a Channel** list and select from one of the following channels:

➤ alt.rock

➤ Classic Rock

➤ Electronica

➤ The 80s

➤ Y! Classical

➤ Y! Country

➤ Y! Jazz

➤ Y! Oldies

➤ Y! R&B Jamz

After a few seconds, the channel you selected should start playing. You can adjust the volume with the slider control in the upper-left corner; click the button under the slider to stop the music.

165

Dealing with Bad Sound

If you're dissatisfied with either the sound quality or the "reception" of your Yahoo! Radio stations, you probably need a better (that is, *faster*) Internet connection. Because the music (which requires a lot of bandwidth) has to be piped down the same Internet connection you use for email and Web browsing, the slower or busier your connection, the more gaps and glitches you'll encounter. One way to "speed up" your *current* connection is to halt all other Internet activity—especially file downloading—while you're listening to Yahoo! Radio. If your Internet connection is slow or congested, however, you probably won't like what you hear from Yahoo! Radio or Yahoo! Broadcast.

Listen to Just About Anything—*Online*—at Yahoo! Broadcast

If Yahoo! Radio doesn't offer enough selection for you, go to the site's big brother— Yahoo! Broadcast (www.broadcast.com). Formerly known as Broadcast.com, Yahoo! Broadcast offers Internet broadcasts of audiobooks, CDs, radio stations, television stations, and on-demand video programming.

Got Extra Bandwidth? Use It!

If you have what is called a *broadband* connection to the Internet—via DSL, cable modem, or a T1 line—you can take advantage of that additional bandwidth for higher-quality audio/video playback. Click the **Broadband** link on the Yahoo! Broadcast page to view available high-bandwidth programming. Many corporations have broadband connections, so if you can play music in your cubicle or office, you might be able to get it from the Internet.

As you can see in Figure 17.2, Yahoo! Broadcast offers programming in a variety of different categories and media. Some Yahoo! Broadcast programs require the use of the RealPlayer G2, while others use the Windows Media Player. Some broadcasts are live, while others are downloaded or buffered versions of archived programming. Still other programming comes from compact discs or audiobooks and is available for either "live" online playback or (for a charge) downloading for future listening.

Figure 17.2

Listen to radio, CDs, or audiobooks online at Yahoo! Broadcast.

To find programming, click through the categories until you find what you're looking for. When you find a program, you'll see a page like that shown in Figure 17.3. In the left column you'll see the requirements for listening to or watching this broadcast; if you don't have the right software installed on your system, click the appropriate link to download and install it *before* you begin listening. Some broadcasts give you a choice of format; click the right button to start playback in the chosen format. In the case of some audiobooks and CDs, you can listen online for free, or download (and keep!) the programming for an additional charge. Click the appropriate button to start your playback software and start listening.

Figure 17.3

Choose a playback format and start listening!

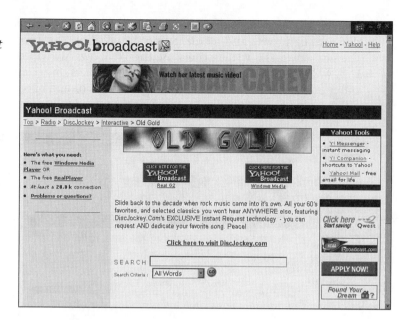

Download for Keeps—and Better Quality

If you encounter a lot of bandwidth problems when listening to broadcasts—pauses and skips and glitches—you might want to *download* the programming instead of listening to it "live," which you can do with some prerecorded broadcasts. When you play back the programming from your PC's hard disk, you bypass all the Internet connection bandwidth problems that contribute to poor "reception" in online broadcasts.

Yahoo! Digital

For the best selection of the latest music—for both "live" listening and downloading to your PC—go to Yahoo! Digital (`digital.yahoo.com`). Yahoo! Digital (shown in Figure 17.4) lets you download clips and songs directly to your hard disk, many in near–CD-quality MP3 format. After you've downloaded a song, you can listen to it on your PC or include it in any homegrown CD compilations you create.

Figure 17.4

Create your own music collection at Yahoo! Digital.

To take full advantage of Yahoo! Digital's music resources, you'll need some or all of the following media players installed on your PC:

➤ Beatnik Player

➤ Liquid Audio Player

➤ MP3 Player (any)

➤ MusicMatch Jukebox

➤ RealPlayer G2

➤ Windows Media Player

For more information about downloading these and other players, click the **Tools** link in the Help section of the Yahoo! Digital home page.

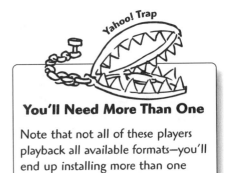

You'll Need More Than One

Note that not all of these players playback all available formats—you'll end up installing more than one player if you want to listen to all types of broadcasts.

After you have the proper players installed, it's a simple matter to choose a featured selection, or click the **Browse More Audio** (or **Browse More Video**) link to search Yahoo! Digital's Music Archive. When the Music Archive page appears, you can browse by either artist (alphabetically) or genre (Blues, Classical, Country, and so on). After you find the item you want, click the song title to display the individual listing page shown in Figure 17.5. For most clips you have the option of previewing the song online for free, or downloading (sometimes in a choice of formats) for a fee. Click the option you prefer—and start listening!

Figure 17.5

Buy and download your favorite songs—often in the popular MP3 format.

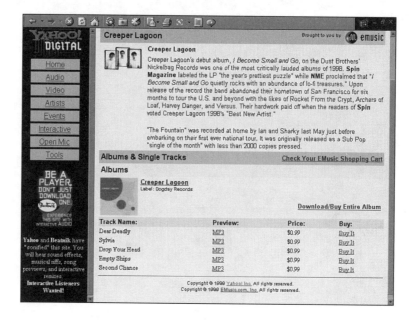

The Least You Need to Know

➤ Go to Yahoo! Radio (radio.yahoo.com) for a quick and easy playback of selected Internet radio stations.

➤ Go to Yahoo! Broadcast (www.broadcast.com) for a comprehensive selection of live and prerecorded Internet radio, video, CD, and audiobook programming.

➤ For CD-quality downloads in MP3 format, go to Yahoo! Digital (digital.yahoo.com).

Chapter 18

Stay Healthy—and Stay Young—with Yahoo! Health and Yahoo! Seniors' Guide

---

In This Chapter

➤ Discover one of the Internet's largest databases of drugs and diseases at Yahoo! Health

➤ Learn how to search for doctors and specialists in your area

➤ Find topics of interest to older users at the Yahoo! Seniors' Guide

---

When you're sick, you want to get well—fast. And as you grow older, you need to look out for yourself more carefully. It makes sense, then, for Yahoo! to create special sites containing both general health information and topics of specific interest to older Internet users. Read on to learn more about Yahoo! Health and Yahoo! Seniors' Guide.

Get Well—and Stay Healthy—with Yahoo! Health

Whether you're researching a potential medical condition, looking for a cure for a specific illness, exploring nutrition and fitness programs, or just searching for a doctor in your neighborhood, you can find the information you need at Yahoo! Health (health.yahoo.com). As you can see in Figure 18.1, Yahoo! Health includes the following health resources:

➤ **Health Research**—Search or browse for information about a specific disease, condition, or general health topic, or for information about a specific medication or drug. The disease/condition/topic pages are comprehensive yet understandable, and include a definition; causes, incidence, and risk factors; prevention information; symptoms; signs and tests; treatments; expectations (prognosis); and complications. The medication/drug pages are written for the layperson, and include brand names drugs are sold under, when you shouldn't take medicines, how to take and store medicine, drugs and foods to avoid while taking medicine, warnings, and potential side effects.

➤ **Alternative Medicine**—Learn all about natural health and healing methods.

➤ **Ask the Doctor**—Get online medical advice from Dr. Dean Edell and Dr. Nancy Snydermann.

➤ **Find a Doctor**—Search by zip code or location, HMO, doctor name, or specialty to find the right doctor near you.

➤ **Nutrition & Fitness**—Explore different foods and recipes, weight-loss issues and programs, and fitness regimens.

➤ **Personal Health Test**—Take an online test to determine your life expectancy and greatest health risks.

➤ **Talk About Health**—Take part in Yahoo!'s health-related chats, events, message boards, and clubs.

➤ **Today's Health News**—Read the latest health-related news from Associated Press and Reuters.

Figure 18.1

Search for health information and answers at Yahoo! Health.

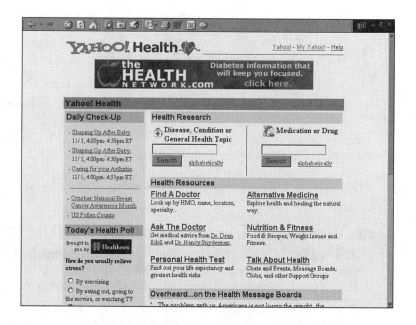

It's hard to imagine any health-related question for which you *can't* find an answer at Yahoo! Health. Whether you're looking for preventive information or a specific cure, Yahoo! Health is an essential site for all your online health needs!

Finally, a Site with Older Users in Mind: Yahoo! Seniors' Guide

Let's face it—older users have different needs and interests than do younger users. If you're over 50, you're probably less interested in downloading the latest MP3 hip-hop files, and more interested in exploring travel, health, or genealogy topics. If you find yourself gravitating toward the latter topics, check out the Yahoo! Seniors' Guide (seniors.yahoo.com), shown in Figure 18.2.

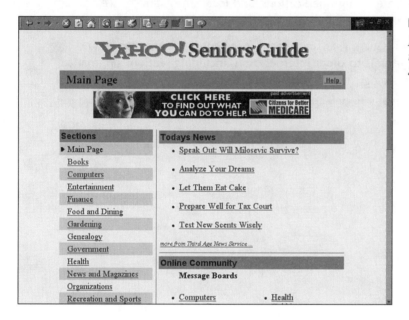

Figure 18.2

Find the topics you're interested in at the Yahoo! Seniors' Guide.

The Yahoo! Seniors' Guide gathers news and information on topics of particular interest to today's active seniors. Here you'll find sections devoted to

➤ Books

➤ Computers

➤ Entertainment

➤ Finance

➤ Food and Dining

➤ Gardening

➤ Genealogy

➤ Government

➤ Health

➤ News and Magazines

➤ Organizations

➤ Recreation and Sports

➤ Travel

173

The Yahoo! Seniors' Guide also includes links to seniors-focused message boards, chat rooms, and Yahoo! Clubs rooms. If you're more attracted to tap than rap, check it out!

The Least You Need to Know

➤ Yahoo! Health (health.yahoo.com) contains comprehensive databases of conditions/diseases, drugs/medications, and local physicians—as well as resources for alternative medicine, nutrition, and fitness.

➤ Yahoo! Seniors' Guide (seniors.yahoo.com) contains information and resources of interest to older Internet users, including sections on finance, gardening, genealogy, health, and travel.

Part 5

Buy and Sell Online: Yahoo! Auctions and Shopping

Want to be a winning bidder—without spending a fortune? Or do you need to do a little shopping from the comfort of your computer terminal? Or maybe you're in the mood for a new car or a new house—and you want to avoid the hassle of traditional big-ticket shopping? Whatever you want to buy—or sell—turn to this section for expert advice!

Chapter 19

Buy Low, Sell High, with Yahoo! Auctions

In This Chapter

➤ Learn how place an item up for auction

➤ Find out how to place bids on items at Yahoo! Auctions

➤ Discover winning bid strategies—such as sniping

➤ Learn about the entire online auction process, from listing to shipping

---

Online auctions are the hottest things going on the Internet today. With an online auction, you can buy or sell just about anything—from Beanie Babies to sports cards to used computer equipment to antiques—through an automated auction process. A seller puts an item up for auction, and over the course of a week or so, bidders place electronic bids on the item. At the end of the auction, the highest bidder wins—and purchases and receives the merchandise. The entire process is automated, so its both easy and fun to participate.

Yahoo! Auctions is one of the largest online auction sites on the Internet, with more than 1 million items up for bid on any given day. Read this chapter to find out how to buy and sell at Yahoo! Auctions—without losing your shirt.

How an Online Auction Works

Never participated in an online auction before? Well, don't get nervous—Yahoo! Auctions makes it easy to join in on the fun. You'll need to register first (unless you've already created a Yahoo! ID), and then you're ready to jump in and join the bidding—or pull some old stuff out of the attic and try to sell it.

More Online Auction Tips—By the Book!

For a comprehensive look at a variety of online auction sites—including tips and secrets for successful selling and bidding—read my book *The Complete Idiot's Guide to Online Auctions.* You can find this book wherever computer how-to books are sold or purchase it online at `www.molehillgroup.com/cig-auct.htm`.

The Seller Places an Ad

The way an auction starts is that someone has something he or she wants to sell. It could be something big, or it could be something small—it really doesn't matter as long as there's a market for it.

The seller enters Yahoo! Auctions and clicks the **Submit Item** link. The seller has to choose a category for this auction and then complete an item information form. After a seller has entered all appropriate information about the item to be sold, he or she clicks the **Done** button and the item is automatically listed for sale.

The Buyer Searches for an Item

Now let's turn our attention to the potential buyer. A buyer looking for something in particular can try to find it either by browsing through the master list of categories or by searching all the items for sale for items matching a specific query or keyword.

If the buyer is new to all this, the browsing option is probably best—it's a good way to get a feel for all the different types of merchandise available. All you have to do is click through the categories and subcategories of items as you do when browsing the main Yahoo! Web directory.

More experienced buyers, however, learn to search for specific things they want. For example, let's say the buyer wants to find a gray-colored Furby. The buyer would enter the query `gray Furby` into the Find Auction box and then click the **Search** button. Yahoo! Auctions then returns a list of gray Furbies currently up for auction.

When a buyer finds an item that looks interesting, he or she clicks the link for that item. This displays a full description of the item for sale, including a picture (if the seller posted one), the initial bid, the current bid, and how much time is left on this particular auction.

If the buyer isn't interested in that item, no harm done—clicking the browser's **Back** button takes the buyer back to the master list with no bid registered. If the buyer is interested, however, we move to the next step.

The Buyer Makes a Bid

To make a bid, the buyer has to enter his or her Yahoo! ID and password, and the *maximum bid* he or she is willing to make.

Maximum Bids

Now, you might be asking, why would you enter a *maximum* bid when the listing is displaying the current *minimum* bid?

Think about it this way: The buyer enters the maximum amount he or she is willing to pay—even though the buyer hopes the bidding doesn't go up that high. Here's an example: Let's say the seller has listed a minimum bid of $20 for an item. The potential buyer reads the listing and determines that the item is actually worth $30—so the buyer enters $30 as the maximum bid. The automated bidding software, however, enters the buyer's bid as $20, which is the minimum *required* bid. If no one else bids on this item, the buyer gets it for $20—and doesn't have to spend the entire $30 he or she was willing to pay. However, if another bidder enters the fray and bids, let's say, $25, then the initial bidder's bid will be automatically increased to meet and beat the competing bid—up to the $30 maximum that was specified.

After the buyer enters a maximum bid amount, he or she clicks the **Preview Bid** button and then confirms the bid. The bid is registered and a new current bid is displayed on the item's listing screen.

The potential buyer gets immediate feedback as to whether he or she was the high bidder from the Preview page. It's possible that a previous bidder registered a higher maximum bid than did this buyer, so the buyer's bid was immediately and automatically outbid. (That is, it's possible to bid the current asking price and find out you didn't bid high enough.) If this happens—and the buyer still wants the item—it's time to make another, higher bid and see what happens.

The Bidding Continues...

Now the waiting begins. Other potential buyers might read the item's listing and place competing bids—or maybe no one else bids. In any case, the auction continues until its time expires.

Automated Bidding Explained

This automated bidding procedure is called *proxy bidding*. If you're a bidder, proxy bidding can save you time and help you get the items you want. Proxy bidding operates via *agent software* that is authorized to act in your place—but with some predefined bidding parameters. You define the maximum amount you are willing to bid, and then the "robot" agent takes over and does your bidding for you. The proxy robot bids as little as possible to outbid new competition, up to the maximum bid you specified. If it needs to up your bid $1, it does. If it needs to up your bid $5, it does—until it hits your bid ceiling, where it stops and bows out of the bidding.

What happens when someone outbids the current minimum bid? Well, several things can happen. First, however, Yahoo!'s automated bidding software automatically adjusts the initial buyer's bid to outbid the new bidder—unless the new bidder's maximum bid exceeds the initial buyer's maximum bid, or until the current minimum bid exceeds the maximum bid specified by the initial buyer. At the point where the initial buyer is outbid, he or she is notified (via email) that he or she no longer has the high bid. In this case, the initial bidder has a choice. He or she can choose to return to the site and place a new, higher bid on the item, or to bow out of the bidding completely, with no other actions necessary.

Bidding in Increments

If you know what the current bid is, how do you figure out what the next higher bid should be? It's easy—Yahoo! Auctions calculates an official *bid increment* for each bid. This bid increment varies by price point; the bid increment is lower when the current bid price is lower and higher when the current bid price is higher. For example, a $5 bid might have a $.50 bid increment (making the next bid $5.50), while a $50 bid might have a $1 bid increment (making the next bid $51) and a $100 item might have a $5 bid increment (making the next bid $105).

The High Bidder Wins

Days go by. The auction runs its course, and at the appointed time the highest bid is recognized as the official winning bid.

Of course, it's not that simple. The final few minutes of any auction often see a flurry of activity, with several bidders trying to get in on the action at the last minute. For that reason, many bidders monitor the final minutes of any auction they're really serious about.

Going, Going...and Still Going?

Sellers at Yahoo! Auctions can choose to have bidding continue beyond the stated auction close if there is bidding activity in the five minutes prior to the original close of the auction. This automatic extension feature tends to minimize the impact of bid *sniping* (discussed later in this chapter), which is the practice of placing a "snipe" bid at the very last second of an auction.

When the auction is finally over, both the seller and the winning bidder are notified via email of the final status of the auction. It is their responsibility to contact each other to arrange payment and shipping. (It's common for the seller to make the initial contact with the winning bidder, although it's okay for either to initiate communication.)

Typically, the seller notifies the buyer of the final *total* price of the item, including shipping and handling. Sometimes shipping and handling has to be negotiated, but more often than not the seller has a firm cost—and often states it up front in the item's description.

The Buyer Pays, the Seller Ships

After the total price is disclosed, the buyer then sends the seller a personal check, cashier's check, or money order. (If the seller is actually a business, the buyer might be able to pay with a credit card; most individuals cannot process credit-card transactions.)

After the seller receives payment (and, in the case of personal checks, waits for the check to clear), the seller then packs and ships the merchandise to the buyer. The buyer receives the merchandise a few days later, and—assuming it all arrives in one piece as described—another online auction is successfully concluded.

Use Escrow for Credit Cards

Individuals can accept credit card payments for items by using an *escrow service.* Escrow services are also good ways for buyers and sellers to protect themselves during a transaction, as the service acts as a "middleman," ensuring that both payment and shipment are made.

One last thing: Yahoo! Auctions encourages users to provide *feedback* about the people they deal with. So if you're a buyer, you should provide feedback—positive or negative, depending on your experience—about the seller and vice versa. You can get a good gauge on the reliability of a buyer or seller by observing his or her overall feedback ratings, gathered from multiple transactions.).

All About Yahoo! Auctions

Yahoo! Auctions is one of the top auction sites on the Internet. More than a million items are available in thousands of different categories; it's easy to find something to bid on and easy to list something for bid. And, unlike some online auction sites, there is no charge to either the buyer or seller—listing and bidding are completely free.

Read the Guides

For detailed instructions about how to use Yahoo! Auctions, click either the **Bidder Guide** or the **Seller Guide** links on the Yahoo! Auctions page.

You access Yahoo! Auctions by clicking the **Auctions** link on the Yahoo! home page, or by going directly to auctions.yahoo.com. As you can see in Figure 19.1, you can search for items up for auction (using the Find Auctions box) or browse for items by category. You submit an item for auction by clicking the **Submit Item** link; you can track the status of items you're selling or bidding on by clicking the **My Auctions** link.

Figure 19.1

Search or browse for items at Yahoo! Auctions.

Bidding to Win

To place a bid on a Yahoo! Auction item, follow these steps:

1. From the Yahoo! Auctions home page, search or browse for a specific item.
2. When the list of items matching your query is displayed (see Figure 19.2), click an individual item listing to see more details.

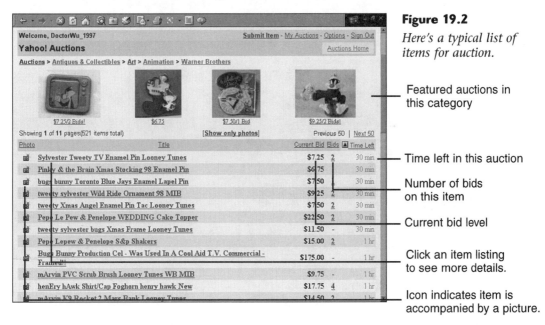

Figure 19.2

Here's a typical list of items for auction.

Featured auctions in this category

Time left in this auction

Number of bids on this item

Current bid level

Click an item listing to see more details.

Icon indicates item is accompanied by a picture.

183

3. When the item listing page appears (see Figure 19.3), review the information and decide whether you want to place a bid.

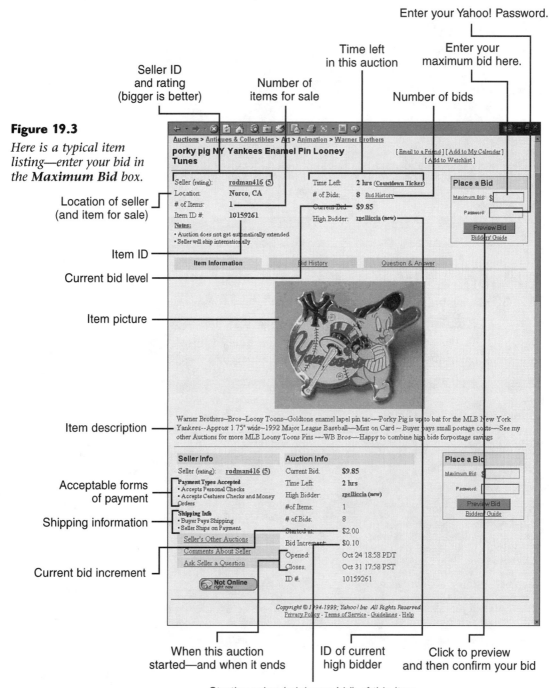

Figure 19.3

*Here is a typical item listing—enter your bid in the **Maximum Bid** box.*

Enter your Yahoo! Password.

Enter your maximum bid here.

Time left in this auction

Number of bids

Seller ID and rating (bigger is better)

Number of items for sale

Location of seller (and item for sale)

Item ID

Current bid level

Item picture

Item description

Acceptable forms of payment

Shipping information

Current bid increment

When this auction started—and when it ends

ID of current high bidder

Click to preview and then confirm your bid

Starting price (minimum bid) of this item

184

4. Enter your maximum bid for this item in the **Maximum Bid** box.

5. Enter your Yahoo! password in the **Password** box.

6. Click the **Preview Bid** button.

7. When the Preview page appears, confirm your bid.

When you click the **Preview Bid** auction, you see the Preview page, which will contain either a High Bid Confirmation (if your bid is the new high bid) or an Outbid Confirmation (if a previous bidder's maximum bid—via automatic bidding—is higher than your maximum bid).

If you get outbid in the course of an auction, you will be notified via email. At this point, you can return to the item listing page and place a new maximum bid—or you can lick your wounds and move on to another, more affordable item.

Submitting an Item for Auction

To submit an item for auction, follow these steps:

1. From the Yahoo! Auctions page, click the **Submit Item** link.

2. If you have not yet registered and submitted your credit card information, you'll be prompted to do so now.

You Need a Card to Play

To list or bid on items at Yahoo! Auctions, you need to register and supply credit card information. Because there are no listing or bidding fees at Yahoo! Auctions, your credit card is not charged; Yahoo! uses this information simply to verify your age and identity.

3. When the Choose a Category page appears, click the category where you want to place your item listing.

4. When the Submitting an Item page appears (as shown in Figure 19.4), verify that you've chosen the proper category.

5. Enter the title for your item listing in the **Title** box.

6. Enter a detailed description for your item in the **Description** box; this will become your main listing text.

Figure 19.4

Fill in all the blanks to properly list your item for auction.

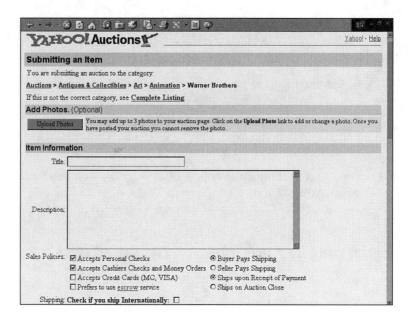

Spice Up Your Listings with HTML

Yahoo! Auctions lets you use HTML codes in your item listings to "punch up" otherwise plain-text listings. You can use just about any HTML code pairs, including **bold** and <i>*italic*</i>. For more information on HTML codes, see Chapter 30, "Create Sophisticated Pages with HTML."

7. Determine what forms of payment you want to accept and then check the appropriate options in the **Sales Policies** section.

8. Determine your shipping policy, then check the appropriate options in the **Shipping** section.

9. In the **Quantity of Item** box, enter the number of items you're selling *in this listing only*. (Typically, this is "1.")

10. Enter the starting price (or *minimum bid*) for your item in the **Starting Price** box.

11. Select how many days you want your auction to last from the **Length of Auction** list. (Longer is generally better, unless you're in a hurry to get things over with.)

12. If you only want to accept bids from higher-quality bidders, select a value from the **Minimum Bidder Rating** list. Any bidders not meeting your minimum rating will be required to submit a credit card before their bids are accepted.

13. If you want your auction to be automatically extended by five minutes if there are last-minute bids placed, check the **Auto Extension** box.

14. If you want to be able to close your auction early, check the **Allow Early Close** option.

15. If you want to specify a *reserve price* for your auction, enter that value in the **Reserve Price** box.

Reserve the Option to Reserve

A *reserve price* is a price above the starting (minimum bid) price that is the lowest price you're willing to take for the item. If no bids come in above the reserve price (which is hidden from bidders), then you're not obligated to sell the item. Sellers sometimes use a reserve price on high-end items if they want to make sure the market does not undervalue what they are selling. Bidders seem to universally dislike hidden reserves, and putting a reserve price on your item can actually discourage bidders from bidding on your item.

16. If you want your auction to automatically end when a set price is met, enter that price in the **Buy Price** box.

17. Pull down the **Closing Time** list and enter the hour of day you want your auction to end. (Note that these hours are Pacific Time—make sure you translate to your local time.)

18. If you want to automatically relist your item if your auction closes without receiving any bids, select a value from the **Auto Resubmit** list.

19. To include a photograph with your listing, click the **Upload Photos** button. When the Upload Photos page appears, click the

Store Your Photos with Yahoo!

Unlike other online auction sites, Yahoo! Auctions stores your photos on its own Web site. You can upload up to three photos (for a total of 1.5Mb) for any item listing.

Browse button to locate photos on your hard disk. When the location of your photo file is listed in the Step 1 box, click the **Add Photo** button. To add more than one photo, repeat these steps; click the **Done** button when you're finished.

20. When you're done entering information and making choices, click the **Continue** button.

21. Yahoo! now displays a preview of your item listing. Examine this page carefully; if you want to make changes, use the **Back** button on your browser to go back and re-enter information on the Submitting an Item page.

22. When your auction listing is in final form, click the **Submit** button.

As soon as you click the **Submit** button, your auction goes "live"—and the auction begins!

Managing Your Auctions-in-Progress

You can manage all your in-progress auctions—whether you're buying or selling—from the My Auctions page. From here, you can do the following:

➤ **Track any open auction**—Even if you're not bidding on an auction, you can track its progress by clicking the **Watchlist** link.

➤ **Track items you're selling**—To track your in-progress items up for auction, click the **Selling** link.

➤ **Track items you're bidding on**—To track the progress of auctions in which you've placed a bid, click the **Bidding** link.

➤ **Review your winning bids**—To display a list of auctions in which you were the winning bidder, click the **Won** link.

➤ **Review your old auctions**—To display a list of items you had up for auction that have since closed, click the **Closed/Sold** link.

When you click the **Selling** link on the My Auctions page, you also access Yahoo!'s Auction Manager. This is a tool that provides various services to sellers; from here you can cancel your auction, close your auction, cancel bids, edit your item's description, and edit your "blacklist" of people you don't want bidding in your auctions.

How to Win an Auction—by Sniping

Experienced auction bidders know that the key to winning an auction is to hide your interest until the very last moment—and then strike swiftly and with authority. With this strategy, stealth and subterfuge are required to disguise your interest, as is the patience to hold your bid until the last possible moment. No one must know that you want this item, no one can suspect what you are willing to bid, and no one can be prepared for your last-minute strike against the people who've been bidding throughout the life of the auction.

Get Automatic Notification

If you want to be notified—via email, Yahoo! Messenger, or through your pager—when something happens in your auction, click the **Options** button on any Yahoo! Auction page; when the Options page appears, click the **Set Event Notification** link. You can choose to receive notification when an auction is canceled or closed, when a bid has been placed on one of your auctions, when you've been outbid on an item, or when you've received feedback from another user.

The thinking behind this strategy is simple. By not disclosing your interest, you don't contribute to bidding up the price during the course of the auction. By bidding at the last minute, you don't leave enough time for other bidders to respond to your bid. The late bidder makes one bid only—and makes it count.

This whole process of swooping in at the last possible moment is called *sniping*. Some bidders (those who don't snipe!) despise sniping, saying it takes all the fun out of the auction process. Experienced snipers say that sniping itself is fun, that it can be kind of a game to see just how late you can bid and still make it count before the auction closes.

Let's look at an example of sniping:

1. You find an item you want and make a note of the time the auction closes—to the second. Next, you arrange your schedule so you're free when you need to bid.

2. Five minutes before the auction closes, you log on to the Internet and access the auction in question. You note the current bid price; let's say it's $25. You feel that a $30 bid will safely win the auction, so you prepare a maximum bid of $30.

3. With about 30 seconds left in the auction, you send your bid. You immediately pop up as the high bidder in the auction—and then the auction closes. By the time the former high bidder gets the auction's automatic outbid notice via email, the auction is already over—and you've won.

The experienced sniper doesn't even look at new auctions listed today. Instead, you want to scan the auctions that are closing today. You need to plan the timing of your bid; you'll need to be at your computer, logged onto the Internet and to the auction in question, ready to press the button at just the right moment.

Whether you like it or not, sniping works. After all, if you place a high enough bid at the last second, there's no time for anyone to respond with a higher bid. The last high bidder always wins, and a sniper stands a very good chance of being the last high bidder.

Can you snipe and still lose an auction? Yes, under these scenarios:

➤ First, there might be another sniper in the queue who places a higher snipe than your maximum bid. A last-second bid of $35 will beat out a last-second bid of $30.

➤ Second, your snipe might be too early, allowing time for the previous high bidder to receive an outbid notice and respond with a higher bid.

➤ Third, your snipe might not be high enough to beat out an existing high bid. If the current bid is $25 but the high bid (not known to you) is $35, you'd be beat if you "only" bid $30.

➤ Fourth, you might be participating in an auction that automatically extends the auction close because of last-minute bidding—making your last-minute bid not really a last-minute bid.

If you've ever been outbid on an item at the very last moment, you know that sniping can win auctions. Even if you hate sniping, the only way to beat a sniper is to snipe yourself.

Top 10 Tips for Placing a Winning Bid

Whether you snipe or don't snipe, you can do other things to increase your chances of winning an auction without overpaying for the item in question. Here are 10 tips that can help anyone be a better bidder at Yahoo! Auctions.

Tip #1: Do Your Research

Don't bid blind; make sure you know the true value of an item before you offer a bid. Look around at other auctions of similar items; what prices are they going for? Research the price of similar items offline; sometimes, you can find what you're looking for at a discount store or in a catalog or at another Internet site—where you'll probably get a real warranty and a better return policy. Shop around, and don't assume that the price you see at an auction is always the best deal available.

In addition, you shouldn't bid on the first item you see. With a million items listed on any given day, chances are Yahoo! Auctions has several other items similar to the first item you saw. Look at the entire list of items before you choose which one to bid on. Seldom is the first item you see the one you really want or the best deal.

Tip #2: Know When to Say No

Be disciplined. Set a maximum price you're willing to pay for an item, and *don't exceed it!* It's okay to lose an auction.

Don't automatically rebid just because you've been outbid. It's too easy to get caught up in the excitement of a fast-paced auction. Learn how to keep your cool; know when to say no.

Tip #3: If It Sounds Too Good to Be True, It Probably Is

A rare copy of *Action Comics #1* for only $25? A brand-new Pentium II computer for only $100? There has to be a catch. That *Action Comics* is probably a facsimile reprint (the genuine article, featuring the first appearance of Superman, is worth thousands of dollars), and the brand-new Pentium II is likely a remanufactured unit missing some key parts. Be suspicious of improbable or impossible deals; always ask questions that confirm or reject your suspicions.

Tip #4: Check the Ratings

Check out the seller's rating. Make sure the seller of the item you want has a good rating—and avoid any who don't. You can click the seller's numerical rating to display actual comments from other users who have dealt with this user before. The best way to avoid bad sellers is to find out they're bad sellers beforehand.

Tip #5: Bid in Odd Numbers

When you bid, don't bid an even amount. Instead, bid a few pennies more than an even buck; for example, if you want to bid $10, bid $10.03 instead. That way, your bid will beat any bids at the same approximate amount—$10.03 beats $10 even, any day—without you having to place a new bid at the next whole bid increment.

Tip #6: Keep Track of Your Auctions

Don't let your auction activity get away from you. Use Yahoo!'s My Auctions page to track all your auctions on a daily basis.

Tip #7: Don't Forget Shipping Costs—and Don't Overpay

When you're placing your bid, remember that you'll actually have to pay more than you bid; you have to pay shipping and handling to put the item in your hands. If S/H costs aren't detailed in the item listing, figure them out yourself, or email the seller to get a reasonable estimate. That ultra-cheap $2 item looks pretty expensive if you have to add $5 shipping and handling to the base price.

Not only should you not get taken by surprise by shipping costs, but you also shouldn't be taken advantage of by unrealistic shipping and handling charges. Get a ballpark feel for shipping on a specific item from the seller's location to where you live. Expect a little overage on the seller's part (she has to buy packing materials, labels, and such), but not too much of an overage. If you know shipping should be in the $2 range, accept a $3 charge, but question a $5 charge.

Tip #8: Watch the Finish

Don't get outbid at the last minute. Most auction activity occurs at the very end of the auction. Track the last hour of your most important auctions and be prepared to react quickly to last-second bidders and snipers.

Tip #9: If You Win It, Inspect It

When you receive the item you paid for, open it up and inspect it—*immediately!* Don't wait a month before you look at it and then expect the seller to rectify a situation that was long considered closed. OK the item, and then send the seller an email saying you got it and it's okay. If you sit on it too long, it's yours—no matter what.

Tip #10: If You Get Ripped Off, Tell Yahoo! About It

If you have a problem with a seller, first try working it out between the two of you. If things don't get resolved, then contact Yahoo! with your grievance. Yahoo! Auctions provides a formal feedback form for bad transactions; you can find it at `add.yahoo.com/fast/help/auct/cgi_feedback`. Use this form when you think you've been ripped off.

Top 10 Tips for Increasing Your Auction Revenues

Here are 10 tips that can help anyone be a more profitable seller at Yahoo! Auctions.

Tip #1: Research Your Price

Don't sell without doing your homework first; make sure you know the true value of an item before you put it up for auction. Before you price your item, search for similar items at your chosen auction site. What are they priced? What are their final selling prices? Research the price of similar items offline; sometimes, you can get a feel for relative value if you compare your item to a newer version of the same. Be informed, and you won't set the price too high or too low; you'll set it just right.

Tip #2: Make Your Ad Stand Out

Do everything in your power to make your ad stand out from the two million other ads currently online. Work on both the title and the description, and consider employing HTML to create a more dynamic ad.

Tip #3: Get All the Buzzwords in the Title

Make sure you have the right words and phrases in your title. If your audience looks for "laser discs," then say `laser disc;` if they look for "LDs," then say `LD`. If they look for both, then use both. Use all possible words (up to your auction's character limit) to hit all possible keywords your potential bidders might be searching for—even if some of the words are redundant.

Tip #4: A Picture Says a Thousand Words

Nothing increases your chances of selling an item like including a picture of it in your listing. Take a photo of your item, scan it in, upload it, and include it with your listing.

Tip #5: End in Prime Time

When you end your auction is important, because some of the most intense bidding takes place in the final few minutes of your auction from snipers trying to steal the high bid at the last possible moment. To take advantage of last-minute bidders, your auction needs to end when the most possible bidders are online.

If you end your auction at three in the morning, everyone will be asleep and you'll lose out on any last-minute bids. Instead, try to end your auction during early evening hours, when the greatest number of users are online.

Remember, though, that you're dealing with a three-hour time-zone gap between the east and the west coasts. So if you time your auction to end at 7 p.m. EST, you're ending at 4 p.m. PST—when most potential bidders are still at work. Conversely, if you choose to end at 9 p.m. PST, you just hit midnight in New York—and many potential bidders are already fast asleep.

The best times to end your auction are between 9 and 11 p.m. EST, or between 6 and 8 p.m. PST. (Figure the in-between time zones yourself!) That way you'll catch the most potential bidders online for the final minutes of your auction—and possibly generate a bidding frenzy that will garner a higher price for your merchandise.

Tip #6: Go Long...or Create a Short-Term Frenzy

When it comes time to choose the length for your auction, go for the longest auction possible. The longer your item is up for auction, the more potential bidders who will see it—and the more potential bidders, the better your chances of selling it for a higher price. Don't cheat yourself out of potential sales by choosing a shorter auction.

On the other hand, if you have something really hot, create a bidding frenzy by choosing a very short auction length. If you do this, play it up in your item's title: `3_Days Only!` works pretty well.

Tip #7: There's No Reason to Reserve

I don't know of a single bidder who likes reserve price auctions. Why use something that scares some bidders away? Set a realistic minimum, and get on with it.

Tip #8: Track Your Auctions

Don't let your auction activity get away from you. Use Yahoo!'s My Auctions and Auction Manager features to track all your auctions on a daily basis.

Tip #9: Blacklist Deadbeats

You don't have to sell to just anybody. You want to sell to someone who will actually consummate the transaction and send you payment; bidders with negative feedback are more likely to leave you high and dry.

In your item listing, you can stipulate that you won't sell to bidders with ratings below a certain level. If you receive bids from these potential deadbeats, cancel the bids. If the deadbeats continue to bid (after being warned off via email by you), you can *blacklist* those bidders from this and other auctions.

To blacklist a bidder, click the **Option** link on Yahoo! Auctions page; when the Options page appears, click the **Edit Blacklist** link, then enter the ID of the bidder you want to blacklist.

Tip #10: If Nobody Buys, Resubmit—with a Different Listing

If you didn't sell your item the first time, try it again. Yahoo! Auctions lets you easily resubmit unsold items—but remember that if it didn't sell the first time, there was probably a reason why. Was your asking price too high? Was your description too vague? Was the title too boring? Should you have included a picture or used HTML to spice up the listing? Change something to increase your chances of selling your item the second time around.

The Least You Need to Know

➤ Yahoo! Auctions (auctions.yahoo.com) is one of the top online auction sites on the Internet, with more than a million items for sale on any given day.

➤ There are no fees to either list or bid on items at Yahoo! Auctions, although you will need to register (and supply a credit card number, which won't be charged).

➤ You list an item for sale by clicking the **Submit Item** link on the Yahoo! Auctions page.

➤ You find items to bid on by browsing or by searching; when you find the right item, enter the maximum amount you're willing to pay (no matter what the current bid level is) in the Maximum Bid box; Yahoo!'s automatic bidding software will automatically increase the value of your bid (up to your maximum amount) as other bids increase.

➤ One way to increase your chances of winning an auction is to wait until the last minute and place a "snipe" bid.

➤ After an auction ends, the high bidder and seller are both notified; the buyer typically pays shipping and handling costs.

SWM SEEKS MATE. NO SMOKERS.

ALSO SELLING '72 ORANGE DODGE DART.

TYPE TYPE

Chapter 20

Advertise Your Stuff (and Yourself!) with Yahoo! Classifieds and Personals

In This Chapter

➤ Learn how to buy and sell merchandise and services via online classified ads

➤ Discover how to find a great relationship, online

➤ Find out how to use Yahoo!'s Personals Mailbox to screen replies to your personals ad (or responses to your replies)

Online auctions are fun, but they're pretty much limited to merchandise small enough to ship cheaply and easily. If you have something larger to sell—like a car or a house—or you just don't want to bother with the whole bidding process, then you're probably more comfortable with the traditional classified advertising format.

Yahoo! Classifieds offers the online equivalent of classified ads, with local listings for autos, computers, pets, real estate, rentals, and services. Yahoo! also offers online personal advertising through the Yahoo! Personals service. If you're like most users, you'll find the ability to search and browse through the listings online preferable to the old-fashioned method of literally using your thumbs to thumb through the listings!

Buy and Sell Big Stuff with Yahoo! Classifieds

Yahoo! Classifieds is a great way to buy and sell items you'd normally sell in a newspaper classified ad. You access Yahoo! Classifieds by clicking the **Classifieds** link on the Yahoo! home page, or by going directly to classifieds.yahoo.com.

As you can see in Figure 20.1, the Yahoo! Classifieds page looks a lot like the main Yahoo! page, with classified ad listings arranged by the following major categories:

Figure 20.1

Browse through the online classified ads at Yahoo! Classifieds.

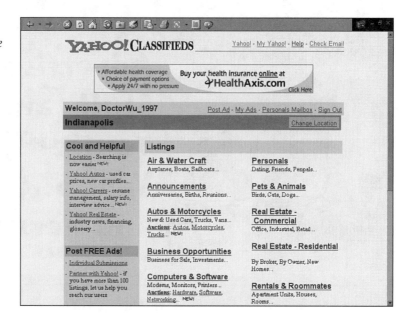

➤ **Air & Water Craft**—(airplanes, boats, JetSkis, and so on)

➤ **Announcements**—(weddings, births, reunions, anniversaries, and so on)

➤ **Autos & Motorcycles**—(see Chapter 23, "New and Used Cars at Yahoo! Autos," for more information on buying automobiles on Yahoo!)

➤ **Business Opportunities**—(investments, businesses for sale, and so on)

➤ **Computers & Software**—(hardware, software, peripherals, and so on)

➤ **Employment**—(see Chapter 26, "Look for a New Job with Yahoo! Careers," for more information on employment resources on Yahoo!)

➤ **General Merchandise**—(antiques, furniture, garage sales, sporting goods, and so on)

➤ **Personals**—(see the "Enhance Your Love Life with Yahoo! Personals" section later in this chapter)

➤ **Pets & Animals**—(birds, cats, dogs, and so on)

➤ **Real Estate—Commercial**—(office, industrial, and retail space)

➤ **Real Estate—Residential**—(see Chapter 24, "Find a New Place to Live with Yahoo! Real Estate," for more information on real estate resources on Yahoo!)

➤ **Rentals & Roommates**—(apartments, rental housing, rooms, and so on)

➤ **Services Offered**—(gardening, carpentry, repairs, and so on)

➤ **Tickets**—(concerts, sporting events, travel, and so on)

When you start browsing or searching the Yahoo! Classifieds listings, you are asked to input your location or zip code. In return, Yahoo! displays those listings closest to your current location. If you want to search the listings in a different locale, click the **Change Location** link and enter a new location or zip code.

Answering a Classified Ad

Just like traditional newspaper classifieds, you don't actually buy anything through Yahoo! Classifieds. Instead, you contact the advertiser directly, via email, and (hopefully) work out a deal between yourselves.

After you find an item or service you're interested in, display the full listing for that item. Each ad listing should include the seller's name, email address, and phone number (optional). The easiest way to proceed is to click the **Reply to This Ad** link next to the person's email address, which automatically prepares an email to the seller. Compose a message expressing interest or asking a question, and send it out. If all goes well, the seller will respond, and the two of you will agree on purchasing arrangements.

Listing Your Stuff in the Classifieds

If you have something to sell, listing your item is *free* in the Yahoo! Classifieds. Just follow these steps to submit a free classified ad:

1. From the Yahoo! Classifieds page, click the **Post Ads** link.
2. When the Submission page appears, click the major category where you want to place your ad.
3. When the "Step 1" submission page for your selected category appears, select a subcategory for your ad.
4. When the "Step 2" page appears, enter your zip code.
5. When the "Step 3" page appears, enter the appropriate information for your item. (This information differs from category to category; the information page for the Computers and Software category is shown in Figure 20.2.)
6. When the "Step 4" page appears, enter your contact information.
7. Click **Submit Entry** to submit your ad.

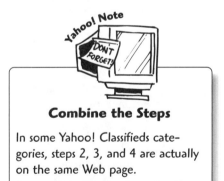

Combine the Steps

In some Yahoo! Classifieds categories, steps 2, 3, and 4 are actually on the same Web page.

After it is submitted, your ad should appear on the Yahoo! Classifieds site within 48 hours. Yahoo! Classifieds lists all ads for 30 days.

If you want to edit, extend, or delete your ad listing, click the **My Ads** link on the Yahoo! Classifieds page. When the list of your ads appears, click the **Edit Ad** link for the ad you want to edit or extend, and then make the appropriate changes.

Figure 20.2

To place a listing, you have to tell Yahoo! Classifieds about what you're selling.

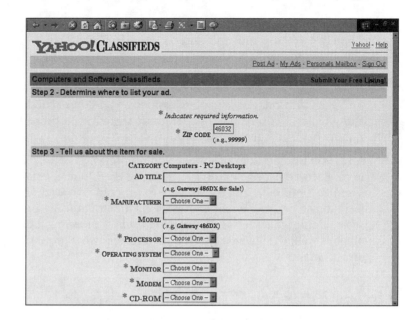

Enhance Your Love Life with Yahoo! Personals

Personal ads are a specialized form of classified ads. In the case of personals, you're not buying or selling a *thing*, you're buying or selling *a person*—or, more precisely, the hope of a relationship with a person. Yahoo! Personals are available for the following gender matches:

➤ Men looking for women (M4W)

➤ Women looking for men (W4M)

➤ Men looking for men (M4M)

➤ Women looking for women (W4W)

For each gender match, Yahoo! lets you post and browse by six different types of relationships:

➤ Long-Term

➤ Short-Term

➤ Penpals/Long Distance

➤ Alternative Lifestyles

➤ Activity Partners

➤ All Relationship Types

Watch Out for Sex-Spam

Unfortunately, sprinkled among the legitimate personals ads on Yahoo! Personals, you'll find a lot of ads for sex sites masquerading as personal ads. This sex-spam is highly annoying, but easily identifiable. Typically, the ad offers something just too good to be true (an 18-year-old girl looking for hot sex with fat 50-year-old married men, for example) and often includes a link to another site. While some legitimate advertisers do have their own personal Web pages (and link to them in their personal ads), most of these links are to fee-based sex sites—not to real people!

You access Yahoo! Personals by clicking the **Personals** link on the Yahoo! main page or the Yahoo! Classifieds page, or by going directly to personals.yahoo.com. As you can see in Figure 20.3, the main personals page lets you browse by relationship type and gender match, or search by username or keywords in the ad.

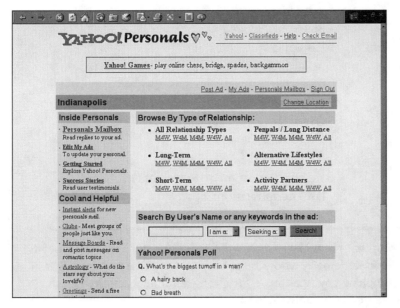

Figure 20.3

Looking for love in all the online places with Yahoo! Personals.

You can browse or search the ads without signing up for the Yahoo! Personals service, but if you want to answer an ad or place your own ad, you are prompted to register and complete a Yahoo! profile. As with Yahoo! Classifieds, placing and responding to Yahoo! Personals is completely free.

BTW, Just What Do All Those Darned Abbreviations Mean?

When you first start reading the personal ads, you'll see a lot of acronyms and abbreviations. If you don't know what they mean, you could end up with a very surprising date! Here's a short list of the more common abbreviations:

Abbreviation	Means This
S	Single
D	Divorced
F	Female
M	Male
W	White
B	Black
H	Hispanic
A	Asian
C	Christian
Bi	Bi-sexual
G	Gay
P	Professional
n/s	Non-smoker
HPTW	Height proportionate to weight
LTR	Long-term relationship
ISO	In search of

So, if you see a listing that reads "SWPF HPTW ISO n/s GAM for LTR," that means a single white professional female, whose height is proportionate to her weight, is in search of a non-smoking gay Asian male for a long-term relationship—which could be the premise of a very funny sitcom!

Found an Ad? Make a Reply!

After you find an ad for someone you think you're interested in, click the **Reply to Ad** link. All replies are handled through the Yahoo! Personals mailbox system, *not* through regular email. When you see the Send a Message page, enter your reply and click the **Send Mail** button.

Play It Safe

Until you get to know someone really well, do *not* enter any personal contact information—including your real email address—in your personal ad replies. Most definitely do not give out your phone number and address to complete strangers!

In general, it's best to be cautious when corresponding with and ultimately meeting people you find through online personal ads. If you decide to physically meet someone after corresponding with them, choose a public place during the daytime, and make sure one of your friends knows where you are. *Don't* meet someone at his or her home on the first date—keep it public, keep it casual, and always have an "escape" planned if things don't turn out as you would like.

Manage Your Mailbox

Replies to personal ads—and responses to replies—are stored in a special Personals Mailbox. You access your mailbox by clicking the **Personals Mailbox** link on the Yahoo! Personals page. Your mailbox lists your Yahoo! ID (or multiple IDs if you created or answered ads under different names), and the number of messages waiting for you. Click your ID to read your waiting responses.

Create Your Own Personal Ad

Creating a personal ad is similar to creating a classified ad, except that all the forms you have to fill in are on a single page. Just follow these steps:

1. From the Yahoo! Personals page, click the **Post Ad** link.
2. When the next page appears, enter your zip code, your identity, a title for your ad, your gender, the gender you're looking for (this is how Yahoo! comes up with the M4W or W4M or whatever designation), your relationship preference, and other information.

You Gotta Be Eighteen

Yahoo! users under the age of 18 are not allowed to post personal ads.

3. Enter the text of your ad—and try to be charming without appearing desperate!—in the **Describe Your Interests** box.

4. Click the **Submit Entry** button to submit your ad.

Your ad should appear on the Yahoo! Personals site within 24 hours, and will remain online for 30 days. You can edit it at anytime before it shows up.

The Least You Need to Know

➤ Yahoo! Classifieds (classifieds.yahoo.com) is a great way to buy and sell merchandise or services unsuited for online auctions—such as automobiles, properties, or pets.

➤ You do not actually purchase merchandise through Yahoo! Classifieds; the buyer contacts the seller (typically via email) and makes purchasing arrangements directly.

➤ Yahoo! Personals (personals.yahoo.com) let you place and respond to personal ads of people in your area for just about any type of gender relationship.

WHOOOP.

Chapter 21

Shop 'Til You Drop with Yahoo! Shopping

In This Chapter

➤ Learn how to make online shopping easier and safer with Yahoo! Shopping

➤ Find out how to consolidate all your online orders through the Yahoo! Shopping Cart

➤ Discover how to speed up your checkout with Yahoo! Wallet

Online shopping doesn't have to be confusing or scary—especially when you use the preferred merchants in the Yahoo! Shopping directory!

Pick a Preferred Provider with Yahoo! Shopping

Virtually every merchant with a cash register and a computer is on the Internet, trying to become an "e-tailer" and make millions online. Many of these wanna-be online merchants won't survive; selling products online is a lot more difficult than it might appear at first blush.

How do you pick the "real" e-tailers from the wanna-be's? And how do you decide *where* to spend your money online?

Yahoo! recognizes your concern and confusion, and has enlisted the best online merchants to participate in the Yahoo! Shopping directory. Yahoo! Shopping brings you together with thousands of *qualified* online merchants, of all types—traditional retail stores, name-brand catalog companies, small boutiques, and specialty shops. All of these merchants are linked not only to the common Yahoo! Shopping directory, but

How Can *Your* Store Become a Part of Yahoo! Shopping?

Yahoo! makes it easy to make your retail business an online business. See Chapter 27, "Put Your Business Online with Yahoo! Small Business," for more information.

also to the Yahoo! Shopping Cart, a single place to finalize your purchases from multiple merchants.

When you want safe and sane online shopping from qualified merchants, there is only one place to turn—Yahoo! Shopping!

Shop the Shops

You access Yahoo! Shopping by clicking the **Shopping** link on the Yahoo! home page, or by going directly to shopping.yahoo.com. As you can see in Figure 21.1, Yahoo! Shopping lets you browse stores by merchandise category, or search for stores that sell specific merchandise.

Figure 21.1

Browse or search the stores at Yahoo! Shopping.

The Yahoo! Shopping directory lists merchants in the following major categories:

➤ Apparel and Accessories
➤ Arts and Collectibles
➤ Baby Care
➤ Bath and Beauty
➤ Books
➤ Computers
➤ Electronics

- ➤ Flowers, Gifts, and Occasions
- ➤ Food and Beverages
- ➤ Health and Wellness
- ➤ Home and Garden
- ➤ Movies and Video
- ➤ Music
- ➤ Office
- ➤ Sports and Fitness
- ➤ Toys, Games, and Hobbies
- ➤ Travel

After you enter a specific store, browse through the merchandise and follow the individual store instructions to place an order for a specific product.

Buy—and Pay

When you make a purchase at a Yahoo! Shopping store, your order is sent to the Yahoo! Shopping Cart. Actually, your Shopping Cart page will have *multiple* shopping carts listed, because each store has its own shopping cart. But your orders for all stores are listed on the same page, and access the same check-out/purchasing information.

When it's time to check out—and pay for your merchandise—go to the Yahoo! Shopping Carts page by clicking the **View Cart/Check Out** link at the top of any Yahoo! Shopping page. From the Yahoo! Shopping Carts page, follow the onscreen instructions for checking out and paying for your merchandise.

Within 24 hours after you check out, you should receive an email confirmation for each order you placed. This email should contain information about who to contact if there is a problem with your order.

Yahoo! Shopping Is Secure

You don't have to worry about potential credit card theft or fraud when using Yahoo! Shopping. Yahoo! uses secure servers to protect all of your personal information, including your name, address, and credit card information—which makes your Yahoo! Shopping experience safer than giving that same information over the telephone!

207

Remember, just because you're using the Yahoo! Shopping Cart (and directory), that *doesn't* mean you're actually buying from Yahoo!. When you make a purchase through Yahoo! Shopping, you're still purchasing from an individual merchant—and that merchant is handling all fulfillment of your order. This also means that if you have any questions or problems, you need to contact the merchant who sold you the goods, not Yahoo!.

Speed Up Your Checkout—with Yahoo! Wallet

If you get tired of entering your credit card information at every shopping site you visit, use Yahoo! Wallet to store your credit card information in one place—and then have the individual sites access your wallet, instead of you entering the information separately.

To use Yahoo! Wallet, go to wallet.yahoo.com and click the **Get Started Now!** button. Enter your Yahoo! username and password, create a unique security key (kind of a second password), and then enter your credit card information. Once this information is entered, you can use Yahoo! Wallet to speed up checkout at any store at Yahoo! Shopping—and it's completely secure!

The Least You Need to Know

➤ Yahoo! Shopping is a directory of thousands of qualified online merchants recommended by Yahoo!.

➤ All orders placed through Yahoo! Shopping merchants are consolidated in a single Shopping Cart and check out process.

➤ The orders you place are fulfilled by the individual merchants—*not* by Yahoo!—and they're responsible for your satisfaction.

➤ Yahoo! Wallet can be used to speed up your checkout at any Yahoo! Shopping merchant by storing your credit card information in a central location accessible by each merchant.

Chapter 22

Book Your Next Vacation with Yahoo! Travel

In This Chapter

➤ Learn how to use Yahoo! Travel to plan for your next business trip or vacation

➤ Find out how to book your own flight, rental car, and lodging reservations online

➤ Discover how to generate a map for any location—as well as driving directions to get you there

Everything you used to use a travel agent for—and more—is now available online, from Yahoo! Travel. Whether you need to research destinations, make reservations, or get driving directions you can do it—easily—with Yahoo! Travel.

Yahoo! Travel: Your Online Travel Agent

Yahoo! Travel is the central hub for most of Yahoo!'s travel-related information and services. As you can see in Figure 22.1, Yahoo! Travel focuses on reservations (for air travel, car rental, hotel rooms, complete vacation packages, and cruises) and trip planning (by destination, activity, or lifestyle).

Figure 22.1

Use Yahoo! Travel for all your personal and business travel needs.

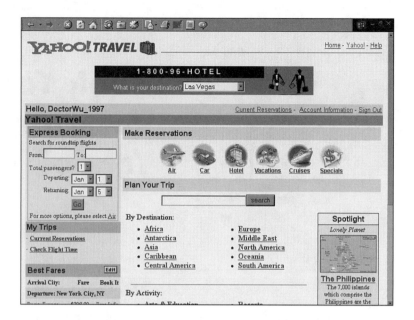

You access Yahoo! Travel by clicking the **Travel** link on the Yahoo! home page, or by going directly to travel.yahoo.com.

Plan Your Trip with Yahoo! Destinations

Before you decide where to go on your next vacation, it pays to do a little research. Yahoo! Destinations includes information for thousands of different destinations, provided by National Geographic Traveler, Rough Guides, Fodor's, and other sources. You can find information on any destination by searching (using the **Plan Your Trip** box on the Yahoo! Travel page) or by browsing, by destination, activity (resorts, cruises, sports & adventure, and so on), or by lifestyle (business travel, families, singles, seniors, and so on).

When you access a destination page, you'll find some or all of the following information:

➤ Dining

➤ Local events

➤ Lodging

➤ Nightlife (including bars, clubs, theater, and so on)

➤ Points of interest (museums, zoos, parks, and so on)

➤ Sports and outdoors (camping, cycling, and so on)

➤ Travel resources (guides, tours, maps, and so on)

➤ Weather conditions and forecast

Many destination pages also include background and articles about the destination, as well as links to Yahoo!'s reservation services.

Get the Resort Report with Yahoo! Ski & Snow

If you're planning a vacation in the white stuff, check out Yahoo! Ski & Snow (snow.yahoo.com). This site includes information for snow resorts around the world, from the Rocky Mountains to the Swiss Alps. You'll also find links to skiing and snowboarding gear and equipment here.

Go Camping with Yahoo! Parks

If you prefer a camping vacation, take a look at Yahoo! Parks (parks.yahoo.com). This site features in-depth information about state, national, and international parks. With information provided by the National Park Service and other sources, this is the place to go to find out about operating hours and seasons, campsite reservations, climate, recommended clothing, and more.

Sleep and Eat with Yahoo! Lodging and Restaurants

Wherever you go, you need a place to sleep—and something to eat. When it comes time to research hotels and restaurants, turn to two superb Yahoo! sites: Yahoo! Lodging and Yahoo! Restaurants.

Find the Perfect Place to Stay with Yahoo! Lodging

No matter where you prefer to stay—including affordable motels, luxury hotels, quaint bed and breakfasts, or extended-stay lodging—Yahoo! Lodging helps you find the perfect place. When you go to Yahoo! Lodging (lodging.yahoo.com) you can search for motels, hotels, and bed & breakfasts by city or state. When you drill down to a specific property, you'll find contact information, current rates, nearby restaurants and attractions, and in-depth descriptions from Fodor's and other sources. If you want to make a reservation at a particular property, just click the **Make Reservation** link to jump to the Yahoo! Travel reservation system.

From Fast Food to Fine Dining with Yahoo! Restaurants

Whether you're on vacation or just out for a night on the town, use Yahoo! Restaurants to find the best place to eat. When you access the Yahoo! Restaurants page (restaurants.yahoo.com), you start by choosing a state or metropolitan area. After you drill down to a specific area, you can search for restaurants by name, price range, or cuisine. You'll end up with a list of restaurants that match your dining criteria; each restaurant listing includes a map and driving directions, price range, and a review by Fodor's or other sources.

Have No Reservations About Making Reservations with Yahoo! Travel

When you decide where you're going, you're only a few clicks away from booking your own reservations, online. Yahoo! Travel partners with Travelocity to offer safe and easy-to-use online reservations for flights, lodging, rental cars, cruises, and more.

Fast Tickets—with Express Booking

If you have simple travel plans and want to make quick flight reservations, you can bypass Yahoo!'s detailed reservation system and use the Express Booking section of the Yahoo! Travel page. Just enter your starting and ending cities, number of passengers, and departure and return dates, and then click the **Go** button. Yahoo! Travel displays a list of matching flights; choose your flight and proceed to purchase your tickets!

To make a reservation, follow these general steps:

1. From the Yahoo! Travel page, click one of the following types of reservations: **Air**, **Car**, **Hotel**, **Vacations**, **Cruises**, or **Specials**.

2. If you're making flight reservations, enter the following information: number of passengers, departure airport, destination airport, departure date, return date, preferred ticket type, preferred airlines (in case you want to pile up the frequent flyer miles on a particular airline!), and whether you want to see the best deals or all available flights. (Figure 22.2 shows the form you have to fill out.)

3. If you're making rental car reservations, enter the following information: city or airport where you'll be picking up the car, total number of travelers, pick up and drop off dates and times, preferred car type, preferred rental company, and corporate discount number (if you have one).

4. If you're making hotel reservations, enter the following information: city, number of guests, number of rooms, check in and check out dates, preferred hotel company, preferred hotel property, type of hotel (all suites, luxury, bed and breakfast, extended stay, motel, resort, and so on), desired amenities, and any special pricing you qualify for.

5. If you're making cruise reservations, enter the following information: region or country you're interested in, desired price per person, number of days for your cruise, and any other pertinent information.

6. Yahoo! Travel now displays a list of matching flights/cars/hotels/cruises. For each item listed, you can click to see more information, or click the **Buy** button to make your reservations.

7. Follow the onscreen instructions to book your reservations.

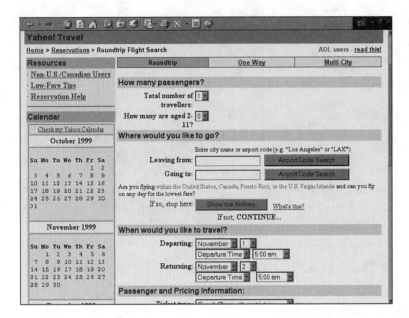

Figure 22.2

Fill out this form to search for flights and make your reservations.

It's really that easy—enter your parameters, make a choice, and book your reservation. And all without leaving the comfort of your computer keyboard!

Get the Lay of the Land—and Directions on How to Get There—with Yahoo! Maps

After you get to where you're going, it helps to have a map of the surrounding area. To generate a map for virtually any location anywhere in the world, go to Yahoo! Maps (maps.yahoo.com). Enter a city, airport code, or specific address, and then click the **Get Map** button; Yahoo! Map generates a map like the one shown in Figure 22.3. You can choose to print this map; use the controls at the top of the map to zoom in or zoom out to show either more detail or a larger region; or click the **Find Nearby Businesses** link to list businesses near the address at the center of the map.

If you need driving directions from one location to another, go to Yahoo! Maps and click the **Driving Directions** link. Enter your starting address and your destination address, and Yahoo! generates turn-by-turn driving directions, complete with a map of your entire route and a map of your destination. Just print out these instructions, and you'll get to where you're going—without getting lost!

Figure 22.3

Map a specific area with Yahoo! Maps.

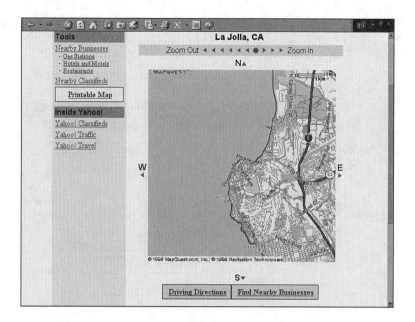

The Least You Need to Know

➤ Yahoo! Travel (`travel.yahoo.com`) includes trip planning information and a system for making online air, car, hotel, and cruise reservations.

➤ You can search for a destination by location, activity, or lifestyle.

➤ Use Yahoo! Lodging (`lodging.yahoo.com`) to search for hotels, motels, and resorts; use Yahoo! Restaurants (`restaurants.yahoo.com`) to search for dining by location and cuisine.

➤ Yahoo! Maps (`maps.yahoo.com`) lets you generate maps for any location, as well as detailed driving directions.

Chapter 23

New and Used Cars at Yahoo! Autos

In This Chapter

➤ Find out everything you need to know before you buy a new car—including the dealer's invoice price

➤ Discover the true value of any used car, as determined by the Edmund's used car pricing guide

➤ Learn everything you need to know to keep your current car running smoothly

---

Yahoo! Autos is one of the best automotive resources on the Internet. From classified ads for used cars to detailed information on new cars—as well as online quotes for auto loans and insurance—you can find everything you need at Yahoo! Autos.

Your Online Automotive Resource: Yahoo! Autos

You access Yahoo! Autos by clicking the **Autos** link on the Yahoo! home page, or by going directly to autos.yahoo.com. As you can see in Figure 23.1, the Yahoo! Autos page is divided into five main sections:

➤ **Buy a Car**—Resources for both new and used car purchases.

➤ **Sell a Car**—Links to the Edmund's used-car pricing guide and the automotive sections of Yahoo! Classifieds and Yahoo! Auctions.

➤ **Finance**—Loan and lease calculators, new-car loan rates and quotes, and quotes for auto insurance.

➤ **Talk Cars**—Links to the automotive sections of Yahoo! Chat, Clubs, and Message Boards].

➤ **Maintain**—Resources for auto repair, troubleshooting, and maintenance.

Figure 23.1

Find a truckload of car-related information and services at Yahoo! Autos.

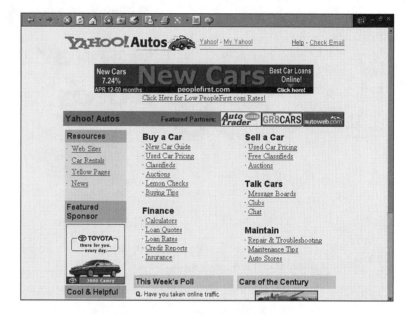

Looking for New Cars at Yahoo! Autos

When you're thinking of buying a new car, turn to these resources at Yahoo! Autos:

➤ **New Car Guide**—Click the **New Car Guide** link and browse by make, class, or price. When you find the car you want, Yahoo! displays an individual New Car Guide, like the one shown in Figure 23.2. Each guide includes basic specs, standard and optional equipment, pricing information (including dealer price!), and the capability to compare this car with any other car in Yahoo!'s database. Click the **Research and Compare** link to pick other cars you're interested in; Yahoo! then prepares a head-to-head comparison of the selected models.

➤ **Buying Tips**—Click the **Buying Tips** link to learn how to find the car of your dreams—and negotiate the best price possible.

➤ **Auto Loans**—Click the **Calculators** link to calculate how much car you can afford; click the **Loan Rates** link to find the current rates on auto loans in your area; and click the **Loan Quotes** link to go to the Yahoo! Loans site (loans.yahoo.com) and apply for a car loan online.

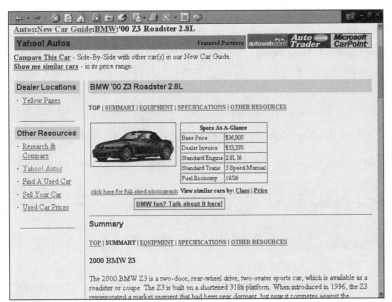

Figure 23.2

Do your research with Yahoo!'s New Car Guides before you head off to the dealership.

Wheels and Deals with Used Cars at Yahoo! Autos

Whether you're selling or looking to buy a used car, check out these sections of the Yahoo! Autos site:

➤ **Used Car Pricing**—Click the **Used Car Pricing** link to access the Yahoo! Used Car Guide, powered by Edmund's, the used-car bible. Select the make and model, check what optional equipment the car has, then enter the car's mileage, and Edmund's will generate the current value of the vehicle.

➤ **Used Car Listings**—Yahoo! has two different sites offering used cars for sale; click the **Classifieds** link to go to the automotive section of Yahoo! Classifieds (discussed in Chapter 20, "Advertise Your Stuff (and Yourself!) with Yahoo! Classifieds and Personals") or click the **Auctions** link to go to the automobile section of Yahoo! Auctions (discussed in Chapter 19, "Buy Low, Sell High, with Yahoo! Auctions").

Keep Your Old Car Up and Running—and Insured

Even if you want to hold on to your old car, Yahoo! Auto offers something for you. Check out these sections of the site:

➤ **Fix Common Problems**—Browse through a comprehensive database of automotive problems when you click the **Repair & Troubleshooting** link; if you need repairs, click the **Auto Stores** list to find a dealer near you.

➤ **Perform Common Maintenance**—Keep your car running smoothly by following the advice displayed when you click the **Maintenance Tips** link.

➤ **Shop for Car Insurance**—When you click the **Insurance** link you jump to Yahoo! Insurance (`insurance.yahoo.com`), where you can shop for the best rates on your auto insurance.

The Least You Need to Know

➤ Yahoo! Autos (`autos.yahoo.com`) includes resources and services for buying and selling new and used cars.

➤ Click the **New Car Guide** link to display detailed information about all new cars on the market.

➤ Click the **Used Car Pricing** link to use the Edmund's Used Car Guide to calculate a price on any used vehicle.

Chapter 24

Find a New Place to Live with Yahoo! Real Estate

In This Chapter

➤ Find out how to compare cities, neighborhoods, and schools at Yahoo! Real Estate

➤ Learn how to browse Yahoo! Classifieds for homes for sale and rent

➤ Discover online mortgage and insurance resources

Moving into a new house is a major life event. You want to do as much research as possible *before* you move, to make sure you've picked the right neighborhood, the right home, and the right mortgage company. Let Yahoo! Real Estate be your guide for all moving-related issues—and things will go as smoothly as possible!

Everything You Need, All in One Place: Yahoo! Real Estate

Yahoo! Real Estate centralizes information and services found at several Yahoo! sites, including Yahoo! Classifieds, Yahoo! Loans, and Yahoo! Insurance. You access Yahoo! Real Estate by clicking the **Real Estate** link on the Yahoo! home page, or by going directly to realestate.yahoo.com.

As you can see in Figure 24.1, Yahoo! Real Estate has the following main sections:

Figure 24.1

Use your mouse to find a house at Yahoo! Real Estate.

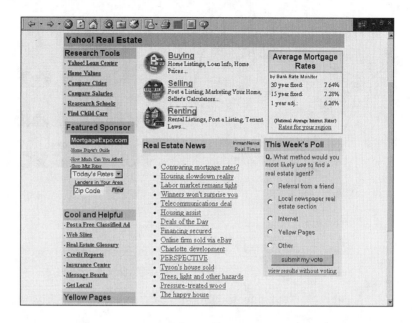

Learn More About Online Real Estate

For the complete skinny on using the Internet in your real estate ventures, check out *The Complete Idiot's Guide to Online Buying and Selling a Home,* by Matthew O'Brien, on sale now.

➤ **Buying**—Click here to access a variety of buyer's tools, including Yahoo! Classifieds real estate listings, home values, finance calculators, and the Yahoo! Loan Center.

➤ **Selling**—Click here to access a variety of seller's tools, including home values, a complete seller's library, and the ability to post a home listing at Yahoo! Classifieds.

➤ **Renting**—Click here to search for house and apartment rentals in your area, compare the benefits of renting versus buying, and access articles in the Renter's Library.

In addition, Yahoo! Real Estate includes a listing of today's national average interest rates for 30-year fixed, 15-year fixed, and 1-year adjustable mortgages, as well as a compendium of real estate news headlines from Inman News and Real Times.

Click for Local Rates

To find out the going rates for loans in your area, click the **Rates for Your Region** link in the Average Mortgage Rates box.

Before You Move—Do Your Research

Yahoo! Real Estate offers several valuable services that help you determine *where* you want to move. These services, found in the Research Tools section of the Yahoo! Real Estate page, include the following:

➤ **Yahoo! Loan Center**—Jump here to research different types of mortgages, calculate how much house you can afford, pre-qualify for a mortgage, and receive a quote on a mortgage for your new house.

➤ **Home Values**—Click this link to display two options: **Search by Location** lets you find all homes sold on a particular street or the sales history of a particular address; **Search by Price Range** finds all homes sold within a certain price range in one city.

➤ **Compare Cities**—Yahoo!'s City Comparison lets you select any two cities in the United States, and then view a side-by-side comparison of cost of living, job growth, taxes, unemployment, median income, home purchase cost, educational performance, quality of life, travel, weather, and other factors.

➤ **Compare Salaries**—Click here to see how much your salary is worth in a different location!

➤ **Research Schools**—Browse to a specific school district to view reports (such as the one in Figure 24.2) detailing number of students, the student:teacher ratio, average class size, SAT and ACT averages, and percent of students moving on to two- and four-year colleges.

➤ **Find Child Care**—Click this link to locate child care providers in a specific location.

Figure 24.2

Compare different school districts—click the district name for even more information.

Yahoo! Real Estate - School Reports

Top: School Reports: Minnesota: Dakota

- Click on the school district name for more detailed information

School District	Total Students	Students : Teacher	Grade 1 Class Size	SAT Avg.	ACT Avg.	% to 4-yr college	% to 2-yr college
Burnsville/Eagan/Savage	10707	14	24	1128	22.5	61%	21%
Farmington	3598	17	26		22.6	52%	30%
Hastings	5154	18	23		22	45%	15%
Inver Grove	4088	16	25		22	49%	27%
Lakeville	8242	16	25	1140	21.6	53%	28%
Randolph	432	14	20		23.8	50%	20%
RAVE-Apple Vly	7978	22	21	1155	22.5	62%	17%
RAVE-Eagan	8764	23	21	1166	23.5	53%	18%
RAVE-Rosemount	9253	23	21	1171	22.2	46%	31%
South St Paul	3571	18	24		22.2	50%	15%
W St Paul/Mendota/Eagan	4029	12	21	1134	21.9	60%	29%
RAVE-Eastview	9734	23	21	1166	22.8	%	%
School District	Total Students	Students : Teacher	Grade 1 Class Size	SAT Avg.	ACT Avg.	% to 4-yr college	% to 2-yr college

Want to learn more? Compare three school districts side-by-side on more than 100 facts at theschoolreport.com. It's FREE.

Go to theschoolreport.com

Browse the Listings—for Houses and Apartments

Yahoo! Classifieds is *the* place to advertise houses for sale and apartments for rent; click the links in the Yahoo! Classifieds section to view the **Homes for Sale**, **Rentals** , and **Commercial Properties** listings. (For more information about Yahoo! Classifieds, turn to Chapter 20, "Advertise Your Stuff (and Yourself!) with Yahoo! Classifieds and Personals.")

All Kinds of Loans at Yahoo! Loans

The Yahoo! Loan Center (loan.yahoo.com) also provides information and services for auto and small business loans, as well as offering online access to your personal credit reports (for a fee).

When You're Ready to Buy— Get a Mortgage, and Get Insured

Click the **Finance Calculators** link to access Yahoo!'s Payment Calculator (to figure out your payment for different loan amounts, terms, and rates), Amortization Calculator (to break down the principal and interest amounts in your loan payments), and Rent vs. Own Calculator (to demonstrate the difference between renting and owning a property).

Click any of the loan links to go to Yahoo! Loan Center—or just go directly to loan.yahoo.com. From here you can obtain mortgage recommendations and custom mortgage quotes, as well as monitor your current mortgage (vis a vis current market rates), browse mortgage rates by region, and prequalify for a new mortgage.

After you're in your new home, you'd better get it insured. For home and renters' insurance, go to the Yahoo! Insurance Center (`insurance.yahoo.com`). Yahoo! Insurance also offers auto insurance, life insurance, and health insurance.

The Least You Need to Know

➤ Yahoo! Real Estate (`realestate.yahoo.com`) offers information and services for home buyers, sellers, and renters.

➤ Yahoo! Loans (`loan.yahoo.com`) offers online application for mortgages and other types of loans.

➤ Yahoo! Insurance (`insurance.yahoo.com`) offers home, renters', auto, life, and health insurance online.

Part 6

Make More Money: Yahoo! Finance and Careers

Did you know Yahoo! has some of the best investor services available online? Do you want to learn more about Yahoo's financial message boards, or portfolio tracking service, or job-hunting sites? Then look here today—and make more money tomorrow!

Chapter 25

Manage Your Personal Finances with Yahoo! Finance

In This Chapter

➤ Discover all the financial resources available at Yahoo! Finance

➤ Learn how to create custom portfolios of your personal stock holdings

➤ Find the best places to get the latest inside company information

➤ Discover how to pay your bills online—from any PC anywhere in the world

---

Most people recognize Yahoo! as a great search site—but how many people recognize it as one of the best resources for financial information on the Internet? All too few.

Truth be told, there are few sites better than Yahoo! when it comes to obtaining stock quotes, in-depth company data, and other financial information. In addition, Yahoo! has one of the most active financial message boards on the Web—a great place to pick up the latest rumors and whispers!

Finding Financial Information at Yahoo! Finance

The home base of all Yahoo!'s financial resources is Yahoo! Finance. You access Yahoo! Finance (shown in Figure 25.1) by clicking the **Stock Quotes** link on the Yahoo! home page, or by going directly to finance.yahoo.com.

Figure 25.1

Yahoo! Finance—for all your financial needs.

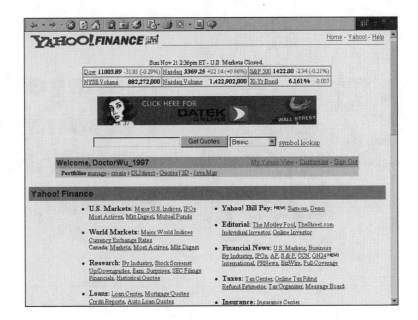

Yahoo! Finance provides links to proprietary information and other Web sites in the following areas:

➤ **U.S. Markets**—Includes major U.S. indices, IPOs, a market digest, and more.

➤ **World Markets**—Includes major world indices, currency exchange rates, a market digest, and more—including much Canada-specific information.

➤ **Research**—Includes research by industry, earnings surprises, SEC filings, company financials, historical quotes, and more.

➤ **Loans**—Includes the Yahoo! Loan Center, mortgage quotes, auto loan quotes, and credit reports.

➤ **The Investment Challenge**—An online investing "game" where you can play the market without investing a penny of your own money.

➤ **Reference**—Includes a company and fund index, glossary, economic and earnings calendars, and more.

➤ **Yahoo! Bill Pay**—A service that enables you to pay all your bills online. (See the "Pay Your Bills Online with Yahoo! Bill Pay" section later in this chapter, for more information.)

➤ **Editorial**—Links to the best advice and commentary on the Internet from The Motley Fool, TheStreet.com, Individual Investor, and Online Investor.

➤ **Financial News**—Links to a variety of market news sources from AP, S&P, CCN, ON24, PRNews, BizWire, and others.

➤ **Taxes**—Includes the Yahoo! Tax Center, online tax filing, refund estimator, tax organizer, and more.

➤ **Insurance**—Includes the Yahoo! Insurance Center, plus quotes for auto, life, health, home, and renters insurance.

➤ **Community**—Includes links to finance-related Yahoo! Message Boards, Chat, Net Events, and Clubs.

In addition, links at the top of the page lead you directly to your personal portfolio, and a search box lets you retrieve current quotes for any security.

International Finance

For country-specific financial information, click the global links at the bottom of the Yahoo! Finance page.

Personalizing the Yahoo! Finance Page

You can redesign the Yahoo! Finance site to include the specific financial information you're looking for on a daily basis. For example, you can choose which sources Yahoo! uses for its financial news headlines and how it displays those headlines. You can also configure the way quotes and charts are displayed on individual quotes pages.

To redesign Yahoo! Finance, follow these steps:

1. From the Yahoo! Finance page, click the **Customize** link.

2. When the Customize Finance page appears, click the element you want to customize (**Account Information**, **News Headlines**, **Market Summary**, **Portfolios**, **Quote Display**, or **Charts**).

3. Follow the instructions on the individual pages to customize that element of Yahoo! Finance.

Building a Portfolio—and Customizing Your Quotes

One of the most powerful features of Yahoo! Finance is its capability to create multiple stock portfolios for each user—and then display the stocks in each portfolio in a variety of custom configurations.

Accessing Your Portfolios

You access your portfolios by clicking the **Quotes** link at the top of the Yahoo! Finance page. Your stocks are displayed in the Basic view, shown in Figure 25.2, which displays the Last Trade, Change, and Volume for each stock in your portfolio.

Figure 25.2

The Basic portfolio view—a great way to track your stocks!

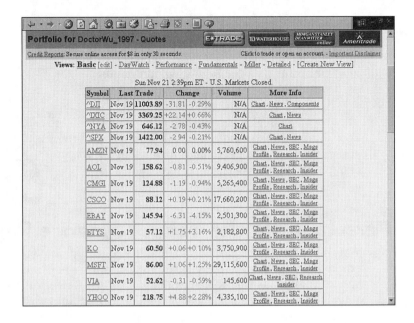

You can select from several other views of your portfolios, including

➤ **DayWatch**—This view displays daily stock performance, including change, volume, and day's range.

Several Smaller Portfolios Makes It Easier

Most users find it easier to track several smaller portfolios than one humongous one. If you have accounts at several different brokerages, create a different portfolio for each account. Break out your 401(k) or IRA into a separate portfolio. You might even want to divide your securities by type or industry for easier tracking.

➤ **Performance**—This view focuses on key metrics for the performance of your individual portfolio, based on the number of shares owned and original and current value.

➤ **Fundamentals**—This view includes details about the companies behind the stocks, presenting market cap, earnings per share, price/earnings ratio, and similar metrics.

➤ **Detailed**—This view displays the entire gamut of information for each stock, including a one-year performance chart.

Creating and Editing Portfolios

Yahoo! Finance lets you create multiple portfolios; each portfolio can contain multiple stocks, securities, and market indices. You can choose to track actual portfolio performance (after you enter shares owned and price paid) or simple stock performance.

Create a Custom View

You can also create a custom view of your portfolios by clicking the **Create New View** link. When the Edit Your Portfolio Views screen appears, you can select up to 16 different fields to display, in any order. These fields include

➤ **Basics**—Symbol, Name, Last Trade With Time, Last Trade Price Only, Change & Percent, Change, Volume, and Average Daily Volume.

➤ **Details**—Bid, Ask, Previous Close, Open, Day's Range, and 52-Week Range.

➤ **Fundamentals**—Earnings/Share, P/E Ratio, Dividend Pay Date, Ex-Dividend Date, Dividend/Share, Dividend Yield, and Market Capitalization.

➤ **Portfolios**—Shares Owned, Price Paid, Commission, Holdings Value, Day's Value Change, Holdings Gain & Percent, Holdings Gain, High Limit, Low Limit, and Notes.

To create a new portfolio, follow these steps:

1. From the Yahoo! Finance page, click the **Create** link in the Portfolios section, at the top of the page.

2. When the Edit Your Portfolio page appears, go to the **Step 1: Portfolio Basics** section and enter a name for your portfolio, then pull down the **Portfolio Currency** list and select the currency (dollars, yen, and so on) you want to use to track your portfolio.

3. Go to the **Step 2: Ticker Symbols** section and enter the ticker symbol for each of the stocks and securities you want to track. Separate multiple symbols with a space; don't bother alphabetizing the list, because Yahoo! can do that for you.

4. Still within the **Step 2: Ticker Symbols** section, check which market indices you want to include in your Portfolio. Click the **More U.S. Indices** or **More International Indices** links to select from a larger list.

Look 'Em Up

If you don't know the symbol for a particular security, click the **Look Up Symbol** link to search for the symbol by company name.

5. Go to the **Step 3: Basic Features** section and check those features you want to enable. You can choose to sort symbols alphabetically, to *not* show the total value of your portfolio, and to use a small font (when displaying extended information)—as well as which view you want to use for this portfolio.

6. Go to the **Step 4: Advanced Features** section and select the additional information you want to display about each stock in your portfolio. You can choose to display Shares Owned, Purchase Price/Share, Trade Date, Commissions, Upper Limit, Lower Limit, or Notes. When you choose one or more of these options, click the **Enter More Info** button to enter the specific information for each item.

7. When you're done configuring your portfolio, click the **Finished** button.

To edit an existing portfolio, click the **Manage** link in the Portfolios section of the Yahoo! Finance page.

Taking Stock: Other Ways to View Your Stock Performance

Yahoo! provides five other ways (beyond the normal Quotes page) to view the current performance of your portfolio: through your My Yahoo! page, the Yahoo! News Ticker, Yahoo! Messenger, 3D Stock Viewer, and the Java Portfolio Manager.

Personal Portfolios at My Yahoo!

My favorite way to track my stocks' performance is on the My Yahoo! Page. You can organize your page to display your portfolio at the top of the left column, so it's the first thing you see when you access your personal page. (My Yahoo! automatically picks up the portfolio contents and preferences you select on the Yahoo! Finance site.)

Your Own Personal Stock Ticker with Yahoo! News Ticker

If you choose to install the Yahoo! News Ticker on your desktop, it automatically includes the current prices for the stocks and securities in your portfolios as part of its scrolling display. If you have a constant connection to the Internet, this is the next best thing to having a real-time stock ticker in your office.

More About My Yahoo!

Learn more about My Yahoo! in Chapter 2, "Create Your Own Personal Yahoo! with My Yahoo!."

More About Yahoo! News Ticker

Learn more about Yahoo! News Ticker in Chapter 15, "Headlines, Forecasts, and Scores with Yahoo! News, Weather, and Sports."

Current Quotes with Yahoo! Messenger

Yahoo! Messenger is another way to put current quotes on your desktop. In addition to displaying quotes for the stocks and securities in your portfolios, Yahoo! Messenger can also be configured to display alerts when selected stocks hit an upper or lower limit, or reach a certain volume limit.

Real-Time Performance with 3D Stock Viewer

Yahoo! offers a special Java applet specifically designed to keep track of the stocks in your portfolio over the course of a trading day. The 3D Stock Viewer offers a three-dimensional view of critical information, and enables you to see both the performance of your stocks (on a percentage basis from the previous day's closing price) as well as their volatility over the past year.

To launch the 3D Stock Viewer, click the **3D** link in the Portfolio section at the top of the Yahoo! Finance page. Figure 25.3 shows the 3D Stock Viewer in action.

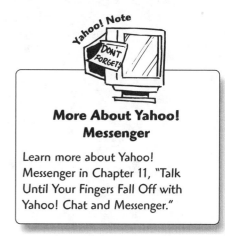

More About Yahoo! Messenger

Learn more about Yahoo! Messenger in Chapter 11, "Talk Until Your Fingers Fall Off with Yahoo! Chat and Messenger."

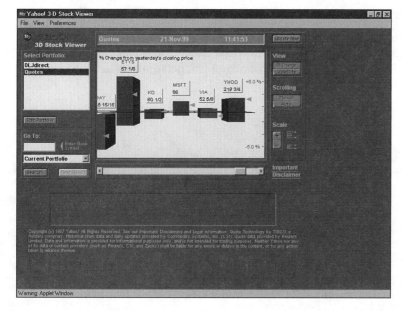

Figure 25.3

Get a real-time interactive view of your portfolio with Yahoo! 3-D Stock Viewer.

"Live" Portfolio Editing with the Java Portfolio Manager

Yahoo! offers another Java applet, called the Java Portfolio Manager, which lets you edit your portfolio while you're viewing it. This "WYSIWIG"—what you see is what you get—editing is a lot faster and more convenient than accessing a separate editing page, as is the case with the normal Yahoo! portfolio pages. To launch the Java Portfolio Manager, click the **Java Mgr** link in the Portfolio section at the top of the Yahoo! Finance page.

More About Yahoo! Message Boards

Learn more about Yahoo! Message Boards in Chapter 12, "Join the Discussions at Yahoo! Clubs and Message Boards."

Get the Inside Scoop—and the Latest Gossip—at Yahoo! Message Boards

These days it seems like *everybody* is talking about stocks. Everyone you meet seems to have some inside information, whispers, rumors, or opinions about one or another companies, all guaranteed to predict tomorrow's stock price. The biggest gathering place for all this "information" is at Yahoo!'s financial Message Boards. You'll find individual message boards dedicated to thousands of stocks; just access a company's message boards to read the latest gossip and rumors.

You access Yahoo!'s financial Message Boards by clicking the **Message Boards** link in the Community section on the Yahoo! Finance page. From there you can search for or navigate through the thousands and thousands of financial boards on the Yahoo! Message Board system.

The Best on the Net

Many financial sites—such as The Motley Fool—have their own message board systems. None compare to Yahoo!'s in terms of volume of messages, and—in my opinion—quality of information. You still have to wade through a lot of uninformed opinions, but the signal/noise ratio on Yahoo! Message Boards is higher than at most other financial sites.

Throw Away Your Checkbook—and Pay Your Bills Online—with Yahoo! Bill Pay

One of the newest features on Yahoo! is Yahoo! Bill Pay. This useful service lets you pay all your bills online from any Web browser. Your transactions are secure and guaranteed by CheckFree; you access Yahoo! Bill Pay by clicking one of the Yahoo! **Bill Pay** links on the Yahoo! Finance page or by going directly to bills.yahoo.com.

Yahoo! Bill Pay, like any online bill paying service, isn't free. You'll pay either $2 per month plus $.40 per payment (for unlimited payments), or $7 per month for 25 payments without the $.40 per-payment charge (however, every additional payment after the first 25 costs $.40 each).

The Least You Need to Know

➤ Yahoo! Finance (finance.yahoo.com) provides a wealth of financial resources for the personal investor.

➤ You can create multiple portfolios to track the performance of selected stocks and securities.

➤ Your custom portfolios also are accessible from your My Yahoo! page, Yahoo! News Ticker, and Yahoo! Messenger.

➤ Yahoo!'s financial Message Boards are a great source of insider information and gossip.

➤ Use Yahoo! Bill Pay (bills.yahoo.com) to pay all your bills online from any computer.

SEARCH FOR SIX FIGURED POSITION IN A RETAIL OUTLET--

TYPE TYPE

Chapter 26

Look for a New Job with Yahoo! Careers

In This Chapter

➤ Discover all the job-related resources at Yahoo! Careers

➤ Find out where to view over a half-million job listings (hint: try Yahoo! Classifieds)

➤ Learn about Yahoo!'s resume-posting services

Tired of slaving away all day at a low-paying job—or are you looking for exciting new opportunities in today's tight job market? Hate to go looking for a new job? Despise the process of creating a new resume?

Then turn to Yahoo! Careers—the easy way to go job hunting, right from your own personal computer!

Access Great Career Resources at Yahoo! Careers

Yahoo! Careers offers a variety of career-related resources, including job listings and a resume-posting service. You can access Yahoo! Careers, shown in Figure 26.1, by clicking the **Employment** link on the Yahoo! home page, or by going directly to careers.yahoo.com.

Figure 26.1

Get great career advice—and look for a new job—at Yahoo! Careers.

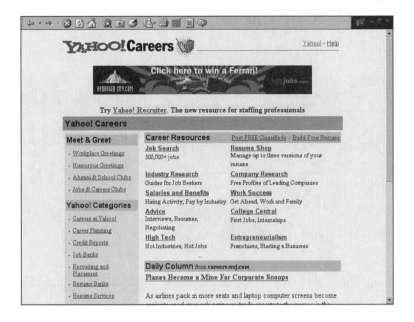

Among the many resources at Yahoo! Careers, you'll find:

➤ **Job Search**—More than a half-million jobs are listed online.

➤ **Resume Shop**—Post up to three different versions of your resume in Yahoo!'s online resume database.

➤ **Industry Research**—Find out which industries are hot—and which are cold—with these detailed research reports.

➤ **Salaries and Benefits**—Do your homework before the interview—and learn about hiring activity, pay by industry, and more.

On the Other Side of the Table

If you're in the recruiting or human resources industries, check out Yahoo! Recruiter, a new resource for employers and staffing professionals.

➤ **Advice**—Get top-notch career advice from the pros about interviews, resumes, negotiating, and more.

➤ **High-Tech**—Find out about the hottest high-tech industries and jobs.

➤ **Company Research**—Get free in-depth profiles of major companies—so you'll know where to apply.

➤ **Work Success**—Find out how to lead a successful life—combining both work *and* family.

➤ **College Central**—A wealth of resources for upcoming and recent college grads, including first jobs and internships.

➤ **Entrepreneurialism**—Learn all about starting your own business—including the best franchises in your area.

➤ **Columns and Features**—Daily and weekly advice and comment from Wall St. Journal Careers, Ask the Headhunter, Walking Wounded, WetFeet.com, and more.

➤ **Relocation Resources**—After you get the job, then what? Turn here for salary comparisons, city comparisons, city profiles, city maps, school reports, and more.

Go Job Hunting in Your Underwear with Yahoo! Job Search

When you click the **Job Search** link on the Yahoo! Careers page, you jump directly to Yahoo!'s employment classifieds. Yahoo! includes over 500,000 job listings in its database in the following job categories:

➤ Administrative

➤ Consulting

➤ Creative

➤ Education

➤ Engineer

➤ Finance

➤ General Management

➤ Health Care

➤ Human Resources

➤ Information Systems

➤ Internships

➤ Legal

➤ Marketing

➤ Operations

➤ Other/Not Specified

➤ Sales

➤ Scientific

➤ Service

➤ Training

➤ Work at Home

You can also search the listings, both within your community and nationwide. You can search by Function, Company, Job Title, or other Keywords. (For example, you could search for `programming` or `copywriting` or `internet`.) When you find a listing you're interested in, use the information on that page to contact the employer directly—typically via email.

Let Employers Look for You at Yahoo! Resumes

More and more employers are searching Yahoo! for prospective employees. Yahoo! helps the process along with Yahoo! Resumes, accessible by clicking the **Resume Shop** link on the Yahoo! Careers page.

Yahoo! Resumes let you post up to three different versions of your resume. You can create an online resume from scratch or by using Yahoo!'s structured template. In addition, Yahoo! Resumes offers a variety of sample resumes and top-notch resume advice. It's a great way to get your name out—on the world's most popular Web site!

The Least You Need to Know

➤ Yahoo! Careers (`careers.yahoo.com`) offers a wealth of career-related resources and advice.

➤ If you're looking for a job, Yahoo! Classifies offers more than 500,000 job listings.

➤ Yahoo! Resume lets you post up to three different versions of your resume online.

Chapter 27

Put Your Business Online with Yahoo! Small Business

In This Chapter

➤ Discover small business information and services at Yahoo! Small Business

➤ Learn how to create a Web site for your business at Yahoo! Site

➤ Find out how to build a complete e-tailing presence with Yahoo! Store

---

Yahoo! is a great end-user site—but it also offers a number of resources for businesses, especially small businesses. From package tracking to Web site building, turn to Yahoo! for all your small business needs!

Access a Web of Resources for Your Business at Yahoo! Small Business

Yahoo! offers a special site just for small business owners. As you can see in Figure 27.1, Yahoo! Small Business—accessible at smallbusiness.yahoo.com—offers the following information and services:

➤ **Small Business Solutions**—Includes the Yahoo! Postal Center (a virtual post office), Web site services, file sharing and access (via Yahoo! Briefcase), and more.

➤ **Advice and Information**—Listed in the Business Guide, Featured Business Tools, and Featured Articles sections, a variety of guides and articles on buying and running a business from Office.com, Inc.com, and other sources.

Figure 27.1

If you run a small business, turn to Yahoo! Small Business for a variety of resources.

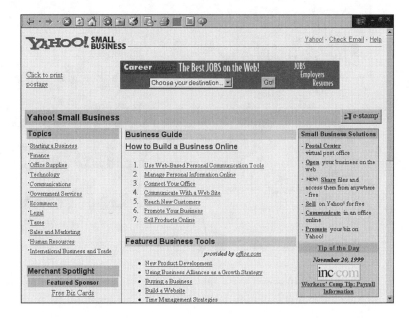

➤ **Package Tracking**—Links to track your Airborne Express, FedEx, UPS, and Postal Service packages online.

➤ **Conventions and Shows**—Finds tradeshows in your industry or community.

➤ **Services**—Links to Yahoo! Calendar, Get Local, Yellow Pages, Maps, and People Search.

Put Your Business Online with Yahoo! Site

Yahoo! Site (site.yahoo.com) is a convenient way to create a Web site for your small business. A combination of authoring tool and hosting service, Yahoo! Site enables you to do the following:

➤ Build your own Web site using a point-and-click editing interface—no other software required. (Figure 27.2 shows a site created with Yahoo! Site.)

➤ Host your Web site on the Yahoo! servers.

➤ Acquire your own unique domain name (in the form of www.*yourname*.com), or use a site.yahoo.com/*yourname*/ address.

➤ Update your site whenever you want.

Figure 27.2

Use Yahoo! Site to create a Web site like this one.

Yahoo! Site is a cost-effective Web hosting service, at just $29.95 per month. There is no startup fee, and you can cancel your site whenever you want.

Yahoo! Site Versus Yahoo! Store

If you want a marketing or informational Web site—and don't need to sell items directly from your site—Yahoo! Site is your best choice for the money. If, however, you want to sell merchandise online—taking orders directly on your site—you need to go with Yahoo! Store. Yahoo! Store has e-commerce capability; Yahoo! Site doesn't.

243

Make Your Site Pay for Itself with Yahoo! Store

If you want to create an online retailing presence, check out Yahoo! Store (store.yahoo.com). Yahoo! Store enables you to create an Internet store capable of accepting orders online.

It's Not Just for the Little Guys...

Some of the largest names in e-tailing use Yahoo! Store to create and host their online presence. For a good example of a sophisticated Yahoo! store, check out the FAO Schwarz site at store.yahoo.com/faoschwarz/.

Here's what you get with Yahoo! Store:

➤ Point-and-click Web site creation—no software necessary

➤ Complete hosting services with fast T3 network connection to major Internet backbones

➤ A unique domain name (either www.*yourname*. com or store.yahoo.com/*yourname*/)

➤ Online credit card processing

➤ Secure order transactions using Secure Sockets Layer (SSL) encryption

➤ Web-based or fax-based order transmittal to your office

➤ Inclusion in the Yahoo! Shopping directory

➤ Comprehensive site traffic and sales data reporting

➤ Capability to upload your own database files to use as your Yahoo! Store merchandise listings

Yahoo! Store costs more than Yahoo! Site, but offers complete e-tailing capability. If you have 50 or fewer items for sale, you'll pay $100 per month for your Yahoo! store. For $300/month you can offer up to 1,000 items for sale. Each additional 1,000 items cost $100/month.

The Least You Need to Know

➤ Yahoo! Small Business (smallbusiness.yahoo.com) offers a variety of information and services tailored for the small business owner.

➤ Yahoo! Site (site.yahoo.com) offers site creation and hosting services for small businesses.

➤ Yahoo! Store (store.yahoo.com) enables you to build a complete online retailing site, capable of accepting credit card orders over a secure connection.

Part 7

Create Personal Web Pages: Yahoo! GeoCities

Yahoo! GeoCities is the world's largest community of personal Web pages. Turn here to learn how to create your own personal Web page—and publish it online, at GeoCities!

Chapter 28

Learn to Homestead with Yahoo! GeoCities

In This Chapter

➤ Discover the world's largest community of personal home pages

➤ Learn how to locate other homesteaders in GeoCities neighborhoods

➤ Find out the many ways to create a Web page at Yahoo! GeoCities

---

Do all your friends have their own personal Web pages? Do *you* want to get in on the community of folks displaying their own Web handiwork, but don't know where to start? Then you need to learn about Yahoo! GeoCities—the Web's largest home page community.

Find a Home for Yourself Online with Yahoo! GeoCities

Yahoo! GeoCities is one of the newest parts of Yahoo!, but it's also one of the oldest and largest home page communities on the Internet. That's because GeoCities had been an established Web site for several years when Yahoo! acquired the site in mid-1999. Renamed Yahoo! GeoCities (and given a new URL—geocities.yahoo.com), the site now is part of the Yahoo! family.

The Yahoo! GeoCities home page is shown in Figure 28.1. From here you cruise like a user or become a developer and start building your own Web pages.

Edit an existing page.

Upload files
and manage
your Web site.

Figure 28.1

Build your own page or cruise the neighborhoods of others' pages at Yahoo! GeoCities.

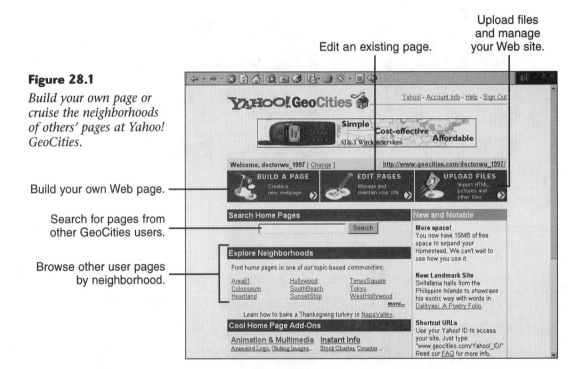

Build your own Web page.

Search for pages from other GeoCities users.

Browse other user pages by neighborhood.

The Old Address Still Works

If you're a veteran GeoCities user, the old www.geocities.com URL is still active, so you don't have to redo any bookmarks or links.

Just What Is GeoCities, Anyway?

Yahoo! GeoCities is, essentially, a really big collection of personal Web pages. At the time of this writing, Yahoo! GeoCities hosted pages from more than five million different users—regular users, just like you and me. GeoCities hosts these Web pages free, and even provides easy-to-use tools you can use to create your own Web pages.

GeoCities pages are organized into *neighborhoods*, which are loosely grouped by theme. For example, the Hollywood neighborhood hosts pages related to film and television, while the Enchanted Forest neighborhood is home to children's pages. When you build a page, you decide which neighborhood you want to "live" in; as a user, you can cruise or search the neighborhoods for interesting pages to visit.

Yahoo! GeoCities offers several different ways to create your own Web pages. Inexperienced Web page designers can use the built-in Yahoo! PageBuilder

248

application; more experienced users can code their own HTML with the Advanced Editor. You can even upload pages created with other applications (such as Microsoft FrontPage) by using GeoCities' File Manager.

If the Pages Are Free, How Do They Make Money?

Normal GeoCities users don't pay a thing to create and post their Web pages on the GeoCities site. (There is a "plus" service with a slight fee, discussed later in this chapter, but it has few subscribers.) Yahoo! makes its money by selling advertising, which is displayed in pop-up windows whenever anyone accesses a page hosted on the GeoCities site. When you jump to a GeoCities user page, a second (smaller) browser window opens on your desktop, containing a message from a Yahoo! advertiser. Kind of annoying, but it keeps the pages free for millions of users.

The five million+ users with pages at GeoCities are called *homesteaders*. Many home-steaders bond together in their neighborhood communities, creating newsletters and linking to each other's pages. There are even chat rooms and email mailing lists specifically for GeoCities homesteaders. When you look at all these activities, you'll agree that Yahoo! GeoCities is truly a *community* of users!

You Get What You Pay For

Whichever method you use to create your pages, you get up to 15MB of space for storage of your pages and accompanying files at no charge—and, for most users, 15MB should be more than enough. If you need more space, however, you can get additional space in 5MB chunks. Each additional 5MB will cost you $2.50 per month.

In addition, Yahoo! offers a premium plan they call GeoPlus. With GeoPlus you get 25MB of basic space, five subdirectory levels, access to CGI and Java Applet libraries (for advanced Web page features), automatically generated site statistics, and dedicated online support. You'll pay $4.95

Help Is Just a Click Away

If you need help with any part of Yahoo! GeoCities—from finding a user to creating your own page—visit GeoCities Help Central at geocities.yahoo.com/help/.

per month for a GeoPlus membership, with additional storage space available in 5MB chunks (at $2.50 per 5MB).

Get Your Own Unique URL

Regular GeoCities homesteaders get assigned a URL that looks something like this: www.geocities.com/*neighborhood/suburb/number/yourname*.html. GeoPlus members have the option of obtaining a unique URL (what Yahoo! calls a *virtual URL*), in the form of www.*yourname*.com, for a $5 monthly fee (plus setup charges).

For most folks, the 15MB provided with the standard GeoCities membership is more than enough space. However, if you have a lot of large graphics, multiple pages, or the need for really sophisticated script-based features, check out what GeoPlus has to offer—it's the perfect service for power Web page developers!

Members Only—But Membership Is Free!

To post a page at Yahoo! GeoCities, you first have to sign up for membership. If you already have a Yahoo! username and password, you're already signed up. If not, you'll have to join the GeoCities site, which is completely free.

How Yahoo! Works with GeoCities

Before Yahoo! acquired GeoCities, you had to sign up for a GeoCities membership separate from your Yahoo! membership. Now that GeoCities is part of the Yahoo! network of sites, your Yahoo! membership provides free access to GeoCities. In fact, your Yahoo! username and password are all you need to start creating your own pages at the GeoCities site.

If you already had a GeoCities membership, you had to renew that membership after Yahoo! acquired the site. This was because Yahoo! was merging the two separate member databases, and the merging required a confirmation of your previous membership. It's no big deal; you can continue to use your old GeoCities membership name, or you can use your Yahoo! membership name—either one works just fine. (If you choose to use your GeoCities name, that becomes your username across the other Yahoo! sites as well.)

Cruise the Neighborhoods at Yahoo! GeoCities

With more than five million users in the GeoCities communities, you can imagine the variety of Web pages available on the GeoCities site. Many of these pages are personal in nature, but others are focused on specific topics, hobbies, or areas of interest. GeoCities organizes its pages into *neighborhoods* of interest, as detailed in Table 28.1.

Table 28.1   GeoCities Neighborhoods

Neighborhood	Area of Focus
Area51	Science fiction and fantasy
Athens	Education and philosophy
Augusta	Golf
Baja	SUVs and 4WD
Bourbon Street	Southern culture
Broadway	Theater and musicals
CapeCanaveral	Science, space, and aviation
CapitolHill	Government and politics
CollegePark	University life
Colosseum	Sports and recreation
Enchanted Forest	Kids' stuff—for and by kids
Eureka	Small business
FashionAvenue	Beauty and fashion
Heartland	Hometown values
Hollywood	Film and television
HotSprings	Health and fitness
Madison Avenue	Advertising
MotorCity	Cars and trucks
NapaValley	Food and wine
Nashville	Country music
Paris	Romance literature and poetry
Pentagon	Military
Petsburgh	Pets
PicketFence	Home improvement
Pipeline	Extreme sports
RainForest	Environment
ResearchTriangle	Future technology
RodeoDrive	Shopping

continues

Table 28.1   Continued

Neighborhood	Area of Focus
SiliconValley	Computer hardware and software
SoHo	Bohemian arts and literature
SouthBeach	Chatting and hanging out
SunsetStrip	Rock and punk music
TelevisionCity	Television
TheTropics	Vacations and resorts
TimesSquare	Games and role-playing
Tokyo	Anime and Asian culture
Vienna	Classical music
WallStreet	Investing and finance
Wellesley	Women
WestHollywood	Gay and lesbian
Yosemite	Hiking and outdoors

Yahoo! Tip

Neighborhood Addresses

You can go directly to a neighborhood home page by adding the neighborhood name to the end of the www.geocities.com URL. For example, go to the TelevisionCity neighborhood page by entering www.geocities.com/TelevisionCity/.

Find a Neighborhood

You can browse the neighborhoods by clicking the appropriate links in the Explore Neighborhoods section of the Yahoo! GeoCities home page. When you click the **More** link (or go directly to www.geocities.com/neighborhoods/), you get a complete list of GeoCities neighborhoods; click a link to go directly to a neighborhood home page.

You can also search for any homesteader's page directly from the Yahoo! GeoCities home page. Just enter a search query (the user's name or interests) in the **Search Home Page** box, and then click the **Search** button. Yahoo! searches the five million+ member pages and returns those that match your query.

Move to the 'Burbs

Each GeoCities neighborhood is divided into several smaller *suburbs*. For example, the TelevisionCity neighborhood includes the following suburbs: Lot, Network, Satellite, Set, Stage, Station, Studio, and Taping. You can browse a neighborhood's suburbs by selecting a suburb from the **Explore the Suburbs** list found on every neighborhood home page.

Each suburb is comprised of *blocks* of sites. One hundred homesteaders reside in each block; each homesteader has a unique address within each block. Blocks are numbered sequentially, typically starting with 1000 (then 1100, 1200, 1300, and so on) .

Visit the Neighborhood Club House

When you visit a neighborhood, you're greeted with the neighborhood's home page, which should look something like the one shown in Figure 28.2. This page is kind of like a club house for the neighborhood; practically every activity available in the neighborhood is accessible from this page.

Chat with your neighbors.　　　　　Cruise the suburbs.

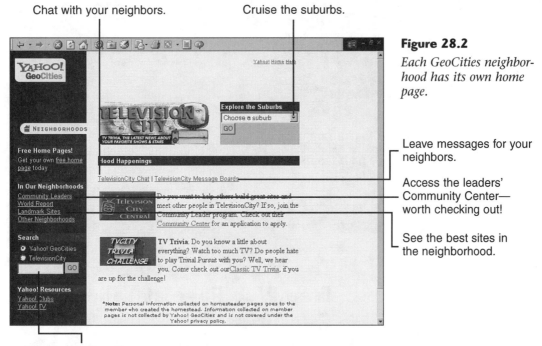

Figure 28.2
Each GeoCities neighborhood has its own home page.

Leave messages for your neighbors.

Access the leaders' Community Center— worth checking out!

See the best sites in the neighborhood.

Search for other sites.

There's a Lot to Do in Your Neighborhood

Each neighborhood page includes links to many different features and services, just for your neighborhood. These features include

➤ **Chat**—Talk with your neighbors at a special Yahoo! Chat room, just for your neighborhood.

➤ **Message Boards**—Leave messages for your neighbors at special neighborhood Yahoo! Message Boards.

➤ **Newsletter**—Subscribe to a regular neighborhood email newsletter, complete with news, contests, promotions, events, and chats.

➤ **Landmark Sites**—Visit the best sites in your neighborhood.

➤ **Community Center**—This is a special page for the leaders in your community. From here you can become a volunteer community leader, get help for any neighborhood-related problems, make your site part of the neighborhood's WebRing, and access other deluxe features. Figure 28.3 shows a typical Community Center page.

Figure 28.3

Access special neighborhood features from the Community Center page.

Round and Round in a Ring of Webs

A WebRing is a collection of Web sites, all devoted to a common topic. Sites within a WebRing link to all other sites in the ring; users can easily jump from site to site to site within the WebRing.

The Many Ways to Get a Free Web Page at Yahoo! GeoCities

Yahoo! GeoCities offers several ways to build a page; we'll take a brief tour of the site's page-building features.

More Than You Ever Wanted to Know About Creating Web Pages

Before we start, however, let's talk a little bit about Web pages themselves. A Web page is nothing more than a computer file, a *document* composed in a certain language or *code*. Just like a word processing document, a Web page document consists of lines of text, with other elements (pictures, sounds, and links) thrown in as appropriate.

The code used to create a Web page document is called *HTML*, which stands for Hypertext Markup Language. The codes in HTML work in the background to define what you see when you view a Web page from your WebTV unit.

Anybody can create a simple Web page, and there are enough sophisticated codes in HTML to enable professional Web page developers to create more complex and lively pages. For a Web page to be viewed by other users, however, that page must reside on a *Web server*, a computer continuously connected to the Internet. When a Web page is *hosted* by a server, that page receives its own specific address (*URL*, or *Uniform Resource Locator*); any user entering that address can view the corresponding page. Yahoo! GeoCities' Web server hosts millions of individual Web pages, each with its own specific URL.

When you have more than one page together on a server, you have a *Web site*. Again, anybody can create a Web site; the pros just build bigger and fancier sites than do we mere mortals.

After you decide to create your own personal Web page, what should you put on it? Some users put personal information on their pages; some use their pages to promote their hobbies; others just list a lot of links to other pages they are particularly partial to. In essence, you can put anything you want on your personal Web page—that's why it's *personal!*

Build a Simple Page—Simply—with Yahoo! PageBuilder

The easiest way to build a personal Web page is with Yahoo! PageBuilder. PageBuilder is a Java-based application that runs on your desktop while you're online and provides a template-driven page-building environment. As you can see in Figure 28.4, you pick a neighborhood and a template for your page, and then modify the template for your own personal needs. (Learn more about Yahoo! PageBuilder in Chapter 29, "Create a Basic Web Page with Yahoo! PageBuilder.")

The Old PageBuilder—GeoBuilder

Before there was PageBuilder, there was GeoBuilder. Like PageBuilder, GeoBuilder was a Java-based page-building application, although it wasn't as easy to use or as robust as PageBuilder. GeoBuilder is being phased out by Yahoo!; if you need to edit a page built with GeoBuilder, that page will be automatically converted to a PageBuilder-compatible page.

Crack the Code with the Advanced Editor

If you want to create more sophisticated Web pages, you have to get down and dirty with the underlying HTML code. Yahoo! GeoCities provides the Advanced Editor just for this purpose. As you can see in Figure 28.5, you can enter HTML code directly into the Advanced Editor window; GeoCities converts that code into a finished Web page. (Learn more about the Advanced Editor in Chapter 30, "Create Sophisticated Pages with HTML.")

Figure 28.5

Build your own page from scratch using HTML code—and the Advanced Editor.

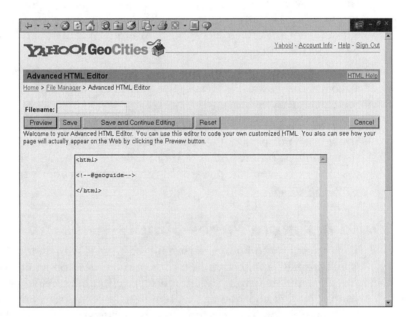

Manage Your Site with File Manager

After you've created your Web site, you can manage the files in your site through GeoCities' File Manager. As you can see in Figure 28.6, you can also use File Manager to upload pages created in other Web page editor programs, such as Microsoft FrontPage. (Learn more about the File Manager in Chapter 31, "Upload Files and Manage Your Site with File Manager.")

Learn All About HTML by the Book

To learn more about using HTML to create a Web page, check out *The Complete Idiot's Guide to Creating a Web Page, Fourth Edition,* from my old pal Paul McFedries. You can find it wherever computer books are sold!

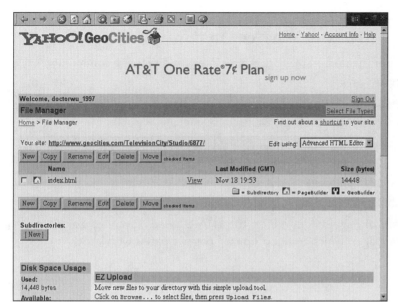

Figure 28.6

Keep your site up-to-date with the powerful features of File Manager.

Every Neighborhood Has Its Standards

When you post pages to the GeoCities site, you have to adhere to the GeoCities page content guidelines. Basically, your pages can't contain nudity, pornography, or other harmful content, nor can they display outside sponsorship banners. In addition, you can't use your pages to sell anything—you can post personal pages, but not commercial pages. (If you need a host for your business pages, check out Yahoo! Site and Yahoo! Store, both described in Chapter 27, "Put Your Business Online with Yahoo! Small Business.") To read GeoCities' complete policies and guidelines, go to www.geocities.com/help/guidelines.

The Least You Need to Know

➤ Yahoo! GeoCities (geocities.yahoo.com) is the world's largest community of personal Web pages.

➤ The Web pages you build at GeoCities are hosted free, although additional server space and functionality is available for a price.

➤ GeoCities pages are organized into topic-oriented neighborhoods; you can browse homesteader pages by neighborhood, or use Yahoo!'s search function to search for specific pages.

➤ GeoCities offers three different ways to create your own Web pages: the easy-to-use Yahoo! PageBuilder editor; the HTML-based Advanced Editor; and the File Manager, which lets you upload pages created with other programs.

WOW!

Chapter 29

Create a Basic Web Page with Yahoo! PageBuilder

In This Chapter

➤ Discover the *easy* way to create a Web page—no HTML coding required!

➤ Learn how to build your Web page based on a pre-designed template

➤ Find out how to personalize your page with a variety of formatting and add-on elements

Yahoo! GeoCities makes building Web pages as easy as clicking and dragging, thanks to Yahoo! PageBuilder. PageBuilder is an easy-to-use tool that lets you build Web pages without learning HTML, based on pre-built templates you customize for your own site. Best of all, you create the page entirely online with no coding knowledge or additional software required.

Your Own Personal Web Page Editor: How PageBuilder Works

Yahoo! PageBuilder is an application that runs while you're online, in its own window on your desktop. It isn't software you install on your hard disk; the program actually runs in your browser, thanks to Java technology.

When you open PageBuilder, it takes a few minutes for the application to download to your computer. (Depending on the speed of your Internet connection, the loading

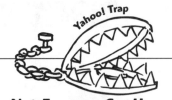

Not *Everyone* Can Use PageBuilder

PageBuilder works only with those Web browsers that support Java applications (versions 4.0 or above of Internet Explorer or Netscape Navigator) and it works only on computers running Windows 95, Windows 98, Windows NT, or Windows 2000. It will *not* work with Macintosh computers or with WebTV Internet terminals.

time can run anywhere from 15 seconds to 5 minutes.) Because the program doesn't permanently reside on your hard disk, you have to load PageBuilder again every time you visit the Yahoo! GeoCities site.

If your Web browser supports Java applications, using PageBuilder is a cinch. All you have to do is pick a neighborhood, pick a predesigned template, and then—when the template is displayed in the PageBuilder window—edit those elements you want to change. Click the **Save** button, and—voila!—you have a great looking Web page.

Ten Steps to Success: Creating Your First Page with PageBuilder

Getting started with PageBuilder is easy. Just follow these general steps:

1. From the Yahoo! GeoCities page, click the **Build a Page** link.

2. If you haven't yet registered or signed in, you are prompted to do so. The first time you register, you are asked to pick a neighborhood for your home page; the neighborhood you click from this list will be the community to which your site will be assigned.

3. On your first visit, you are also asked to provide some additional information about the page you'll be building; fill in as much or as little info as you're comfortable with and then click the **Submit** button to proceed.

Be a Good Neighbor

To learn more about GeoCities neighborhoods, see Chapter 28, "Learn to Homestead with Yahoo! GeoCities."

4. Yahoo! GeoCities now shows a page displaying your account information and the address (URL) for your new page. (Simultaneously, you should receive an email from Yahoo! providing additional information about your new GeoCities page.) Write down your page's address, and then click the **Build Your Page Now!** link to start building your page.

5. When the Build Pages page appears, shown in Figure 29.1, click the template you want to use for your page. PageBuilder offers a number of different themed templates, ranging from Advice Column to Family Tree to My Hobby to Tribute Page.

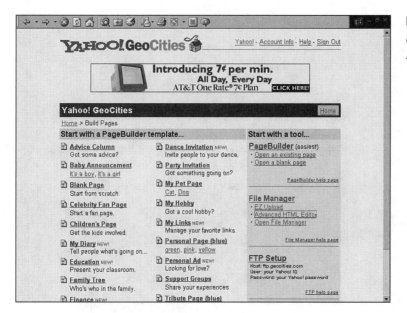

Figure 29.1

Get started by choosing a PageBuilder template.

6. When the Start with a template page appears, shown in Figure 29.2, confirm that this is really the template you want to work from. (If it isn't, click the **Back** button on your browser to return to the Build Pages page and choose another template.) When you're ready to proceed, click the **Launch PageBuilder** link to start loading the PageBuilder application.

7. Yahoo! now opens a small Yahoo! PageBuilder Loading window on your desktop. *Don't close this window!* It's through this window that PageBuilder's Java code is loaded. Be patient—it takes a few minutes for the entire program to download to your computer.

8. After a few minutes, the Yahoo! PageBuilder window—shown in Figure 29.3—opens on your desktop with your selected template displayed. You can now edit the page using the tools on the toolbar and on the **Format** menu, as described in the next section of this chapter.

9. When you're done editing, click the **Save** button to open the Save and publish Page dialog box, shown in Figure 29.4. Select or enter a name for your page, and then click the **Save** button.

Too Many Templates!

If you're not sure which template to pick, go with Personal Page—it's a good all-around template to work from.

Figure 29.2

Is this the template you want? If so, get ready to launch PageBuilder!

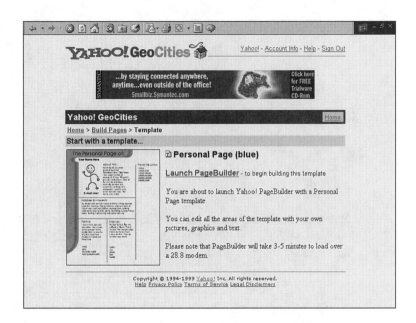

Save
this page.

Add
new text.

Insert an
add-on element.

Create a
new page.

Modify a
selected element.

Create a
hyperlink.

Display
PageBuilder Help.

Figure 29.3

This is where you create your Web page—in the Yahoo! PageBuilder window.

Open an existing page.

Preview this page in
your Web browser.

Copy a selected element.

Delete a selected element.

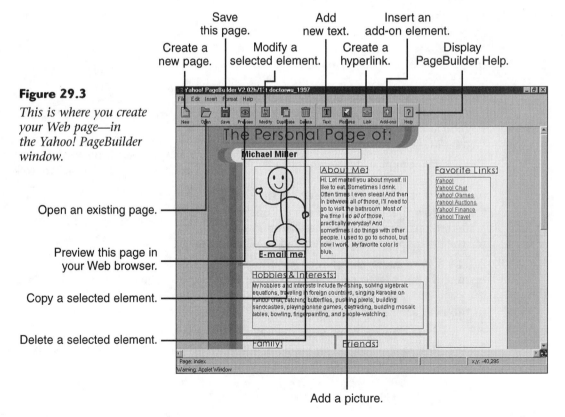

Add a picture.

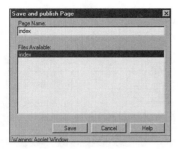

Figure 29.4

Getting ready to save your page...

10. After you page has been saved, PageBuilder asks whether you want to view your page. Click **Yes** to view your saved page in your Web browser, or **No** to return to the PageBuilder window. Figure 29.5 shows what a finished page looks like in your Web browser.

Although creating a Web page is relatively quick, you'll want to spend a little more time *editing* your page to make it look just the way you want. Read on to learn how to edit a page based on the PageBuilder template.

Your Home Page Is the Index

The first page on your site—the *home page*—should always be saved with the filename index.

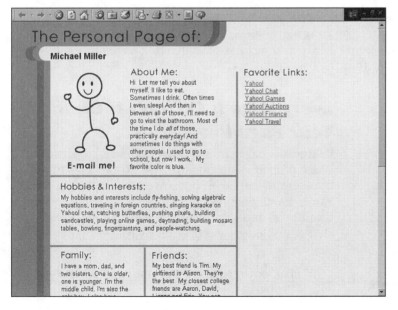

Figure 29.5

Your finished page, ready for viewing on the Web.

263

What's My Address?

If you're not sure of the Web address of your GeoCities site, go the GeoCities File Manager and click the **Enter the File Manager** button. At the top of the next page, just under the words Yahoo! GeoCities File Manager (in large bold type—you can't miss it!) will be the neighborhood, suburb, and number of your page. When you tack www.geocities.com onto the front of this, (like this: www.geocities.com/*neighborhood*/*suburb*/*number*/), you have your address. Even easier, Yahoo! GeoCities now provides a *second* address for your page that uses your Yahoo! ID. Just add your Yahoo! username to the end of www.geocities.com to create a URL that looks like this: www.geocities.com/*yourID*/.

Making Your Page *Your* Page: Modifying Your PageBuilder Template

The real key to creating your own Web page with PageBuilder is modifying the template you started with. You can change virtually everything about the page you're presented with—from basic text to pictures to underlying page properties—and you do it all from within the PageBuilder window.

Edit the Code

If want to make changes to the underlying page's HTML code (to the Head, Body Tag, or Body codes), pull down the **Format** menu and select **Advanced Page Properties** to display the Advanced Properties dialog box.

Every Page Is Different: Change Your Page Properties

Behind the page you see is a set of page properties. These properties include the title that appears in the browser title bar when others view your page, the keywords search engines use to index your page, and the default size and colors used on your page. You can change any of these properties by following these steps:

1. Pull down the **Format** menu and select **Page Properties**.
2. When the Page Properties dialog box appears, make any appropriate changes.
3. Click **OK** to apply your changes.

264

Move It or Lose It: Move, Resize, and Delete Page Elements

Everything on your page—every picture, every block of text, every table or line—is a separate element. You edit and format each element individually.

Among the changes you can make to *any* element are

➤ **Moving the element**—To move an element, select it and use your mouse to drag it to a new location.

➤ **Resizing the element**—To resize an element, select it and grab one of the *handles* around the outside of the element, then drag the handle to a new position.

➤ **Deleting the element**—To delete an element from your page, select it and click the **Delete** button on the PageBuilder toolbar.

➤ **Duplicating the element**—To make a copy of an element on your page—which you can then edit separately—select the element and click the **Duplicate** button. The copy now appears next to the original element; move it or resize it as appropriate.

➤ **Reformatting the element**—To change any other properties of an element, select the element and click the **Modify** button. When the next dialog box appears—and different types of elements will display different dialog boxes—make the appropriate changes and then click **OK**.

If You Don't Like What It Says (Or How It Looks), Change It: Edit and Format Your Text

Your template-based Web page comes complete with a bunch of "dummy" text. You'll want to edit this text to be a tad more personal, and perhaps even delete some of the elements on your page.

All text on your page is enclosed in text boxes. Each text box is a separate element; you edit, format, or delete each text box individually.

To edit the text in a text box, position your cursor within the text box and then use your keyboard to insert and delete text as you would with any word processor. To delete an entire text box, just select the text box (*not* the text within!) and press the **Delete** key on the keyboard.

To reformat the text within a text box, double-click the entire text box. The toolbar at the top of the PageBuilder window changes to look like the one in Figure 29.6. Use the buttons on this toolbar to change the font, font size, alignment, color, and formatting of the text.

Figure 29.6

Select a text box to display the text formatting toolbar.

To add a new text box, click the **Text** button on the PageBuilder toolbar. To delete an entire text box, select the text box and then click the **Delete** button.

Fewer Fonts

Like most Web browsers, PageBuilder can only display Courier, Helvetica, and Times Roman fonts—which means you should limit your font choices to these fonts whenever possible. However, if you apply a font other than these *and* a user's Web browser is configured to display that font, then the correct font will be displayed when your page is viewed with that browser.

Pretty Pictures Pretty Fast: Add Pictures to Your Page

Web pages are, by nature, graphical. If you have to choose between text and pictures, you should probably go with the pictures—it's what other Web users expect.

PageBuilder makes it easy to add your own pictures to your Web page. Just follow these steps:

1. Click the **Pictures** button on the PageBuilder toolbar to display the Select Pictures dialog box (shown in Figure 29.7).

2. To select a picture from the GeoCities library of images, pull down the **Collection** list, choose a collection, and then select a picture from the **Picture List**.

3. To upload your own picture, click the **Upload** button. When the next dialog box appears, locate and select the picture file from your hard drive, and then click the **Upload File** button to return to the Select Picture dialog box.

4. To attach a hyperlink to this picture, enter the URL to link to into the **Link to a location** box.

5. To display a screen tip when a user's mouse hovers over this picture, enter the text for the tip in the **Screen Tip** box.

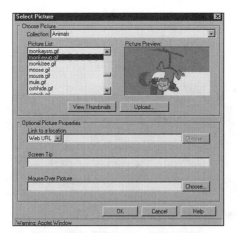

6. To display a different picture when the user's mouse hovers over this picture, click the **Choose** button and select a different picture or file.

7. Click **OK** to insert the picture into your document.

After the picture is inserted on your page, you can move it and resize it as necessary.

It's Not Always What's Up Front That Counts: Change Your Page Background

One of the easiest things you can personalize about your page is its background. You can accept the standard white background for your page, you can choose a different color, or you can select a picture to display in the background.

To change your page's background, follow these steps:

1. Pull down the **Format** menu and select **Background** to display the Background Properties dialog box.

2. To change the background color for your page, click the **Set Background Color** button and choose a new picture from the next dialog box.

3. To use a picture from the GeoCities library of images for your page background, pull down the **Collection** list, choose a collection, and then select a picture from the **Picture List**.

4. To upload your own picture to use for your page background, click the **Upload** button. When the next dialog box appears, locate and select the picture file from your hard drive, and then click the **Upload File** button to return to the Background Properties dialog box.

5. Click **OK** when done.

Make Your Own Muzak with Background Music

You can also use the Background Properties dialog box to add music to your site; this background music plays whenever anyone accesses your page. Just click the **Choose** button in the Background Music section of the Background Properties dialog box, and then select a music file. If you want the song to play continuously, check the **Loop** option in the Background Music section.

Get Jumping: Link to Other Web Pages

One of the most-encountered characteristics of a Web page is the *hyperlink*. This is the underlined text (or outlined graphic) that, when clicked, jumps you to another page or site on the Web. You can create links for any text or graphic on your page by following these steps:

1. Select the text or image you want to link from.

2. Click the **Link** button on the PageBuilder toolbar to display the Hot Link dialog box, shown in Figure 29.8.

Figure 29.8

Create links to other Web pages from the Hot Link dialog box.

3. To link to a Web page on another site, pull down the **Link to a location** list, select **Web URL**, and then enter the full address for the other page. (Make sure you enter the "http://" as part of the address.)

4. To link to another page on your GeoCities site, pull down the **Link to a location** list, select **My Page**, and—when the next dialog box appears—select one of the listed pages. Click **OK** to return to the Hot Link dialog box.

5. To create a Mailto: link (that, when clicked, opens a new preaddressed email message), pull down the **Link to a location** list, select **E-Mail**, and then enter the email address you want to link to.

6. To link to another file (*not* a Web page!) on your site, pull down the **Link to a location** list, select **My File**, and—when the next dialog box appears—select a file to link to. Click **OK** to return to the Hot Link dialog box.

7. To link to a non-Web location on the Internet (such as an FTP site or newsgroup), pull down the **Link to a location** list, select **Other**, and then enter the link's address.

8. Click **OK** to insert the link.

Cool Stuff with a Click: Use PageBuilder Add-Ons

PageBuilder includes a variety of other elements you can insert into your Web page. Normally, these elements would have to be inserted with complex HTML code or fancy scripts, but PageBuilder has pre-assembled these elements for easy insertion.

You can choose from the following types of elements:

➤ **Basics**—Includes text, pictures, backgrounds, background music, buttons, bullets, horizontal lines, and counters.

➤ **Fun and Games**—Includes Game Cheats, Recipe of the Day, Tic-Tac-Toe, Love Test, Birthday Countdown, Video Poker, Beanie Babies Trivia, and Current Events Trivia.

➤ **Animation**—Includes animated logos, fading images, gliding images, rotating images, and random images.

➤ **Instant Info**—Includes Time and Date Stamp, Yahoo! Search Box, Stock Charter, Yahoo! Maps, Yahoo! Directions, and Yahoo! Mortgage Calculator.

➤ **Interactive**—Includes links to your Yahoo! Messenger (when you're online) and Yahoo! Message Boards.

➤ **Forms and Scripts**—Includes buttons, check boxes, list boxes, and text fields.

To insert one of these add-on elements, follow these steps:

1. Click the **Add-Ons** button on the PageBuilder toolbar.

2. When the Add Stuff to Your Page! dialog box appears, pull down the **Category** list and select the type of element you want to add.

3. Double-click an element to insert it into your page.

4. Click **Cancel** to close the dialog box.

Get Really Fancy: Write Your Own HTML Code

Although PageBuilder was designed to let you create a Web page without using any HTML, you can still insert HTML code into your page when you want to incorporate more sophisticated formatting or elements. To add HTML code to your PageBuilder page, follow these steps:

1. Click the **Add-Ons** button on the PageBuilder toolbar.

2. When the Add Stuff To Your Page! dialog box appears, pull down the **Category** list and select **Forms and Scripts**.

269

3. Double-click the **HTML Code** icon.

4. When the next dialog box appears, enter the appropriate HTML code.

5. Click **OK** when done.

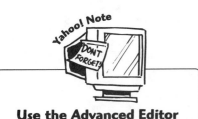

Use the Advanced Editor for HTML Editing

If you want to use HTML to create a complete page, use the GeoCities Advanced Editor discussed in Chapter 30, "Create Sophisticated Pages with HTML."

Put More Stuff on Your Site: Upload Supporting Files

On occasion you might want to upload files to your site that aren't attached to a specific Web page. (For example, you may want to store images for an eBay auction listing in your GeoCities directory—and then link to it from your auction listing.) To upload files directly to your GeoCities directory from within PageBuilder, follow these steps:

1. Pull down the **File** menu and select **Upload/Import Images and Files.**

2. When the next dialog box appears, locate and select the file(s) you want to upload from your hard disk.

3. Click the **Upload** button to begin uploading.

You Built It, You Manage It

If you built a page with PageBuilder, you can edit it—at any time—with PageBuilder. If you want to manage the files on your site—upload, delete, rename, and so on—you use the GeoCities File Manager tool.

Editing with PageBuilder

To reopen PageBuilder and modify an existing file, follow these steps:

1. From the Yahoo! GeoCities home page, click the **Edit Pages** link.

2. When the Edit Pages page appears, click the **Launch PageBuilder** link.

3. When PageBuilder launches, you can select which pages on your site you want to edit—or you can click the **New** button to start creating another Web page.

Managing with File Manager

To open File Manager from the Yahoo! GeoCities home page, follow these steps:

1. Click the **Edit Pages** link.

2. When the Edit Pages page appears, click the **Open File Manager** link.

You can also access File Manager from within PageBuilder. Just pull down the **File** menu and select **File Manager**; your browser automatically jumps to the File Manager page, where you can manage all the files on your site.

The Least You Need to Know

➤ Yahoo! PageBuilder lets you build Web pages without directly using HTML coding.

➤ When you first log on to PageBuilder, you choose which neighborhood you want your site to reside in.

➤ You base your new page on a predesigned template, which you then modify to your own personal tastes.

➤ PageBuilder lets you add all kinds of elements to your page, including text, graphics, hyperlinks, background music, and a variety of prebuilt controls and applets.

Chapter 30

Create Sophisticated Pages with HTML

In This Chapter

➤ Discover the two HTML editors at Yahoo! GeoCities

➤ Find out how HTML codes work

➤ Learn how to use HTML codes to insert and format elements on your Web pages

---

As you learned in the last chapter, Yahoo! PageBuilder is an extremely easy way to create Web pages—just point, click, and drag, no complicated coding required. As easy as PageBuilder is, however, it is somewhat limited in its capability to create really sophisticated Web pages. In addition, not all users can use PageBuilder—if you can't run Java applications, you can't run PageBuilder.

So if you want to create more sophisticated Web pages—or if you can't run Java applications—you need to use a different Web page editor, one that lets you enter HTML code directly. Fortunately, Yahoo! GeoCities supplies two HTML editors—the Basic HTML Editor and the Advanced HTML Editor.

Web Pages from the Ground Up—Using the GeoCities HTML Editors

An HTML editor lets you enter raw HTML code to create your Web pages. When you manipulate the underlying code, you get precise control over what appears in a Web browser. Of course, to write HTML code you have to *know* HTML code, which means

Borrow from the Best

One way to create instant HTML code is to "borrow" ideas from existing Web pages. Most Web browsers let you display the underlying code for the pages you visit; you can then copy this code into GeoCities' HTML Editor to replicate the existing Web page—and then edit it for your personal needs.

Use PageBuilder Once, Use It Again

If you created a page using PageBuilder (or its predecessor, GeoBuilder), you can't edit it with either the Basic or Advanced HTML Editors. Any page created with PageBuilder has to be edited with PageBuilder.

true beginners should start with something a little more automated and a lot easier, such as Yahoo! PageBuilder.

That said, GeoCities' Basic HTML Editor is designed for beginning HTML coders. You still have to have some basic knowledge of HTML, but the Basic HTML Editor automates some of the coding process for you. For example, the Basic HTML Editor lets you specify your page's background color by selecting a color from a pull-down list; it automatically inserts the code for you, based on your selection.

If you're more experienced with HTML, you should use the GeoCities Advanced HTML Editor. The Advanced HTML Editor is essentially a big blank box where you enter the entire HTML code for a Web page. Nothing is automated; you have to do everything by hand.

Within Yahoo! GeoCities, the default editor is the Advanced HTML Editor. You can, however, select which editor you want to use from GeoCities' File Manager page. To open one of these HTML editors, follow these steps:

1. From the Yahoo! GeoCities home page, click the **Edit Pages** link.
2. When the Edit Pages page appears, click the **Open File Manager** link.
3. When the File Manager page appears, pull down the **Edit Using** list and select either **Basic HTML Editor** or **Advanced HTML Editor**.
4. To create a new page, click the **New** button. To edit existing pages, check the page(s) you want to edit, and then click the **Edit** button.

HTML Coding with Some of the Pain Removed—Using the Basic HTML Editor

The Basic HTML Editor lets you create a Web page by filling in a few blanks, making a few selections from some pull-down lists, and entering whatever specific HTML code you're comfortable with. As you can see from Figure 30.1, the Basic HTML Editor page looks somewhat like a form page; fill in the form to create your page.

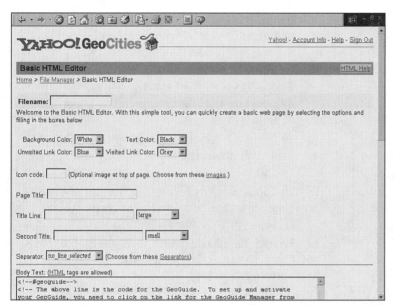

Figure 30.1

Use the Basic HTML Editor when you know a little HTML code—but not enough to create a page totally from scratch.

To create a new page with the Basic HTML Editor, follow these steps:

1. Enter the filename for this page in the **Filename** text box. (If this is to be the home page for your site, name your page index.html.)

2. Pull down the **Background Color** list and select your page's background color.

3. If you want to change the text, link, or unvisited link colors, pull down the appropriate lists and make your selections. (In most cases you should use the default colors for these elements.)

4. To add an optional image at the top of your page, enter the icon code for that image. You can browse the available images—and obtain their codes—by clicking the **Images** link.

5. Enter a title for your page in the **Page Title** box. (This is the title that appears in the title bar of Web browsers when your page is accessed.)

6. Enter the main headline for your page in the **Title Line** box. Pull down the corresponding list to select a type size for your headline.

7. If you want to display a subhead on your page, enter the subtitle in the **Second Title** box and then pull down the corresponding list to select the type size.

8. To insert a horizontal line between your headline/subhead and the rest of your page, pull down the **Separator** list and choose a line style.

9. Enter the main text for your page in the **Body Text** box. This box is also where you insert any dedicated HTML coding for your page, including links, graphics files, and the like.

**You Don't *Have* to
Enter Any HTML**

If you don't want to use fancy HTML codes for a page, you don't have to. You can enter plain text into the **Body Text** box; just make sure you separate each paragraph with the <p> code.

10. To insert a horizontal line between your body text and the rest of your page, pull down the **Separator** list and choose a line style.

11. To create a list of Web site links, enter each site's address in the **Link to URL** boxes, followed by the site's name in the **Description of Link** boxes.

12. To insert a horizontal line after the list of Web sites, pull down the **Separator** list and choose a line style.

13. To add a block of text at the bottom of your page, enter the text in the **Footer Text** box. HTML coding is allowed in this box.

14. To include a Mailto: link to your email address, check the **Include E-Mail Address on Page** option.

15. To insert a horizontal line at the very bottom of your page, pull down the **Separator** list and choose a line style.

16. To preview your page in your Web browser, click the **Preview** button.

17. To save your Web page and return to the File Manager, click the **Save** button. To save the current state of your page and stay in the Basic HTML Editor, click the **Save and Continue Editing** button. To cancel all your work so far, click the **Reset** button and then return to the File Manager by clicking the **Cancel** button.

As you can see in Figure 30.2, you can create a basic Web page without entering a line of HTML code. Just by filling in the blanks, you get a presentable page containing a handful of key elements.

For more sophisticated pages, however, you'll need to use the Advanced HTML Editor discussed in the following section.

Write Your Own Code from Scratch—Using the Advanced HTML Editor

If you're serious about writing HTML code, you want to use the Advanced HTML Editor. As you can see in Figure 30.3, the Advanced HTML Editor is pretty much a big empty box. You enter all your HTML code into this box, and then preview and save the results.

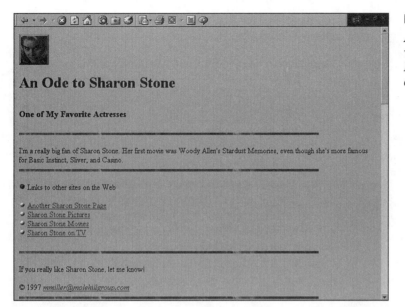

Figure 30.2

A basic Web page created with the Basic HTML Editor—and no HTML codes entered!

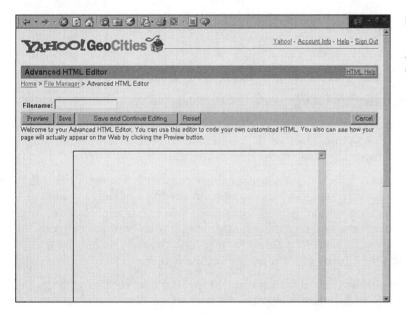

Figure 30.3

Use the Advanced HTML Editor to enter all your code by hand.

277

Use Your Own HTML Editor

You can use any HTML editor or Web page creation program—such as Microsoft FrontPage—to create the pages you post on Yahoo! GeoCities. Just create the files on your hard disk and then *upload* them into your GeoCities directory. See Chapter 31, "Upload Files and Manage Your Site with File Manager," for more details.

To create a new page from the Advanced HTML Editor, follow these steps:

1. Enter the filename for this page in the **Filename** text box. (If this is to be the home page for your site, name your page `index.html`.)

2. Enter your HTML code into the big blank text box.

3. To preview your page in your Web browser, click the **Preview** button.

4. To save your Web page and return to the File Manager, click the **Save** button. To save the current state of your page and stay in the Advanced HTML Editor, click the **Save and Continue Editing** button. To cancel all your work so far, click the **Reset** button and then return to the File Manager by clicking the **Cancel** button.

This sounds easy—*if* you know your way around HTML. To learn more about writing HTML code, keep reading!

All the Codes You Need to Know: The Complete Idiot's HTML QuickStart

HTML is really nothing more than a series of *codes* that tell Web browsers how to display different types of text and graphics. The codes are embedded in a document, so you can't see them; instead, you see the results of the codes.

HTML coding might sound difficult, but it's really fairly easy. First, know that HTML is nothing more than text surrounded by instructions in the form of simple codes. Codes are distinguished from normal text by being enclosed within angle brackets. Each particular code turns on or off a particular attribute, such as boldface or italic text. Most codes are in sets of "on/off" pairs; you turn "on" the code before the text you want to affect, and then turn "off" the code after the text.

For example, the code **<h1>** is used to turn specified type into a level-one headline; the code **</h1>** turns off the headline type. And the code **<i>** is used to italicize text; **</i>** turns off the italics. (As you can see, an "off" code is merely the "on" code with a slash before it, **</like this>**.)

Any text *not* surrounded by code uses HTML's default formatting—normal Times Roman text. The same with tables and other elements; if no code is applied, they default to standard formatting.

To create more interesting Web pages, then, you need to learn some of the basic HTML codes.

That's Not All, Folks

I'll only present a handful of the huge number of HTML codes available to you. If you want to learn more about these and other HTML codes, I recommend you go to the Web Diner (www.webdiner.com), Webmonkey (www.webmonkey.com), or HTML Goodies (www.htmlgoodies.com) Web sites. You can also pick up a copy of *The Complete Idiot's Guide to Creating a Web Page, Fourth Edition*, by Paul McFedries, a great primer for creating your own Web pages with HTML, wherever good books are sold.

Codes to Get Started

When you first create a new Web page, you have to insert some codes to identify the document as an HTML document. These codes are mandatory; you should get used to typing them in whenever you start to work on a new Web page.

In fact, the best way to think of these codes is as a "shell" into which you insert the rest of your text and other codes. For a typical document, here's the shell you use:

```
<html>
<head>
<title>insert the title of the document here</title>
</head>
<body>
insert your entire document—including other HTML codes—between the
<body> and </body> tags
</body>
</html>
```

So you enter the **<html>** and **<body>** codes, and insert everything else between them—including the **<head>** and **<title>** codes.

Codes for Backgrounds

The **<body>** code can be expanded to define document-wide attributes for your Web page. The most common use of these **<body>** attributes is to assign a background color to your Web page.

279

You assign a background color by adding a special **bgcolor** code *within* the "on" **<body>** code, like this:

```
<body bgcolor="xxxxxx">
```

Of course, you still have to use the **</body>** "off" code at the end of your document; that doesn't change.

In the **bgcolor** code, you replace the *xxxxxx* with the six-digit code for a specific background color—surrounded by quotation marks. Table 30.1 lists some basic color codes.

Table 30.1   Common Color Codes

Color	Code
White	FFFFFF
Red	FF0000
Green	00FF00
Blue	0000FF
Magenta	FF00FF
Cyan	00FFFF
Yellow	FFFF00
Black	000000
Light gray	DDDDDD

Get the Codes—in Color!

For a complete listing of the literally hundreds of different HTML color codes, go to the Web Design Group's RGB Color Values site at www.htmlhelp.com/cgi-bin/color.cgi.

As an example, suppose you wanted to set the background color for your document to light gray. You would enter the following code:

```
<body bgcolor="DDDDDD">
```

Pretty simple.

Codes for Text Formatting

Now you enter the text of your Web page between the **<body>** codes, which creates a document that contains nothing but plain text—which looks pretty plain. If nothing else, you should boldface or italicize some of your important text, which is some of the easiest HTML coding you can do.

Here are some of the common HTML codes that format the way selected text looks in your listing:

<h1>formats text as the largest headline**</h1>**

<h2>formats text as the second-largest headline**</h2>**

<h3>formats text as the third-largest headline**</h3>**

****boldfaces text****

<i>italicizes text**</i>**

<u>underlines text**</u>**

<tt>creates monospaced, or typewriter-style text**</tt>**

<blink>creates blinking text**</blink>**

<center>centers text**</center>**

<pre>displays text as "preformatted" for when you want to preserve line breaks and such**</pre>**

Just insert the "on" code right before the text you want formatted, and insert the "off" code right after the selected text. For example, if you had a sentence where you wanted to boldface a single word, it would look like this:

This is the sentence with the ****highlighted**** word.

It's really that simple—just add the **** and **** codes around the text you want boldfaced. The rest of your page looks as normal as it did before.

Codes for Fonts

You don't have to settle for the standard font used by default on many Web pages; you can make your page stand out with your own special font face.

To specify a different font face for a piece of text, use the following code:

```
<font face="xxxx">text</font>
```

Replace *xxxx* with the name of the font you want. For example, if you wanted to change the font to Garamond, you would enter this code:

```
<font face="Garamond">text</font>
```

If you want to change the *size* of your text, use this code:

```
<font size="xx">text</font>
```

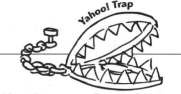

Yahoo! Trap

Use Common Fonts, Please

Just because you specify a font doesn't necessarily mean that all the other users who'll be viewing your Web have the same font available to them. If you change fonts on your page, change to a common font, such as Arial, Helvetica, or Times Roman; going more obscure could ensure an unpredictable display for your listing for many users.

Replace the *xx* with the size you want, from 1 to 7, with 1 being the smallest and seven the biggest. (That's the exact opposite of the way the header codes work... go figure!)

That's right—you don't specify the exact point size, just the *relative* size displayed onscreen. For example, if you want really tiny type, go with size 1 and enter this code:

```
<font size="1">text</font>
```

You can also string these font codes together. Let's say you wanted to change your text to the largest possible Times Roman; you would enter this code:

```
<font face="Times Roman" size="5">text</font>
```

Be careful about changing fonts within your description. Too many different fonts look garish. This may be something you want to set at the beginning of your description and leave it the same throughout the entire listing. (If so, just remember to put the **</font>** code at the very end of your description!)

Codes for Color

Adding color to your text works much the same as changing the font face or size. The code you use looks like this:

```
<font color="#xxxxxx">text</font>
```

As with the **bgcolor** code, replace the six *x*'s with the code for a specific color. Suppose you wanted to color some text red. You would use this code:

```
<font color="#FF0000">red text</font>
```

Color is a good way to highlight important parts of your page. You can put headings or subheadings in a different color, or highlight selected words or phrases in the same manner. Try not to use too many colors, however; if your page starts to look like a rainbow, the color loses its impact.

Codes That Insert Things

So far I've shown you codes that format text. There are other codes that insert items into your document. These codes don't have "on/off" pairs; they're freestanding. These types of codes include

<p> inserts a paragraph break

**
** inserts a line break

<hr> inserts a horizontal rule

So if you wanted to separate two paragraphs, you would insert a **<p>** between the two blocks of text. If you wanted to put a line between the two paragraphs, you would insert a **<hr>**. Sometimes it's good to use horizontal rules between different sections of your page.

Codes for Graphics

Inserting pictures and other graphics really adds some excitement to an otherwise boring Web page. If you want to add a graphic to your page, you need to know the address of that graphic (in the form of a Web page URL), and then use the following code:

```
<img src="URL">
```

There is no "off" code for inserted graphics. Note that the location is enclosed in quotation marks—and that you have to insert the **http://** part of the URL.

As an example, if your graphic was the file **graphic01.jpg** located at www.web-server.com/mydirectory/, you would insert this code:

```
<img src="http://www.webserver.com/mydirectory/graphic01.jpg">
```

Codes for Links

Web pages are all about hyperlinks to other Web pages. If you want to include a hyperlink to another Web page, use the following code:

```
<a href="URL">this is the link</a>
```

The text between the on and off codes appears onscreen as a typical underlined hyperlink; when users click that text, they are linked to the URL you specified in the code. Note that the URL is enclosed in quotation marks, and that you have to include the **http://** part of the address.

Here's what a representative hyperlink code looks like:

```
<a href="http://www.webserver.
com/mydirectory/mypage.htm">This is a
link to my Web page</a>
```

Find Graphics on the Web

If you see a graphic you like on a Web page, you can easily save that file to your hard disk for your own personal use. Just right-click the graphic and select the **Save Picture As** option from the pop-up menu. Also, don't forget to use the Yahoo! Image Surfer (discussed in Chapter 8, "Search for Pictures with Yahoo! Image Surfer") to search the Web for pictures to add to your pages.

You can also add a Mailto: link on your page; users click this link to send email to you. Here's the code for a Mailto: link:

```
<a href="mailto:yourname@domain.com">click here to email me</a>
```

So if you wanted to include a Mailto: link to my email address (author@molehillgroup.com), the code would look like this:

```
<a href="mailto:author@molehillgroup.com">Click here to email the
author</a>
```

Codes for Lists

If you have a list of items somewhere on your page, you might want to format them in a bulleted list. Using HTML codes, it's easy to create a neatly bulleted list.

First, enclose your bulleted list with the **<ul>** and **</ul>** codes. Then precede each bulleted item with the **<li>** code. (There's no "off" code for bulleted items, by the way.)

So the code for a typical bulleted list would look like this:

```
<ul>
   <li>item one
   <li>item two
   <li>item three
</ul>
```

A bulleted list is a great way to run through a list of items—it's a lot cleaner than just listing a bunch of stuff within a long text paragraph.

Code for Tables

In addition to making pretty text and inserting links and graphics, one of the other interesting things you can do with HTML is add a table. Yeah, I know, tables sound boring, but lots of information looks better in a grid of rows and columns—and you make a grid with a table.

The code to create a table, although it looks complex, is quite simple—at least in theory. You start off by enclosing your table with **<table>** and **</table>** codes. Then you enclose each individual row in the table with **<tr>** and **</tr>** codes, and each cell in each row with **<td>** and **</td>** codes.

A basic table with two rows and two columns (four cells total) would be coded like this:

```
<table>
   <tr>
      <td>row 1 cell 1</td>
      <td>row 1 cell 2</td>
   </tr>
   <tr>
      <td>row 2 cell 1</td>
      <td>row 2 cell 2</td>
    </tr>
</table>
```

Figure 30.4 shows the table created by this code (with a table border added, which you'll learn how to do later).

Figure 30.4

Create a table to hold text or pictures—or just organize your page a little.

Within any individual cell you can insert any type of item—plain text, formatted text, bulleted lists, background shading, even graphics. One neat effect is to use a simple two-column, one-row table to create the effect of two columns on your page. You can even shade the background of one of the cells/columns to set it off; it's a nice way to include more detailed information about your item.

You can format both the table as a whole and the cells within a table to some degree:

Indent for Clarity

When you're dealing with complex coding like this, it's sometimes easier to visually understand what's going on if you indent different levels of the code.

➤ To dictate the width of the table border, use the `<table border="xx">` code, where *xx* is in pixels.

➤ To shade the background of a cell, use the `<td bgcolor="#xxxxxx">` code (which works like the color code for text).

➤ To dictate the width of a cell, use the `<td width="xx%">` code, where *xx* is a percentage of the total table width.

These codes are ganged together with the standard `<table>` and `<td>` codes in the table.

Add Yahoo! Search to Your Web Page

Yahoo! enables you—and *encourages* you—to put a Yahoo! search form on your own personal page. Here's the HTML code you use to add a Yahoo! search field:

```
<!— Begin Yahoo Search Form —>
<form method="GET" action="http://search.yahoo.com/bin/search">
    <img src="http://us.yimg.com/i/recip/1yahoo.gif" width=104
height=21 align=top alt="[ Yahoo! ]">
    <input type="text" name="p" value="" size=18>
    <input type="submit" name="name">
    <font size=1>
```

```
    <a href="http://search.yahoo.com/search/options">options</a>
    </font>
</form>
<!— End Yahoo Search Form —>
```

When you insert this code in your Web page, you get something that looks like
Figure 30.5.

Figure 30.5

*Insert a Yahoo! search
button and box on your
own personal Web page.*

Yahoo! also has code available to let you insert other Yahoo! elements on your page,
including Yahoo! News Search, Yahoo! Maps, Yahoo! Yellow Pages, Yahoo! Weather,
and up-to-the-minute stock prices. Go to Yahoo! To Go (`docs.yahoo.com/docs/
yahootogo/index.html`) to learn more.

The Least You Need to Know

➤ Yahoo! GeoCities offers two different HTML editors, the Basic HTML Editor
and the Advanced HTML Editor.

➤ HTML codes are used to format and insert items on your Web page.

➤ HTML codes are enclosed within angle brackets (**< >**); most instructions have
separate "on" and "off" codes.

➤ Yahoo! supplies its own code that enables you to insert a Yahoo! search form
on your page.

Upload Files and Manage Your Site with File Manager

In This Chapter

➤ Discover how to manage the files on your GeoCities site

➤ Learn how to upload files from your personal computer to your GeoCities directory

➤ Find out how to create new subdirectories on your site

After you've created your Web pages, your work is done—right?

Wrong.

Web pages quickly turn into "living" things that require constant oversight and maintenance. Before much time passes you'll find yourself updating your existing pages, adding new pages to your site, and deleting less-popular pages.

To perform this site maintenance, you use Yahoo! GeoCities' File Manager tool. File Manager—not to be confused with the File Manager utility included with older versions of Microsoft Windows—lets you manage your existing files, upload Web pages and other files directly from your PC, and create and organize subdirectories for your site.

Edit, Rename, and Delete: Managing Your Existing Files with File Manager

You access File Manager by following these steps:

1. From the Yahoo! GeoCities home page, click the **Edit Pages** link.
2. When the Edit Pages page appears, click the **Open File Manager** link.

After the File Manager page appears as shown in Figure 31.1, you see a list of all the files on your site. If you have subdirectories within your main directory, those subdirectories are also listed. To perform file management operations, just select a file and click the appropriate button.

Figure 31.1

Use File Manager to edit, rename, and delete your Web pages.

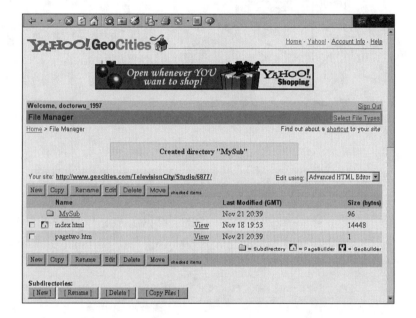

Viewing Files

To view a file from within your Web browser, follow these steps:

1. From within File Manager, locate the file you want to view.
2. Click the **View** link.

Editing Files

When you choose to edit a file on your site, you have the option of using either PageBuilder or one of GeoCities' two HTML editors. If your page was created with PageBuilder, you should use PageBuilder to edit the page; see Chapter 29, "Create a Basic Page with Yahoo! PageBuilder," for more details.

If your page was created by any editor *except* PageBuilder, follow these steps to edit the file:

1. Check the file you want to edit.
2. Pull down the **Edit using** list and select either **Advanced HTML Editor** or **Basic HTML Editor**.
3. Click the **Edit** button.

The editor you selected now opens, with the selected page loaded and ready for editing. See Chapter 30, "Create Sophisticated Pages with HTML," to learn more about GeoCities' Basic and Advanced HTML Editors.

You Have to Use PageBuilder for PageBuilder Pages

If you created a page using PageBuilder (or its predecessor, GeoBuilder), you can't edit it with either the Basic or Advanced HTML Editors; GeoCities displays a warning message if you try. To edit pages created with PageBuilder, you have to use PageBuilder again.

Renaming Files

You can use File Manager to rename any file on your site. Just follow these steps:

1. Check the file you want to rename.
2. Click the **Rename** button.
3. When the Renaming Files page appears, enter the new filename in the **New Name** box, and then click the **Rename Files** button.

Deleting Files

To delete a file from your site, follow these steps:

1. Check the file(s) you want to delete.
2. Click the **Delete** button.
3. When the confirmation page appears, click the **Delete Files** button.

After you delete a file from your site, it's gone—there's no getting it back. The only way to restore a deleted file is to upload a copy of the file from another source, such as your hard disk.

Creating New Files

To create a new file using one of GeoCities' two HTML editors, follow these steps:

1. Pull down the **Edit using** list and select either **Basic HTML Editor** or **Advanced HTML Editor**.
2. Click the **New** button.

The selected editor now appears, with a new blank page ready for your input.

Get Organized: Working with Subdirectories

You can construct your site so that "subsites" or subsidiary page reside in their own separate subdirectories. (You can also have all your pages stored in the same main directory; however, too many files in a single directory can be a little unwieldy to maintain.)

Creating New Subdirectories

To create a new subdirectory on your site, follow these steps:

1. Go to the Subdirectories section of the File Manager page and click the **New** button.
2. When the Create Subdirectory page appears, enter a name for the subdirectory in the **New Subdirectory Name** box.
3. Click the **Create Subdirectory** button.

Use PageBuilder? Then No Subdirectories!

If you use PageBuilder to create your pages, you can't use subdirectories. PageBuilder only recognizes files stored in your main directory; use subdirectories only if you use one of the two HTML editors, or if you upload completed files from your PC.

Moving Files to a Subdirectory

After you've created a new subdirectory, you can either upload files directly to that subdirectory, or move or copy files from your main directory into the new subdirectory.

To move existing files, follow these steps:

1. Check the file(s) you want to move.
2. Click the **Move** button.
3. When the Moving Files to a Subdirectory page appears, pull down the **Subdirectory** list and select the subdirectory where you want to move the file(s).
4. Click the **Move Files** button.

Copying Files to a Subdirectory

To copy existing files, follow these steps:

1. Check the file(s) you want to copy.
2. Click the **Copy Files** button (in the Subdirectories section of the File Manager page).
3. When the Copy Files to a Subdirectory page appears, pull down the **Subdirectory** list and select the subdirectory where you want to copy the file(s).
4. Click the **Copy Files** button.

You can also copy files *within* a single directory or subdirectory. When you do this, you have to assign the copy a different filename. Follow these steps:

1. Check the file(s) you want to copy.
2. Click the **Copy** button.
3. When the Copying Files page appears, enter a new filename for each file in the **New Name** box.
4. Click the **Copy Files** button.

Building a Site from Offsite: Using EZ Upload

Even though GeoCities supplies three different Web page editors, you don't have to use any of these tools—you can create Web pages using HTML editing software installed on your own PC, and then upload those files to your GeoCities directory. (GeoCities doesn't care where your pages come from.) There are two ways to upload files to GeoCities—using GeoCities' EZ Upload utility, or using your own FTP software.

Uploading Files the EZ Way

To upload files with EZ Upload, follow these steps:

1. From the EZ Upload page (shown in Figure 31.2), enter the location and name for each file you want to upload. (To locate a file on your hard disk, click the **Browse** button.)
2. If you want to automatically convert the filenames of your files to lowercase (which is, more or less, the Internet convention), check the **Automatically convert filenames to lowercase** option.
3. To change .HTM files to .HTML files (another Internet convention), check the **Automatically change ".htm" extensions to ".html"** option.
4. Click the **Upload Files** button.

291

Figure 31.2

Use EZ Upload to transfer files from your hard disk to your GeoCities directory.

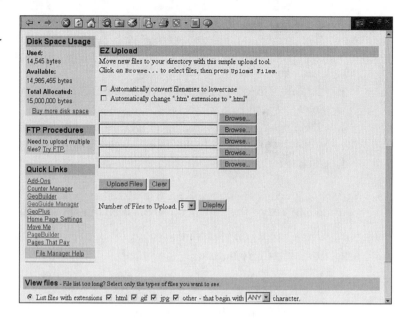

Upload As Many As You Want

By default, EZ Upload displays boxes for 5 files. To upload more than 5 files at a time (up to 20 files), select another value from the **Number of Files to Upload** list, and then click the **Display** button.

By default, EZ Upload uploads your files to your main GeoCities directory. To upload files to a subdirectory, you first have to switch to that subdirectory, and then use EZ Upload from that subdirectory page.

Uploading Files with FTP

Another way to upload files to your GeoCities directory is by using a separate FTP program. Some FTP programs, such as WS-FTP, offer more functionality than is available with EZ Upload; in some instances, FTP also provides faster uploading speeds.

FTP = Faster Than Poop

FTP stands for File Transfer Protocol, and is an older—and sometimes faster—technology used to upload and download files to and from servers on the Internet. You can use FTP programs both to upload and to download files to and from your GeoCities directory.

Each FTP program works a little differently, so I can't provide precise instructions for uploading here. However, you will need to configure your FTP program for your GeoCities directory; the key settings are described in Table 31.1.

Table 31.1 GeoCities FTP Settings

Option	Setting
FTP server	ftp.geocities.com
Username	Your Yahoo! GeoCities member name
Password	Your Yahoo! GeoCities password

When you enter information into your FTP software, make sure you use all lowercase letters.

If You Don't Watch It, It'll Fill Up: Managing Your Disk Space

File Manager is also where you monitor the disk space used by your GeoCities site. Remember, you get 15MB of space at no charge—if you start bumping up against that limit, you'll either need to delete some files or purchase additional space (at $2.50 per month for each 5MB block).

You monitor your space by scrolling down the File Manager page to the Disk Space Usage section (typically next to the EZ Upload section). You'll see the following information:

➤ Disk space used

➤ Disk space available

➤ Total disk space allocated

If you want to purchase additional space, click the **Buy More Disk Space** link and follow the instructions there.

The Least You Need to Know

➤ Use File Manager to edit, rename, and delete files on your GeoCities Web site.

➤ You can also use File Manager to create subdirectories on your site and to monitor your disk space usage.

➤ Use EZ Upload to upload files from your PC to your GeoCities directory.

Make a Better Site with Home Page Add-Ons

In This Chapter

➤ Learn how to add graphic, interactive, and multimedia elements to your Web pages

➤ Find out how to choose what types of advertisements appear on your Web pages

➤ Discover how you can earn cash from your pages with the Pages That Pay program

In the previous chapters you learned how to create and manage your own personal Web pages at Yahoo! GeoCities. Let's wrap up this section with a look at some of the cool and fun things you can add to your pages—from pictures to stock tickers to interactive games!

Add More Stuff to Your Pages with GeoCities Add-Ons

GeoCities offers a variety of *add-ons* that you can plug directly into your Web pages. These add-ons are predesigned elements that can be copied directly into any Web page—whether you built your pages with PageBuilder, the Advanced HTML Editor, or another HTML editing program.

You access all these add-ons from the Yahoo! GeoCities home page in the Cool Home Page Add-Ons section on the left side.

Make a Picture-Perfect Page with Art Add-Ons

GeoCities offers a large library of images you can add to any GeoCities Web page. Among the types of art available are the following:

➤ Arrows

➤ Bullets

➤ Buttons

➤ Clip art

➤ Icons

➤ Lines

You can add any of these images to your page by following these steps:

1. From the Yahoo! GeoCities home page, click the **Art** link.

2. When the Art page appears, click the type of image you want to add.

3. GeoCities now launches a separate Free Image Library window. Navigate through the image categories in this window until you find the image you want to use.

4. Use your mouse to select the code for the selected image.

5. Right-click the selected code to display the pop-up menu, and then select **Copy**.

6. Switch to your HTML file and paste the copied code into your page code.

If you used PageBuilder to create your page, you can access this art library from within the PageBuilder window. Just click the **Picture** button to display the **Select Pictures** dialog box, pull down the **Collection** list to choose an image type, and then select a specific image from the Picture list.

Get Really Animated with Animation and Multimedia Add-Ons

When you click the **Animation & Multimedia** link on the Yahoo! GeoCities home page, you see a list of various high-tech add-ons you can install on your Web page. When you add one of these add-ons to your page, the result is a lively, moving, never-look-the-same-way twice kind of effect—definitely more interesting than static, text-only pages!

Other Sites for Cool Graphics

There are numerous sites on the Web that contain libraries of graphic images you can use in your Web pages. Many of these sites provide their pictures at no charge; others require a subscription for access or charge a per-picture fee. These sites include the following:

➤ Art Today (www.arttoday.com)

➤ Barry's Clip Art Server (www.barrysclipart.com)

➤ ClipArtConnection (www.clipartconnection.com)

➤ ClipArtNow (www.clipartnow.com)

➤ Corbis (www.corbis.com)

➤ Free Graphics (www.thefreesite.com/freegraphics.htm)

➤ Icon Bank (www.iconbank.com)

➤ Mediabuilder (www.mediabuilder.com)

GeoCities offers the following animation and multimedia add-ons:

➤ **Animated Logo**—This add-on lets you create single images that display multiple images, for a quick-and-easy animation effect.

➤ **Drop-Down Menu**—Insert menus that drop down when users slide their mouse over them.

➤ **Fading Images**—Insert Modify your images to fade in and out of your page.

➤ **Gliding Images**—Turn your static images into presentation-style displays, with several different transition styles.

➤ **Horizontal Site Menu**—Add a fit-to-size site menu along either side of your page.

➤ **Image Highlight Menu**—Create a menu that combines text and graphics— where buttons change when hovered over or selected.

➤ **Random Image**—Make your page look different on every visit by rotating between a group of different images.

➤ **Rotating Image**—Create a 3D rotating banner.

➤ **Scrolling Text and Images**—Make your text and images scroll across your screen.

➤ **Things**—Use the GeoThingMaker (a free software tool) to create your own unique interactive buttons, navigation widgets, animated characters, interactive games, and streaming media. You can also choose from libraries containing hundreds of predesigned Things, such as South Park Things and NFL Things.

➤ **Streaming Media**—Subscribe to Yahoo!'s GeoMedia service, which lets you create and publish your own streaming audio and video files. Using RealNetworks' RealProducer G2 software, you can add your favorite video clips and audio clips to your GeoCities Web page.

➤ **Vertical Menu**—Add a simple site menu along the top or bottom of your page.

Build an Online Playground with Fun & Games Add-Ons

Click the **Fun & Games** link on the Yahoo! GeoCities home page to add any of the following games and other fun elements to your Web page:

➤ **Baby's Birth Countdown**—Display an online countdown to your upcoming blessed event.

➤ **Baseball**—Display schedule, stats, and game results from your favorite baseball teams.

➤ **Basketball**—Display schedule, stats, and game results from your favorite NBA teams.

➤ **Beanie Babies Trivia**—Display random Beanie Babies trivia questions, as shown in Figure 32.1.

Figure 32.1

Let your visitors entertain themselves with Beanie Babies trivia.

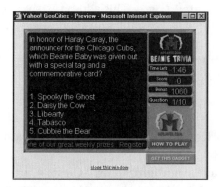

➤ **Birthday Countdown**—Display an online countdown (in days and seconds) to an upcoming birthday.

➤ **Computer Games Trivia**—Display random trivia questions about new and classic computer games.

➤ **Current Events Trivia**—Display random current events trivia questions.

➤ **Entertainment Trivia**—Display random trivia questions about movies, music, television, and more.

➤ **Game Cheats**—Display a box of game cheats on your Web page.

➤ **General Trivia**—Display random general-interest trivia questions.

➤ **Indulgence Advisor**—Display a fun little tool that recommends specific indulgences for when you've had a particularly bad day.

➤ **Love Compatibility Test**—Display the romantic possibilities between two selected star signs.

➤ **Slot Machine**—Display an interactive slot machine game on your page.

➤ **Star Trek Trivia**—Display random Star Trek-related trivia questions.

➤ **Star Wars Trivia**—Display random Star Wars-related trivia questions.

➤ **Tic-Tac-Toe**—Display an interactive tic-tac-toe game on your page.

➤ **Video Poker**—Display an interactive poker game on your page.

➤ **Wedding Countdown**—Display an online countdown to the upcoming big event.

Just the Facts, Ma'am, with Instant Info Add-Ons

The add-ons available when you click the **Instant Info** link on the Yahoo! GeoCities home page provide constantly updated information for your Web page visitors. The many Instant Info add-ons include the following:

➤ **Baby's Birth Countdown**—Display an online countdown to your upcoming blessed event.

➤ **Birthday Countdown**—Display an online countdown (in days and seconds) to an upcoming birthday.

➤ **Countdown to the Big Day**—Display an online countdown to any date you specify.

➤ **Counter**—Display a count of visitors to your site—one of the most popular add-ons available. (See Figure 32.2 for a typical counter.)

Figure 32.2

The most popular add-on of them all—a simple visitor counter.

➤ **Crime Watch**—Display a scrolling newsfeed of crime headlines.

➤ **Home Page Headlines**—Display news and sports headlines on your Web page; choose from a variety of news sources.

➤ **Mortgage Calculator**—Display a Mortgage.com mortgage calculator, so users can calculate their monthly mortgage payments under different scenarios.

➤ **Stock Charter**—Display a "live" performance chart for your favorite stock.

➤ **Stock Quote**—Display a form to let users look up current stock prices.

➤ **Wedding Countdown**—Display an online countdown to the upcoming big event.

➤ **Yahoo! GeoCities Search Box**—Display a search box that lets users search for other GeoCities members' Web pages.

Everybody's Talkin' 'Bout Interactive Add-Ons

When you click the **Interactive** link on the Yahoo! GeoCities home page, you access a selection of elements that provide information to and from your site's users, including

➤ **Ad Square**—Described later in the "Banners and Pop-Ups and Squares, Oh My!" section of this chapter.

➤ **Banner Exchange**—Described later in the "Banners and Pop-Ups and Squares, Oh My!" section of this chapter.

➤ **Guestbook**—Lets visitors to your site sign in and leave you personal greetings.

➤ **Yahoo! User Message Boards**—Create your own personal message board for your site. (To learn more about Yahoo! Message Boards, see Chapter 12, "Join the Discussions at Yahoo! Clubs and Message Boards.")

➤ **Yahoo! GeoCities Search Box**—Display a search box that lets users search for other GeoCities members' Web pages.

➤ **Forms**—Add a form that lets users send you messages (via email) directly from your Web page.

It's Payback Time: GeoCities' Ads and Sales Links

As you know, Yahoo! GeoCities lets you post pages on their site for free. They make their money by selling ads that appear when users access member pages.

Although this form of advertising may be annoying, you do have some control over the way advertisements appear on your site. In addition, Yahoo! lets you get in on the act by including links to specific merchants from your page—and get paid from any sales that result!

Banners and Pop-Ups and Squares, Oh My!

Yahoo! GeoCities displays three different types of advertising on their pages:

➤ **Ad Squares**—An Ad Square is a small window that appears in the top-right corner of the Web browser when a user accesses your page. As you can see in Figure 32.3, each Ad Square can include a variety of different elements, all described in Table 32.1. If a user doesn't click any of the options within your Ad Square, the ad eventually collapses to just another item in the Ad Square list. You select which items appear in your page's Ad Square via the Set Up Your Ad Square page (geocities.yahoo.com/members/cgi-bin/adsquare/adsquare/)—although you can't get rid of the ads, of course. Ad Squares, when activated, disable banners and pop-ups.

Figure 32.3

Users can choose from a number of ways to contact you—and either click or ignore the ad—via the options in an Ad Square.

Table 32.1 Yahoo! Ad Square Options

Link	Description
View My Profile	Displays your Yahoo! Profile
Send Me a Message	Sends an instant message, using Yahoo! Messenger
Send Me Email	Sends an email message to your designated address
My Neighborhood	Links to your neighborhood's home page
Sign My Guestbook	Allows visitors to add their names to your Guestbook
Send This Page	Sends this page (via email) to another user

➤ **Banners**—If you choose *not* to display Ad Squares, you can choose to have GeoCities automatically add a banner advertisement to the top of your Web page. The banner ads rotate through a selection of advertiser ads and ads for other member sites. You turn on the banner feature by inserting a GeoGuide into your Web page code, either from PageBuilder or with specific code in either of GeoCities' HTML editors. You can even submit your own banner ads to be used within the Yahoo! GeoCities Banner Exchange. For more information on GeoGuide and the Banner Exchange, go to geocities.yahoo.com/addons/ interact/mbe.html. To set up and manage GeoGuide on your Web page, click the **GeoGuide Manager** link in the Quick Links section of GeoCities' File Manager.

➤ **Pop-Ups**—If you choose *not* to display either Ad Squares or banner ads, then Yahoo! automatically displays a separate pop-up window when users access your page. These pop-up windows contain paid advertisements from Yahoo!'s many advertisers.

Nobody really likes advertisements—except advertisers, of course! Probably the most annoying of GeoCities' three forms of advertising is the pop-up; users *hate* closing that extra window every time they access another GeoCities member page. Although the Ad Square can be equally annoying, at least it offers some user benefit via the links to other site features. Banner ads offer the benefit of not appearing in a separate window, and of sometimes promoting your site and the sites of other GeoCities homesteaders. Which type of ad you choose is up to you, of course—but know that if you make *no* choice, you'll get pop-up ads by default.

How to Choose

To activate pop-ups on your pages, you don't have to do anything—they appear automatically, unless you activate the GeoGuide or Ad Squares. To add a GeoGuide to your page to display banner ads, click the **GeoGuide Manager** link in the Quick Links section of GeoCities' File Manager. To activate an Ad Square for your page, go to `geocities.yahoo.com/members/cgi-bin/adsquare/adsquare/`.

Make Your Pages Pay with GeoCities' Sales Links

If you're tired of Yahoo! and their advertisers making money off your personal pages, you can beat them at their own game by including links to online merchants on your pages—and collecting a commission when your site visitors make purchases from these links. The Pages That Pay affiliates program enables you to make money from your site with little or no effort on your part.

Learn More, Online

Learn more about the Pages That Pay affiliate program by clicking the **Pages That Pay** link on the Yahoo! GeoCities home page, or by going directly to `geocities.yahoo.com/pagesthatpay/`.

It doesn't cost you anything to join the Pages That Pay program. All you have to do is select which merchants you want to link to, and Yahoo! does the rest. You can create links to merchants, products, or product categories—or even include a product search form on your page.

Among the merchants participating in Pages That Pay are the following:

➤ ActionAce.com

➤ Adatom.com

➤ Ancestry.com

➤ Barnesandnoble.com

➤ DigitalWork

➤ Egghead.com

➤ Net2Phone

➤ Netopia, Inc.

➤ Outpost

➤ Proflowers.com

➤ Qwest

➤ Reel.com

➤ Seattle FilmWorks

➤ SmarterKids.com

➤ Tickets.com

➤ Value America

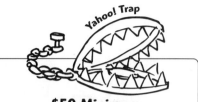

$50 Minimum

Yahoo! cuts you a check only if your commissions due are at least $50. If you haven't earned this much, you don't lose your money, but Yahoo! won't pay you until you earn some more commissions.

You can include links from any or all of these merchants on your pages. You'll be paid a commission specified by the merchant; commissions are paid four times a year (January, April, July, and October).

To add Pages That Pay links to your pages, click the **Pages That Pay** link in the Quick Links section of the GeoCities' File Manager.

The Least Your Need to Know

➤ GeoCities' Add-Ons let you add graphical, interactive, and multimedia elements to your Web pages.

➤ Yahoo! GeoCities will display one of the following types of advertisement when users access your Web page: Ad Square, banner ad, or pop-up ad window.

➤ If you become a member of the Pages That Pay affiliate program, you include links to merchants on your Web page—and make commissions when users click the links and make purchases.

The Yahoo! Glossary

address   The unique identifier for either a Web page or an email recipient. A Web page address is also called a *URL*.

bandwidth   The speed of your Internet connection. The more bandwidth, the better; high-bandwidth connections (100Kbps or more) are necessary to adequately receive many of today's audio and video "Webcasts." High-bandwidth connections are sometimes called "big pipes."

browser   A software program that lets your computer access HTML pages on the World Wide Web. Netscape Navigator and Microsoft Internet Explorer are the two most popular browsers today.

client   A software program that runs on your personal computer and makes requests from another "server" computer.

cookie   A small text file, stored on your computer's hard disk, that is used by a particular Web site to identify you on return visits. Cookies store some amount of personal information, and can be used to track your Web surfing.

dead link   A hyperlink on a Web page that doesn't lead to an active page or site—probably because that page no longer exists.

directory   A search site that collects and indexes Web pages manually, either by user submission or editorial selection. Yahoo! is the Web's most popular directory.

document   A piece of information the user may want to retrieve. Web pages are often referred to as documents.

domain   The name of a computer site on the Internet. Domains are hierarchical, and lower-level domains often refer to particular Web sites within a top-level domain. Examples of domains are .com, .edu, .gov, and .org.

download   The process of transferring a file from an Internet site to your personal computer; the opposite of *upload*.

email   Electronic mail, a means of corresponding to other computer users over the Internet through digital messages.

FAQs   See *Frequently Asked Questions*.

file   Digital information in an identified format. A file can be anything from a picture file to a Microsoft Word file to a collection of names and addresses. Web pages are files in HTML format.

frames   An HTML technique for combining two or more separate HTML documents within a single Web page.

Frequently Asked Questions   Also known as a FAQs, these are documents that answer the most commonly asked questions about a particular topic. FAQs are often found in newsgroups and on some Web sites as a preparatory answer to the common questions asked by new users.

FTP   File Transfer Protocol, an older, non-Web–based convention that enables files to be downloaded from other computers on the Internet.

hit   The results of a search; a measure of the number of Web pages matching a given query.

home page   The initial page screen of a Web site.

host   An Internet server that houses a Web site.

HTML   Hypertext Markup Language, the quasi-programming language used to create Web pages.

HTTP   Hypertext Transfer Protocol, the protocol that enables communication between Web servers and Web browsers.

hyperlink   Special text or graphics on a Web page that, when clicked, automatically transfers the user to another Web page.

index   The database of Web pages maintained by a Web search engine or directory. Sometimes directories are called indexes.

indexing   The process of converting a collection of information or documents into a form suitable for easy search and retrieval.

Internet   The global "network of networks" that connects millions of computers around the world. The World Wide Web and Usenet are both parts of the Internet.

Internet Explorer   Microsoft's Web browser.

Java   An Internet-based programming language that creates applications that run while you're online, using your Web browser. Yahoo! PageBuilder is a Java-based application.

keyword   A word that forms all or part of a search engine query.

mailing list   A discussion group conducted via email.

mirror sites   One or more copies of a Web site, located on different servers. Many sites "mirror" their information on multiple servers to prevent overloading of their main site.

modem   Computer hardware that enables transmission of digital data from one computer to another over common telephone lines.

Netscape Communicator   The software suite that contains the Netscape Navigator Web browser.

Netscape Navigator   Netscape's Web browser.

network   Two or more computers connected together. The Internet is the largest network in the world.

newsgroup   A special-interest discussion group, hosted on Usenet.

plug-in   Any utility used in conjunction with your Web browser that adds functionality to your browser. The RealAudio player used to play Yahoo! Radio is one such plug-in.

portal   A Web site that provides a gateway to the Internet, as well as a collection of other content and services. Most of today's portals—including Yahoo!—started life as search engines or directories.

protocol   An agreed-upon format for transmitting data between two computers.

query   A word, phrase, or group of words, possibly combined with other syntax or operators, used to initiate a search with a search engine or directory.

registration   The process of informing a search engine or directory about a new Web page or site.

relevance   A measure of how well a document or page satisfies the user's query.

search   To look for information in an orderly fashion.

search box   The text box where you enter your search query.

search engine   A Web server that indexes Web pages and then makes the index available for user searching. Search engines differ from directories in that the indexes are generated using *spiders*, where directories are assembled manually. Search engine indexes typically include many more Web pages than are found in directories.

search site   Generic term for a Web site that offers either a search engine, a directory, or both.

search term   See *query*.

server   A central computer that responds to requests for information from one or more client computers. On the Internet, all Web pages are stored on servers.

site   A unified collection of Web pages on the Internet.

snail mail   Traditional U.S. Postal Service mail.

spam   Email or newsgroup messages that are unsolicited, unwanted, and generally irrelevant.

spamdexing   The optimization of a Web page with intent to deceive a search engine's spider and result in higher or misleading placement in query results.

spider   A software program that follows hypertext links across multiple Web pages, but is not directly under human control. A *spider* is a type of robot. Spiders scan the Web, looking for URLs, automatically following all the hyperlinks on pages accessed. The results from a spider's search are used to create the indexes used by search engines.

title   The text corresponding to the formal name of a Web page.

upload   The process of transferring a file from your computer to another computer on the Internet; the opposite of *download*.

URL   Uniform Resource Locator; the address of a Web page.

Usenet   A subset of the Internet that contains topic-specific *newsgroups*.

virus   A malicious computer program, often downloaded unknowingly from the Internet, that can cause damage to your computer files.

Web   See *World Wide Web*.

Web browser   See *browser*.

World Wide Web   A subset of the Internet that contains HTML pages.

Yahoo!   The most popular site on the Internet—and the world's most popular Internet directory—located at www.yahoo.com.

Index

315

317

N